Evaluation Foundations Revisited

EVALUATION FOUNDATIONS REVISITED

Cultivating a Life of the Mind for Practice

Thomas A. Schwandt

STANFORD BUSINESS BOOKS
An Imprint of Stanford University Press
Stanford, California

Stanford University Press
Stanford, California

Special discounts for bulk quantities of Stanford Business Books are available to corporations, professional associations, and other organizations. For details and discount information, contact the special sales department of Stanford University Press.
Tel: (650) 736-1782, Fax: (650) 736-1784

Printed in the United States of America on acid-free, archival-quality paper

Library of Congress Cataloging-in-Publication Data

Schwandt, Thomas A., author.
  Evaluation foundations revisited : cultivating a life of the mind for practice / Thomas A. Schwandt.
    pages cm
  Includes bibliographical references and index.
  ISBN 978-0-8047-8655-3 (pbk. : alk. paper)
  1. Evaluation. I. Title.
  AZ191.S35 2015
  001.4—dc23

                                        2014049326
  ISBN 978-0-8047-9572-2 (electronic)

Typeset by Bruce Lundquist in 10.9/13 Adobe Garamond

Contents

Acknowledgments

Sincere thanks to members of the QUERIES Seminar in the Department of Educational Psychology at the University of Illinois, Urbana-Champaign, for reading drafts of chapters and offering thoughtful comments. I am especially grateful to Jennifer Greene, Emily Gates, Gabriela Garcia, and Nora Gannon-Slater from that group for sharing their reactions to the overall concept of the book as well as for suggesting ways to improve various chapters. Michael Morris and Leslie Goodyear reviewed an earlier draft and offered valuable suggestions for sharpening the focus of the book. My wife was a very patient and engaged listener as I mulled over ideas and fretted over ways to express myself; I have learned much from her. A very special thanks to my editor at Stanford University Press, Margo Beth Fleming, for her encouragement, editorial advice, and her careful attention to this project since it was first proposed. Many of the ideas expressed here were developed, improved, or refined in conversations with colleagues, far too numerous to mention, over many years. What readers may find of value here I owe in large part to those conversations and to the insights and wisdom of my colleagues. Errors, blunders, and ideas that confound rather than enlighten are of course my own doing.

Evaluation Foundations Revisited

Prologue

Evaluation is the act of judging the value, merit, worth, or significance of things. Those "things" can be performances, programs, processes, policies, or products, to name a few. Evaluation is ubiquitous in everyday life. It is evident in annual performance appraisals, the assessment of a good golf swing, scholarly reviews of books, quality control procedures in manufacturing, and the ratings of products provided by agencies such as Consumer's Union. Forensic evaluations by psychiatrists are a common aspect of many court proceedings; teachers evaluate the performance of their students; expert judges assess and score athlete performances in high school diving competitions; drama critics for local newspapers appraise the quality of local theatre productions; foundation officers examine their investments in social programs to determine whether they yield value for money. Evaluation is an organizational phenomenon, embedded in policies and practices of governments, in public institutions like schools and hospitals, as well as in corporations in the private sector and foundations in the philanthropic world. Evaluation and kindred notions of appraising, assessing, auditing, rating, ranking, and grading are social phenomena that all of us encounter at some time or another in life.

However, we can also identify what might be called a "professional approach" to evaluation that is linked to both an identity and a way of practicing that sets it apart from everyday evaluation undertakings. That professional approach is characterized by specialized, expert knowledge and skills possessed by individuals claiming the designation of "evaluator." Expert knowledge is the product of a particular type of disciplined inquiry, an organized, scholarly, and professional mode of knowledge production.

The prime institutional locations of the production of evaluation knowledge are universities, policy analysis and evaluation units of government departments or international organizations, and private research institutes and firms. The primary producers are academics, think tank experts, and other types of professionals engaged in the knowledge occupation known as "evaluation," or perhaps more broadly "research and evaluation."[1] Evaluation is thus a professional undertaking that individuals with a specific kind of educational preparation claim to know a great deal about, on the one hand, and practice in systematic and disciplined ways, on the other hand. This knowledge base and the methodical and well-organized way of conducting evaluation sets the expert practice apart from what occurs in the normal course of evaluating activities in everyday life. Expert evaluation knowledge, particularly of the value of local, state, national, and international policies and programs concerned with the general social welfare (e.g., education, social services, public health, housing, criminal justice), is in high demand by governments, nongovernmental agencies, and philanthropic foundations.

Focus of the Practice

The somewhat unfortunately awkward word used to describe the plans, programs, projects, policies, performances, designs, material goods, facilities, and other things that are evaluated is *evaluands*; a term of art that I try my best to avoid using. It is the evaluation of policies and programs (also often referred to as social interventions) that is of primary concern in this book. A program is a set of activities organized in such a way so as to achieve a particular goal or set of objectives. Programs can be narrow in scope and limited to a single site—for example, a health education program in a local community to reduce the incidence of smoking—or broad and unfolding across multiple sites such as a national pre-school education initiative that involves delivering a mix of social and educational services to preschool-aged children and their parents in several locations in major cities across the country. Policies are broader statements of an approach to a social problem or a course of action that often involve several different kinds of programs and activities. For example, the science, technology, engineering, and mathematics (STEM) education policy, supported by the U.S. National Science Foundation (NSF) (among other agencies), is aimed in part at increasing the participation of students in STEM careers, especially women and minorities. That aim is realized through a variety of different kinds of programs including teacher preparation programs; informal, out-of-school education programs; educational efforts attached to NSF-funded centers in science and engineering; and programs that provide research experience in STEM fields for undergraduates.

However, even if we restrict our focus to the evaluation of programs, there remains an incredible variety including training programs (e.g., job training to reduce unemployment; leadership development for youth programs); direct service interventions (e.g., early childhood education programs); indirect service interventions (e.g., a program providing funding to develop small- and medium-size business enterprises); research programs (e.g., a program aimed at catalyzing transdisciplinary research such as the U.S. National Academies of Science Keck Future's Initiative); surveillance systems (e.g., the U.S. National Security Agency's controversial electronic surveillance program known as PRISM or, perhaps in a less sinister way of thinking, a program that monitors health-related behaviors in a community in order to improve some particular health outcome); knowledge management programs; technical assistance programs; social marketing campaigns (e.g., a public health program designed to encourage people to stop smoking); programs that develop advocacy coalitions for policy change; international development programs that can focus on a wide variety of interventions in health, education, food safety, economic development, the environment, and building civil society; strategy evaluation;[2] and programs that build infrastructure in or across organizations at state or local levels to support particular educational or social initiatives.

Aims of the Practice

Evaluation is broadly concerned with quality of implementation, goal attainment, effectiveness, outcomes, impact, and costs of programs and policies.[3] Evaluators provide judgments on these matters to stakeholders who are both proximate and distant. Proximate stakeholders include clients sponsoring or commissioning an evaluation study as well program developers, managers, and beneficiaries. Distant stakeholders can include legislators, the general public, influential thought leaders, the media, and so on. Moreover, policies and programs can be evaluated at different times in their development and for different purposes as shown in Table 1.

4

Table 1. Types of Evaluation

Implementation evaluation (also called operational evaluation)[a]	Focusing on what happens in the program—its characteristics, participants, staff activities, and so on—to determine what is working and what is not; determining whether the program is operating according to design. Can be undertaken for several purposes including monitoring, accountability (i.e., compliance with program specifications), and program improvement.
Program monitoring	Monitoring/tracking continuously key program data (e.g., participation levels, program completion rates, program costs); often accomplished through the design and operation of a management information system. (A type of implementation evaluation.)
Process evaluation	Examining how the program produces an outcome; searching for explanations of successes and failures in the way the program works; typically requires an examination of how program staff and participants understand and experience the program. (A type of implementation evaluation.)
Outcome evaluation	Focusing on the kinds of outcomes that the program produced in the program participants such as a change in status, behavior, attitudes, skills, and so on; requires the development and specification of indicators that serve as measures of outcome attainment. Outcome monitoring involves examining whether performance targets for program outcomes are being achieved.[b]
Impact evaluation	Examining whether results are actually attributable to the program or policy in question; often focuses not only on the expected and unexpected effects on program participants or beneficiaries attributable to the program (or policy) but also, in the longer run, on the community or system in which the program operates.[c]
Efficiency assessment	Determining whether the benefits produced by the program justify its costs; often determined by using cost-benefit or cost-effectiveness analysis.[d]
Social impact assessment	Measuring the social or public value created by policies, projects, and social interventions.

[a] See Khandker, Koolwal, and Samad (2010: 16–18).

[b] The literature is not in agreement on the definitions of outcome and impact evaluation. Some evaluators treat them as virtually the same, others argue that outcome evaluation is specifically concerned with immediate changes occurring in recipients of the program while impact examines longer-term changes in participants' lives.

[c] Khandker, Koolwal, and Samad (2010); see also the InterAction website for its Impact Evaluation Guidance Notes at http://www.interaction.org/impact-evaluation-notes

[d] Levin and McEwan (2001).

Scope of the Practice

Evaluation of policies and programs in the United States is an important part of the work of legislative agencies and executive departments including the Government Accountability Office, the Office of Management and Budget, the Centers for Disease Control and Prevention, the Departments of State, Education, and Labor, the National Science Foundation, the U.S. Cooperative Extension Service, the Office of Evaluation and Inspections in the Office of the Inspector General in the Department of Health and Human Services, and the Office of Justice Programs in the U.S. Department of Justice. At state and local levels evaluations are undertaken by legislative audit offices, as well as by education, social service, public health, and criminal justice agencies (often in response to federal evaluation requirements).

Professional evaluation of programs and policies is also an extensive global undertaking. Governments throughout the world have established national-level evaluation offices dealing with specific public sector concerns such as the Danish Evaluation Institute charged with examining the quality of day care centers, schools, and educational programs throughout the country or the Agency for Health Care Research and Quality in the U.S. Department of Health and Human Services that investigates the quality, efficiency, and effectiveness of health care for Americans. At the national level, one also finds evaluation agencies charged with oversight for all public policy such as the Spanish Agency for the Evaluation of Public Policies and Quality of Services and the South African Department of Performance Monitoring and Evaluation. These omnibus agencies not only determine the outcomes and impacts of government policies but in so doing combine the goals of improving the quality of public services, rationalizing the use of public funds, and enhancing the public accountability of government bodies.

Evaluations are both commissioned and conducted at think tanks and at not-for-profit and for-profit institutions such as the Brookings Institution and the Urban Institute, the Education Development Center, WestEd, American Institutes of Research, Weststat, and the International Initiative for Impact Evaluation (3ie). Significant evaluation work is undertaken or supported by philanthropies such as the Bill & Melinda Gates Foundation and the Rockefeller Foundation. Internationally, evaluation is central to the work of multilateral organizations including the World Bank, the

Organisation for Economic Co-operation and Development (OECD), the United Nations Educational, Scientific, and Cultural Organization (UNESCO), and the United Nations Development Programme (UNDP); as well as government agencies around the world concerned with international development such as the U.S. Agency for International Development (USAID), the International Development Research Centre in Canada (IDRC), the Department for International Development (DFID) in the United Kingdom, and the Science for Global Development Division of the Netherlands Organization for Scientific Research (NWO-WOTRO).

The scope and extent of professional evaluation activity is evident from the fact that twenty academic journals[4] are devoted exclusively to the field, and there are approximately 140 national, regional, and international evaluation associations and societies.[5] This worldwide evaluation enterprise is also loosely coupled to the related work of professionals who do policy analysis, performance measurement, inspections, accreditation, quality assurance, testing and assessment, organizational consulting, and program auditing.

Characteristics of the Practice and Its Practitioners

The professional practice of evaluation displays a number of interesting traits, not least of which is whether it actually qualifies as a profession—a topic taken up later in this book. Perhaps its most thought-provoking trait is that it is heterogeneous in multiple ways. Evaluators examine policies and programs that vary considerably in scope from a local community-based program to national and international efforts spread across many sites. They evaluate a wide range of human endeavors reflected in programs to stop the spread of HIV/AIDS, to improve infant nutrition, to determine the effectiveness of national science policy, to judge the effectiveness of education programs, and more. This diversity in focus and scope of evaluation work is accompanied by considerable variation in methods and methodologies including the use of surveys, field observations, interviewing, econometric methods, field experiments, cost-benefit analysis, and network and geospatial analysis. For its foundational ideas (for example, the meaning of evaluation, the role of evaluation in society, the notion of building evaluation capacity in organizations), its understanding of the fields in which it operates, and many of its methods, evaluation draws on other disciplines.

The individuals who make up the community of professional practitioners are a diverse lot as well. For some, the practice of evaluation is a specialty taken up by academic researchers within a particular field like economics, sociology, education, nursing, public health, or applied psychology. For others, it is a professional career pursued as privately employed or as an employee of a government, not-for-profit or for-profit agency. There are three broad types of evaluation professionals: (1) experienced evaluators who have been practicing for some time either as privately employed, as an employee of a research organization or local, state, federal, or international agency, or as an academic; (2) novices entering the field of program evaluation for the first time seeking to develop knowledge and skills; and (3) "accidental evaluators," that is, people without training who have been given responsibility for conducting evaluations as part of their portfolio of responsibilities and who are trying to sort out exactly what will be necessary to do the job.[6]

Preparation for the Practice

With only two exceptions (evaluation practice in Canada and Japan), at the present time there are no formal credentialing or certification requirements to become an evaluator. Some individuals receive formal training and education in evaluation in master's and doctoral degree programs throughout the U.S. and elsewhere in the world.[7] However, at the doctoral level, evaluation is rarely, if ever, taught as a formal academic field in its own right but as a subfield or specialty located and taught within the concepts, frameworks, methods, and theories of fields such as sociology, economics, education, social work, human resource education, public policy, management, and organizational psychology.

Perhaps the most significant sources of preparation for many who are "accidental evaluators," or those just learning about the practice while employed in some other professional capacity, are short courses, training institutes, workshops, and webinars often sponsored by professional evaluation associations; certificate programs offered by universities in online or traditional classroom settings;[8] and "toolkits" prepared by agencies and available on the Internet.[9] The rapid development and expansion of these types of training resources are, in part, a response to the demand from practitioners in various social service, educational, and public health occupations to learn the basics of evaluation models and techniques because doing an evaluation has become one of their job responsibilities (perhaps permanently but more often only temporarily).[10]

This trend to "train up" new evaluators is also consistent with broader cultural efforts to scientize and rationalize the professional practices of education, health care, and social services by focusing directly on measurable performance, outcomes, and the development of an evidence base of best practices. In this climate, evaluators function as technicians who, when equipped with tools for doing results-based management, program monitoring, performance assessment, and impact evaluation, provide reliable evidence of outcomes and contribute to the establishment of this evidence base. However, while providing evidence for accountability and decision making is certainly an important undertaking, the danger in this way of viewing the practice of evaluation is that assurance is substituted for valuation. Evaluation comes to be seen for the most part as one of the technologies needed for assuring effective and efficient management and delivery of programs as well as for documenting achievement of targets and expected outcomes.[11] The idea that evaluation is a form of critical appraisal concerned with judging value begins to fade from concern.

At worst, this trend to narrowly train contributes to the erosion of the ideal of evaluation as a form of social trusteeship, whereby a professional's work contributes to the public good, and its replacement with the notion of technical professionalism, where the professional is little more than a supplier of expert services to willing buyers.[12] Focusing almost exclusively on efforts to train individuals to do evaluation can readily lead to a divorce of technique from the calling that brought forth the professional field in the first place. Furthermore, while learning about evaluation approaches along with acquiring technical skills in designing and conducting evaluation are surely essential to being a competent practitioner, a primary focus on training in models and methods (whether intending to do so or not) can create the impression that evaluation primarily requires only "knowing how."

Rationale for the Book

Taking some license with an idea borrowed from the organizational theorist Chris Argyris, we might characterize evaluation training in "knowing how" as a type of single-loop learning. It is learning problem solving, how to apply procedures and rules to be sure we are, in a phrase, "doing things right."[13] In single-loop learning we take the goals, values, norms, and frameworks that underlie why we do what we do for granted. Argyris contrasted the reactive mindset of single-loop learning with the productive mindset of double-loop learning. The latter asks, "Are we doing the right things?" and involves examining and reassessing goals, values, and frameworks by asking "why" and "so what" that help improve understanding. Triple-loop learning goes even further by challenging existing learning frameworks as well as mental models and assumptions. The core question is "What makes this the right thing to do?"[14] This kind of learning involves examining one's professional identity and the aims of one's profession as well as how one's frame of reference, style of thinking, and behavior produce both intended and unintended consequences. It is toward the cultivation of double-loop and triple-loop learning in evaluation that this book is addressed.

This aim reflects my longstanding concern that training in technique in evaluation must be wedded to education in both the disposition and the capacity to engage in moral, ethical, and political reflection on the aim of one's professional undertaking. A few years ago, I encountered a wonderful phrase that captures this idea. In 2002–2003, the Carnegie Foundation for the Advancement of Teaching convened a seminar as part of its continuing examination of education for the professions. In that seminar, participants were invited to discuss pedagogical approaches across the disciplines that would help students develop a "life of the mind for practice." Participants defined this notion as "critical thinking through lived situations that demand action with and on behalf of others."[15] Developing "a life of the mind for practice" certainly involves all three types of learning sketched above. However, the phrase particularly draws our attention to the fact that professional practice requires both a capacity for discretionary judgment (critical thinking that issues in appropriate actions) and a clear realization of the social purpose of the practice (action with and on behalf of others).

To possess a life of the mind for evaluation practice is to recognize that professional practice is a matter of designing means for investigating and rendering a judgment of value that will be effective in light of contextual circumstances, political and ethical considerations, client expectations, and resource constraints. It is to realize that assumptions that evaluation practitioners and the public make about the purpose and roles of evaluation, how and why it is of service to society, the uses to which evaluation knowledge is put, and the evidence employed in arguments about value are almost always contested or contestable and must constantly be revisited in professional practice. A "life of the mind for practice" is required because central to the nature of what we call professional work is the notion that it lacks uniformity in the problems it must contend with and the solutions it must invent. Donald Schön argued that the problems of real-world professional practice are really not problems at all but messy, undefined situations that he called "indeterminate zones of practice—uncertainty, uniqueness, and value conflict—[that] escape the canons of technical rationality."[16] By that he meant that approaches to technical problem solving, the clear-cut application of theories or techniques from the store of professional knowledge, and unambiguous means-end reasoning simply fail to be useful in addressing such problems. To face these kinds of situations and act appropriately, the professional must learn practical reason or the capacity for discretionary judgment.[17]

A vital aspect in the development of a life of the mind for practice is thoughtful, perceptive, and continual engagement with what, for lack of a better term, could be called the contemporary landscape of evaluation issues. These are problems, questions, disputes, and concerns that the professional practice of evaluation, as a particular kind of disciplined inquiry, must always contend with. As one experienced evaluator put it, these issues, "by their very nature, are never finally solved, only temporarily resolved . . . [and they] influence the character of evaluation theory, method, practice, and, indeed, the profession itself."[18]

The landscape encompasses assumptions, principles, values, and ways of reasoning that inform how evaluators define and position their professional activity and argue for the usefulness of their work to society. It includes notions about what comprises evaluative evidence and how that evidence is used to make claims about the merit, worth, or significance of policies and programs. It incorporates perspectives on the ethical conduct, political stance, and professional obligations of evaluation professionals. Moreover, this landscape is inescapably multi- and interdisciplinary with concepts, theories, and empirical findings from social psychology, political science, organizational theory, philosophy, and other fields informing perspectives on key issues. Evaluators inescapably engage features of this landscape as they define and navigate their practice and interact with evaluation funders, clients, and users.

How best to portray this landscape is no small challenge. Several hand-books and other resources provide more encyclopedic coverage than is offered here.[19] My goal is to offer a responsible, but modest, overview in a way that is accessible to novice and accidental evaluators yet inviting of further reflection by seasoned ones. I have taken a cue from an earlier attempt to argue what the field is and ought to be concerned with. In 1991 William Shadish, Thomas Cook, and Laura Leviton offered the first comprehensive effort to map what they referred to as the foundations of program evaluation. They held that their book was "meant to encourage the theoretical dispositions of practitioners by expanding their repertoire of methods, challenging the assumptions behind their methodological and strategic decisions, and creating a broader conceptual framework for them to use in their work."[20] Their expectation was that, upon engaging their analysis of several major theorists' perspectives, readers would be able to better address key questions related to how social programs contribute to social problem solving, why and when evaluations should be done, the evaluator's role, what constitutes credible evaluation knowledge, how judgments of value are to be made, and how evaluation knowledge is used.

While this book is not as thorough an appraisal as theirs, nor organized around the work of evaluation theorists, it shares a similar interest in broadening the conceptual framework of evaluators by portraying a range of key ideas, concepts, and tasks that foreground the professional practice of evaluation as a particular form of disciplined inquiry. Accordingly, I have opted to survey the landscape in such a way that readers can consider the following questions:

- How are we to understand the variability and heterogeneity that characterizes the practice?
- What is the role of theory in evaluation?
- How are notions of value and valuing to be understood?
- What is evaluative evidence and how is it used in evaluative arguments?
- How is evaluation related to politics?
- What does the use of evaluation entail?
- What comprises professional conduct in evaluation, and what might the professionalization of the practice involve?

The term *professional practice* is used intentionally to signify that evaluation is not simply a technical undertaking. Undoubtedly, effective practice requires a wide range of skills for the competent execution of all manner of tasks involved in evaluating including negotiating a contract, preparing an evaluation budget, designing an evaluation, managing an evaluation, choosing or designing instruments and means of data collection, analyzing data, reporting, and so forth. However, in addition to knowing how, evaluation practice requires knowing why. Examining "knowing why" is critical to a life of the mind for practice. The skill of knowing why is cultivated through an engagement with conceptual, practical, and theoretical knowledge that offers resources for answering the questions listed above. Engagement means not simply familiarity with this knowledge, but using it to develop reasoned viewpoints and warranted actions.

The term *disciplined inquiry* is defined much in the same manner as Lee Cronbach and Patrick Suppes used it more than forty years ago. It refers to a systematic, empirical process of discovery and verification, wherein the argument is clear, and the logical processes that link evidence to credible conclusions are apparent.[21] Evaluation is a form of disciplined inquiry concerned with the determination of value. This particular trait distinguishes it from forms of disciplined inquiry that employ social science methods in service of diagnosing, explaining, and solving social problems. Evaluation is concerned with the merits of various approaches to social problem solving and thus shares with those types of inquiry a broad ambition to contribute to social betterment.

Plan of the Book

The chapters aim to present material on the nature and practice of evaluation in such a way as to appeal to two audiences. The expectation is that that those new to the practice might consider what is presented here an invitation to explore the field, while those more seasoned hands might find some new perspectives on familiar material. Chapter 1 briefly introduces the issue of the heterogeneity and variability of evaluation practice by highlighting several fundamental disagreements about the meaning of evaluation, its purpose, methods, and the role and responsibility of the evaluator. Subsequent chapters discuss other ways in which the practice displays significant variations in both its understanding of key concepts and in its self-conception. Chapters 2 through 7 are organized around three broad objectives: to describe the significant dimensions of the topic in question and indicate key issues; to introduce, but not necessarily resolve, controversies and debates in each area; and to suggest, where appropriate, what appears to be gaining traction as a new issue or direction in professional evaluation practice.

Chapter 2 presents a viewpoint on how theory is related to practice in evaluation and explores ways in which theoretical knowledge can be useful to practice. Chapter 3 discusses issues related to values and valuing in evaluation. It seeks to clarify the multiple ways in which the term *values* figures in evaluation (e.g., as the criterion for determining merit, worth, significance; as the perspective of the individual evaluator; as broadly held social values); it examines the common problem of values disagreement among stakeholders to an evaluation; and it discusses ways in which the activity of valuing is performed in evaluation. Chapter 4 is concerned with how evidence and argument are central to evaluation practice. It discusses the properties of evidence and the character of evaluative judgments. Politics in and of evaluation is the topic of Chapter 5, which explores the multiple ways in which relations between evaluation, politics, and policymaking are understood. Evaluation is inherently a political activity in multiple ways. For example, the very activity of conducting an evaluation involves one in the micro-politics of negotiating contracts, access to and control of data, and navigating among the competing views of stakeholders. At a macro-level, the decision to evaluate is a political act and the value of evaluation as a social enterprise is linked to conceptions of how it best serves a democratic society. Chapter 6 addresses the complicated matter of what it means to use evaluation. It expands upon current ways in which use is discussed in the evaluation literature by bringing to bear what we know from a broader literature on knowledge utilization and the relationship between experts and citizens. Chapter 7 is concerned with issues related to the professional obligations and conduct of evaluators. It takes up issues surrounding professional integrity and discusses efforts of the profession to evaluate its own work. The book concludes with some final thoughts about educational preparation for professional practice.

1   Variability in Evaluation Practice

Best practices have become the most sought after form of knowledge.
Not just effective practices, or decent practices, or better practices—but best.[1]

*Patton,
2001*

A focus on best practices, toolkits, practice guidelines, and the like arises fairly naturally in the context of concerns about variation in professional practice. The terms *variation* and *variability*, as commonly used, signify unevenness, deviation, or divergence from norms or standards, discrepancy, or inconsistency.

Every profession is concerned about variability both for reasons of quality assurance and from the standpoint of ensuring that practitioners consistently deliver on the fundamental purpose of the practice regardless of the particular circumstances in which they work.

There are two general views on the nature of variability in professional practice:[2] One holds that variation is a challenge to the rational basis of practice and could be eliminated if practitioners had clear guidelines, including protocols and rules for decision making. Researchers as well as some practitioners who argue that decisions made in practice are too often based on habit and intuition and lack a firm grounding in empirical evidence endorse this view. (One contemporary example of this idea is evident in the book *Moneyball*, the story of Billy Beane, who pioneered the use of sabermetrics—objective knowledge about baseball players' performance based on players' statistics—versus the tradition of relying on the intuitions of a team's scouts to evaluate players.)[3] Concerns about restoring the rational basis of practice are also informed, in part, by nearly fifty years of empirical studies examining whether predictions made by expert clinicians are superior to those made by simple statistical rules or algorithms—about 60% of the studies have shown significantly better accuracy for the statistical rules.[4] Finally, support for this way of thinking also comes from those who argue that practice ought to be primarily technically based; that is, it should consist of the application of scientifically validated knowledge.[5]

A second view holds that variability is inherent in multiple dimensions of the environment where a practice is performed (think of variation in both resources and the composition of patient populations in hospitals in rural versus metropolitan areas, for example) and thus it is always an aspect of normal practice. In this view, by definition, practice involves flexibility and constant adjustments and modifications. Generally, those who hold this view subscribe to a judgment-based view of practice as comprised of actions informed by situated judgments of practitioners.[6] Rather than encouraging the development of practices that are protocol-driven and rule following, advocates of this view of variability support the idea of developing practical wisdom. They also challenge the idea that intuition often employed by practitioners is an irrational, unscientific process and cannot be improved or sharpened, so to speak.[7] However, this perspective on variability as a normal dimension of practice does not necessarily mean that addressing and managing variation in practice is not a problem.

Responses to practice variation encompass a range of different actions. Evidence-based approaches to practice promote the use of protocols, practice guidelines, and in some cases rules (consider rules regarding nursing care for patients with dementia, for example) for how practitioners should provide services.[8] Another response involves developing performance measures for practitioners based on protocols. In order to identify behaviors or actions considered outside practice norms, a practitioner's performance is measured and compared to standards or targets; in other words, professional practice is audited and the results of the audit fed back to the practitioner to change behavior.[9] Still other responses involve developing lists of best practices and toolkits that, while perhaps not intended to achieve complete standardization of practice, aim to help practitioners operate on some common ground with shared understandings of concepts, methods, ethical guidelines, and so on.[10]

As suggested by the broad description of the field in the Prologue, variation in evaluation practice is common. No doubt, heightened awareness of this state of affairs of the practice and the motivation to address it have been fueled by the evidence-based movement that has developed across the professions of nursing, social work, teaching, counseling, and clinical medicine. At the heart of this movement is the idea that practitioners ought to use models and techniques that have been shown to be effective based on scientific research. (However, whether what are often touted as best practices are actually backed by scientific evidence is another matter.) Exactly where and when the idea of best practices that originated in the business world migrated to the field of evaluation is not clear, yet the term is no longer a buzzword confined to business enterprises. The literature is full of best practice approaches for evaluating just about everything, including leadership development programs, faculty performance, think tanks, public health interventions, and teacher education programs, to name but a few targets.[11] Moreover, there is a growing sense in the field that although evaluators operate in a world marked by complex contextual conditions, that world "is not so fluid that meaningful patterns cannot be appreciated and used as a basis for action."[12] Hence, in recent years we have witnessed efforts to develop practice guidelines for matching methods to specific evaluation circumstances, as well as guidelines for choosing appropriate means for determining program value in different contexts.[13]

Multiple sources of variability in evaluation practice will be discussed throughout this book. Here, I focus on four primary sources: how evaluation is defined, what methods an evaluator ought to employ, how the professional evaluator relates to and interacts with parties to an evaluation, and how the purpose of the practice is understood.

Defining "Evaluation"

There is no universally agreed upon definition of evaluation, although there are two primary points of view. The first emphasizes that evaluation is an activity concerned with judging value; the second views evaluation as a form of applied research.

In a precise sense—what one would find in dictionary definitions—evaluation refers to the cognitive activity of determining and judging the value of some object, which could be an activity, event, performance, process, product, policy, practice, program, or person. Evaluation is a matter of asking and answering questions about the value of that object (its quality, merit, worth, or significance).[14] The four-step logic involved in doing an evaluation defined in this way is as follows:

1. Select criteria of merit (i.e., those aspects on which the thing being evaluated must do well on to be judged good).

2. Set standards of performance on those criteria (i.e., comparative or absolute levels that must be exceeded to warrant the application of the word "good").

3. Gather data pertaining to the performance of the thing being evaluated on the criteria relative to the standards.

4. Integrate the results into a final value judgment.[15]

Defenders of this understanding of evaluation argue that unless one is using this logic and employing evaluation-specific methodologies directly concerned with means of determining value—for example, needs and values assessment and evaluative synthesis methodologies (combining evaluative ratings on multiple dimensions or components to come to overall conclusions)—one is literally not doing *evaluation*.[16] In this view, evaluation is a particular kind of critical thinking that follows a specific logic of analysis necessary for appraising value. That logic can be applied to the evaluation of literally anything. A strong statement of this view appears in the *Encyclopedia of Evaluation*, where we find that it is the "judgment about the value of something . . . that distinguishes evaluation from other types of inquiry, such as basic science research, clinical epidemiology, investigative journalism, or public polling."[17]

However, many practitioners of evaluation define it differently as a specific type of applied social science research (i.e., *evaluation research*) concerned with the processes of collecting, analyzing, interpreting, and communicating information about how a program or policy is working and whether or not it is effective.[18] These practitioners employ the standard tools of the social scientist (experiments, surveys, interviews, field observations, econometric methods) to monitor program processes and to answer questions of whether a policy or program works and why. A prominent concern in evaluation research is establishing the causal link between a program or policy and intended outcomes. A strong advocate of this way of understanding evaluation summarized it as follows: "Evaluation is social research applied to answering policy-oriented questions. As such, an important criterion for judging evaluations is the extent to which they successfully apply the canons of social science."[19]

The central issue here is whether this disagreement in definition is a difference that makes a difference, and for whom. From the perspective of many agencies both domestically and internationally that promote and conduct evaluation, it appears that the two perspectives are sometimes combined and broadly interpreted in yet even different ways. For example, the W.K. Kellogg Foundation defines evaluation not as an event occurring at the completion of program but as a process "providing ongoing, systematic information that strengthens projects during their life cycle, and, whenever possible, outcome data to assess the extent of change" and "helps decision makers better understand the project; how it is impacting participants, partner agencies and the community; and how it is being influenced/impacted by both internal and external factors."[20] The United Nations Development Programme (UNDP) Independent Evaluation Office defines evaluation as "judgment made of the relevance, appropriateness, effectiveness, efficiency, impact and sustainability of development efforts, based on agreed criteria and benchmarks among key partners and stakeholders."[21] For the U.S. Government Accountability Office, "a program evaluation is a systematic study using research methods to collect and analyze data to assess how well a program is working and why."[22] Finally, the Department of International Development (DFID) of the U.K. government argues that evaluation is a collection of approaches "focuse[d], in particular, on whether planned changes have taken place, how changes have impacted, or not, on different groups of people and investigates the theory behind the change. . . ."[23]

From another perspective, held by at least some evaluators, it is quite important to take an analytical philosophical approach to answering the question, "What can and should legitimately be called the activity of 'evaluating' irrespective of the circumstances in which it is conducted, the object being evaluated, and expectations for its use?" It is important because defining what is actually "evaluation" is intimately related to establishing one's professional identity as an evaluator as distinct from the identity of others engaged in related pursuits like applied social research, program auditing, organization development, and management consulting. After all, claims to expertise are built around distinctive knowledge, theories, and methods. If evaluators cannot lay claim to and agree on the definition and central purpose of their practice (and their own unique body of knowledge) then their identity as a specific kind of professional practice is at risk.[24] Other evaluation practitioners appear to be less concerned with this matter of professional identity, or at least do not see that the issue depends on resolving this definitional dispute. Many who regard evaluation as the application of social science methods are content to view evaluation as a compendium of approaches, concepts, and methods serving multiple purposes and taught as a specialization within social science fields such as economics, psychology, sociology, and political science.

The definitional problem surfaces in an additional way in the international development evaluation community, where it is not uncommon to find the expression *monitoring and evaluation* (M&E).[25] Many in the evaluation community aim to clearly distinguish monitoring from evaluation. The former is, more or less, the ongoing, routine tracking of a program to diagnose problems in implementation—are we taking the actions we said we would take, delivering the services we said we would deliver, reaching the clients we said we would reach?—and to make adjustments accordingly. It is also a process for tracking performance against stated goals. In this case it is often referred to as *performance measurement* or *performance monitoring.*[26] Monitoring is a management tool that assists in timely decision making, ensures accountability, and provides a basis for learning and for evaluation. However, evaluation focuses on objective, independent judgments of value around outputs, processes, and outcomes. When compared to monitoring, the focus of evaluation is less on the determination of what is being accomplished and more on the value of those accomplishments. The difference is summarized in Table 2.

In this book evaluation is regarded primarily as a practice concerned with judging the value of programs and policies. Those judgments can take several generic forms including those listed below:

- X is good as determined by its performance against a set of criteria.
- X is better (more valuable) than Y as determined by comparing X and Y on a set of criteria.
- X is better (more valuable) than Y because X produces the intended outcome and Y does not.
- X is better (more valuable) than Y because, although they both produce the intended outcome, X is more effective or efficient than Y in producing that outcome.
- X is better (more valuable) than Y because, although they both produce the intended outcome, X is more relevant and sustainable.

Table 2. Differences between Monitoring and Evaluation

Focus	Sample Monitoring Questions	Sample Evaluation Questions
Outputs (Products, services, deliverables, and reach)	How many people or communities were reached or served? Were the targeted numbers reached?	• *How adequate* was program reach? • Did we reach *enough* people? • Did we reach the *right* people?
Process (Design and implementation)	How was the program implemented? Was implementation in accordance with design and specifications?	• *How well* was the program implemented—fairly, ethically, legally, culturally appropriately, professionally, and efficiently? • For outreach, did we use the best avenues and methods we could have? • How well did we access hard-to-reach, vulnerable populations and those with the greatest need? • Who missed out, and was that fair, ethical, and just?
Outcomes (Things that happen to people or communities)	What has changed since (and as a result of) program implementation? How much have outcomes changed relative to targets?	• *How substantial and valuable* were the outcomes? • How well did they meet the most important needs and help realize the most important aspirations? • Were outcomes truly impressive, mediocre, or unacceptably weak? • Were they not just statistically significant, but educationally, socially, economically, and practically significant? • Did they make a real difference in people's lives? • Were the outcomes worth achieving given the effort and investment to obtain them?

Source: Adapted with permission from Jane Davidson, "Monitoring and Evaluation: Let's Get Crystal Clear on the Difference," *Genuine Evaluation,* Jan. 14, 2013. Available at http://genuine evaluation.com/monitoring-and-evaluation-lets-get-crystal-clear-on-the-difference/

Choosing Methods

Almost from its beginnings, the field of evaluation has exhibited considerable variation in (and conflicts over) the choice of evaluation methods. Debates, often quite heated, raged in the 1970s and 1980s over the relative merits and appropriate uses of quantitative data and statistical methods associated with psychological and achievement measurement and experimental designs versus qualitative data as generated in case studies and via the use of ethnographic methods.[27] Method debates are generally proxies for deeper differences surrounding what evaluation should be examining. On the one hand, there are evaluators who view policies and programs as "thing-like" objects with identifiable properties (e.g., inputs, processes, outcomes, impacts) that can be readily defined and measured using methods for collecting and analyzing quantitative data. On the other hand, there are evaluators who view programs as multifaceted compositions of human experiences permeated with multiple meanings. Thus, rather than employing methods suited to a variable- and measurement-oriented approach to evaluation, these evaluators use methods associated with ethnographic work including open-ended or unstructured interviews, field observations, and so forth. These methods are used to generate data and evaluation findings that build upon "experiential, personal knowing in real space and time and with real people" and are "steadfastly responsive to the chronological activity, the perceptions, and the voices of people" associated with what is being evaluated.[28]

Something approaching a détente between advocates of these so-called quantitative versus qualitative evaluation approaches began to emerge in the mid 1990s as mixed-methods thinking began to take hold and support for the idea became more widespread.[29] Mixed methods refers to the intentional or planned use of methodologies for collecting and analyzing both qualitative and quantitative data in the same study.[30] However, the controversy over best methods once again heated up in the early 2000s in view of intensive efforts on the part of several U.S. federal agencies to promote the near-exclusive use of experimental designs in evaluation research and the very influential movement across the world of international development evaluation to focus on impact evaluation via the use of experimental and econometric methods.[31] The tension persists between advocates of designing evaluations using field studies and methods to generate and analyze qualitative data to understand the experience of program participants versus those employing experimental studies and statistical analyses of quantitative data for the purposes of determining causal claims.[32]

While acknowledging that choices of methods follow from the needs and constraints of particular contexts, one notable recent attempt to address (although not necessarily resolve) this tension argues that the field needs to develop an evidence base for methods choice. It also argues that strong causal knowledge should be treated as a public good, thus warranting special attention in evaluation policies to methodologies that yield such knowledge.[33] Here we have yet another example of how to address variability in evaluation practice.

Adopting a Stance as an Evaluator

Within the practice there are differing views on the evaluator's role and responsibilities relative to those who are most intimately involved with a program (stakeholders such as staff, managers, beneficiaries, clients). This variation in the understanding of professional obligation has significant consequences for how one interprets the ethical and political aspects of one's responsibility as an evaluator. Some evaluators regard stakeholders primarily as sources of data—they are "subjects" in the parlance of social science research that employs methods such as survey research and experimentation. In the U.S., relations between evaluators and research subjects are guided in large part by the ethical principles codified in the Federal Policy for Human Subjects (generally referred to as the "Common Rule") that cover such matters as respect for persons, informed consent, assessment of risk of participation, and so on.

In the field of evaluation there are also adherents to what are broadly defined as stakeholder-based or participatory approaches.[34] Although there is considerable disagreement in the field on what falls under the umbrella of "participatory,"[35] one generally accepted view is that in these approaches program stakeholders are involved in decision making related to planning and implementing an evaluation. The extent of that involvement varies, with genuinely participatory or collaborative evaluation signaling a partnership between the evaluator and those who participate in the evaluation. Typically, partnership means the involvement of program staff and participants in setting the focus for the evaluation, instrument development, data collection, interpreting, and reporting. The evaluator works as facilitator and collaborator in the process.[36] Key characteristics of this kind of evaluation include:

- Structures and processes are created to include those most frequently powerless or voiceless in program design and implementation. The participatory process honors human contributions and cultural knowledge.

- Participants commit to work together to decide on the evaluation focus, how it should be conducted, how findings will be used, and what action will result. Often the process requires addressing differences in point of view and conflicts.

- Participants learn together to take corrective actions and improve programs.

- Creative methodologies are used to match the resources, needs, and skills of participants.[37]

A somewhat different notion of partnering is evident in developmental evaluation that is intended to support an ongoing process of innovation within an organization.[38] The developmental evaluator enters a long-term partnering relationship with a team engaged in designing, testing, continuously adapting, and improving these innovative initiatives. In the team, the evaluator's primary function "is to elucidate team discussions with evaluative questions, data and logic, and to facilitate data based assessments and decision-making in the unfolding and developmental processes of innovation."[39]

Of course, the general ethical advice contained in the Common Rule applies in these types of evaluation as well. However, the interactive and dialogical processes that characterize evaluator involvement here raise additional ethical concerns or at least complicate the matter of ethical behavior, a phenomenon widely acknowledged in fields such as participatory action research, community-based research, and collaborative ethnography. Furthermore, many participatory approaches are practiced from an avowed political stance of transforming the social conditions under which program beneficiaries live, and that raises the issue of evaluator objectivity and whether it is legitimate for evaluators to be advocates for particular kinds of social change. The variation in practice here and the issues that it raises echo a long-standing concern in the field about whether "closeness," so to speak, to the concerns of stakeholders on the part of the evaluator and the involvement of stakeholders in decisions about what to evaluate and how will inevitably lead to biased conclusions about the value of a program.[40]

Determining the Purpose of Evaluation in Society

Evaluation is a social practice that occupies a particular place within an organizational or community setting, reflecting the goals, aspirations, and interests of the people in that organization or community. This results in different ideas about the purpose and use of evaluation. Consider, for example, the practice of evaluation as specifically located within indigenous societies (American Indian, Native Alaskan, Maori, Pacific Islanders, etc.) and undertaken by indigenous peoples. The activity of evaluation is grounded here in the traditional ways of knowing and core values of these peoples. Evaluation is used in service of self-determination and to reverse the devastating effects of social and educational practices imposed on indigenous peoples.[41]

Compare that to the purpose of evaluation as reflected in the worldwide Campbell Collaboration dedicated to improving decision making at the levels of both policymaking and practice through providing systematic reviews on the effects of programs in the areas of education, social welfare, crime and justice, and international development. The aim is to achieve an unvarnished, hard-nosed, objective appraisal of what the data reveal regarding what works (and what doesn't). The Campbell Collaboration argues systematic reviews are a first, but not the only, step in building evidence-based policy. There must also be mechanisms to establish and maintain ongoing dialogue between evaluation researchers, policymakers, and end users.

Finally, consider the Rockefeller Foundation's evaluation strategy. It has argued that foundations and development agencies committed to improving the lives of the poor and vulnerable in developing countries must reform evaluations they fund and undertake if they aspire to play a meaningful role in social transformation for rethinking and reshaping evaluation. Rockefeller endorses five principles for repositioning evaluation—principles articulated by African evaluation leaders and policymakers at the January 2012 gathering of the African Evaluation Association's biannual conference in Accra, Ghana. These principles include:

- Hearing, respecting, and internalizing the voices of program beneficiaries in order to effectively evaluate what success should look like for the people we are most concerned about.

- Regarding evaluative knowledge as a public good to be widely shared—not limited to boards and program teams, but shared widely with grantees, partners, and peers.

- Addressing evaluation asymmetries between developed and developing regions. The majority of human and financial resources for evaluation emanate from agencies and foundations based in the developed world with evaluators from developing countries playing a minor role, if any. Many of these evaluators do not get sufficient experience to move into leadership roles where they can conduct and use evaluation results for social transformation.

- Broadening the objects of evaluation to move beyond the individual grant or project to a more strategic assessment of portfolios of investments, policy change, new financing mechanisms, and sector-wide approaches.

- Investing in the development and application of innovative new methods and tools for evaluation and monitoring that reflect multi-disciplinary and systems approaches to problems and complexity, that assess network effectiveness and policy change, and that use new technology to enable stakeholders to provide close to real-time data and feedback.[42]

Each of these sets of circumstances is more than simply a context in which a relatively uniform practice of evaluation unfolds. Each example illustrates that different arrangements of social, political, and cultural circumstances both support and constitute evaluation as a specific kind of undertaking with a particular kind of orientation and a clear preference for specific forms of evidence relevant to appraisals of program value. These and similar variations in conceptions of the practice and its purpose sit rather uneasily alongside one another, for example a service-to-clients orientation with a more critical and transformative stance or a data-analytic orientation characteristic of experimentation next to the demands of a dialogical, engaged participatory approach.[43]

Implications

This chapter has introduced the idea of variability in evaluation practice—a theme that permeates this book. It is not news that all professional practices exhibit variation. In some fields, the variation is so significant and the body of knowledge and techniques so extensive that specializations develop. In law, for example, there are specialties in maritime, corporate, employment, sports, criminal, and environmental law, to name but a few; specialties and subspecialties are well known in the field of medicine. Yet, even taking this kind of practice variability into account, we recognize that practitioners in the long established professions of law, medicine, and accounting share something of a common conception of the social purpose of their respective undertakings as well as a professional identity. Arguably, although the field of evaluation may generally accept the premise that what evaluators do is evaluate, answers to questions about what exactly that means, how it should be done, and what the evaluator's role is and should be in the process display considerable variability.

In 1991, three astute observers of the state of the art of evaluation theory and practice noted that there were several unresolved issues in evaluation, including:[44]

- Should evaluators work as change agents?
- By whose criteria of merit should we judge social programs?
- Should evaluation results be synthesized into a single value judgment?
- What methods should evaluators use?
- What should the role of the evaluator be?
- What values should be represented in the evaluation?

Nearly two decades later, two evaluators with long track records wrote that fundamental issues in evaluation remained, including:[45]

- Why should evaluation be undertaken?
- What is the proper role for the evaluator?
- How should stakeholders be involved in an evaluation?
- What constitutes acceptable evidence for evaluation decisions?
- How should we arrive at the most valid understanding of program quality (e.g., via experimentation, deliberation, phenomenological rendering)?

For present purposes the central issue is how we should interpret this apparently enduring condition of evaluation practice variability. One interpretation is that variation is undesirable and ought to be reduced via the development of best practices, uniform toolkits, and other means such as approved lists of competencies on which to base training programs, certification requirements, and practice standards. Another interpretation holds that variability need not necessarily be a negative appraisal of the state of the practice, for it is entirely possible that evaluation practice is best understood in pluralist terms.

As commonly used, pluralism signifies a multiplicity of views and heterogeneity. It is a type of reaction to the variety of traditions, philosophic orientations, methodologies, political perspectives, cultural views, values, and so on that characterize not simply the current scene in evaluation but life more generally. Pluralism can take several forms: (a) fragmenting pluralism—here one communicates only with one's own group and sees no need to engage with others outside that circle; (b) flabby pluralism—where one poaches ideas and methods from different orientations in a superficial way; (c) polemical pluralism—where different orientations are used as ideological weapons; (d) defensive pluralism—a form of tokenism where lip service is paid to the fact that others do their own thing, but we are already convinced that there is nothing to be learned from them; (e) engaged fallibilistic pluralism, which means taking seriously the weaknesses and shortcomings of one's own position and being genuinely committed to listening to the views of others without dismissing those views as obscure, imprecise, confused or trivial.[46]

A pluralist evaluation practice would recognize and affirm diversity within its ranks and be quite comfortable embracing different understandings of its purpose, means, convictions, and interests. In such a practice, tensions in definitions, debates over methods, arguments about the merits of different evaluator roles, and disagreements over preferences for uses of evaluation stemming from organizational missions and realities are likely never to be resolved. Different views on these matters would simply peacefully (for the most part) coexist or perhaps, at best, meet each other in an engaged fallibilistic way.

Pluralism with respect to the meaning, aims, and means of evaluation is clearly a *descriptive* statement of the way evaluation *is* at present. Whether pluralism also a *normative* claim, a claim about the way evaluation practice *should* be, is an open question and one that the practice as a whole continually wrestles with. If pluralism is to be regarded as the best view of the practice, then it must be defended by demonstrating how, why, and in what contexts it yields a more adequate understanding of the purpose, conduct, value, and use of evaluation practice than can be had by a single view of the practice's aims and means.[47] Whether such a complete defense is forthcoming in the field remains to be seen.

However, we can be confident that it is precisely because the practice as presently understood exhibits such variability that individuals aspiring to become professional evaluators need to cultivate the capacity for thoughtful awareness of and critical reflection on the sources of differences as well as develop their own respective positions on these matters. To navigate the varied topography of evaluation practice, the evaluation practitioner needs more than an *awareness* of the variability sketched in this chapter. The practitioner also needs to develop a reasoned response to that state of affairs. That response is a matter of professional judgment evident in the capacity to engage and take a stance on multiple issues that comprise the core understandings of the practice. One of these issues—how theory is to be understood and used in evaluation practice—is the topic of the next chapter.

2   Evaluation Theory and Practice

> What do we mean by theory? No single understanding of the term is widely
> accepted. Theory connotes a body of knowledge that organizes, categorizes,
> describes, predicts, explains, and otherwise aids in understanding and
> controlling a topic.[1]

Clarifying just what we mean by the terms *theory* and *practice*—or
theoretical and practical knowledge, knowing why and knowing how,
thinking and doing—as well as grasping the relationship between them,
are contested issues in all professions, and evaluation is no exception. We
know that learning does not happen automatically as a result of experience and thus requires theoretical reflection, but we are not quite sure
just how that operates or how it is learned. We know that appeals to
theory—as that underlying, distinctive, general knowledge that defines
the basis of expertise—are located in a broader context of aspirations to
professionalism. But it is the rough ground of everyday, concrete practice
that is most recognized by both practitioners and their clients. At the
same time, we recognize that theory is an important aspect of cultivating
the capacity for autonomous professional judgment that, in turn, distinguishes professional practice from bureaucratic rule following or the
mere application of technique.[2] This chapter offers a perspective on the
meaning of the terms *theory* and *practice* and their relationship in evaluation. In so doing, it takes up several ways in which the notion of theory is
discussed in the field and suggests some new ways of thinking about the
importance of theory.

Theory-Practice Relationship

In the social-behavioral sciences, the term *theory* is usually understood
as scientific theory—an empirically well-confirmed explanation of some

phenomenon that is consistent with the application of scientific criteria recognized within a community of scientists; examples include cognitive theory and behavioral theory in psychology, labeling theory in sociology, and neo-institutional theory in political science. Theoretical knowledge is general knowledge of some phenomenon. It is the kind of knowledge that can be applied over many situations (it is unbiased toward any particular case), and it can be used to understand, explain, predict, or control situations not yet encountered.

As Donald Schön noted several years ago, the idea that dominates most thinking about knowledge for the professions is that practice is the site where this theoretical knowledge is *applied* to solutions to problems of instrumental choice.[3] If we accept this idea, then the professional practice of evaluation would be regarded as the application of the theory (or science) of evaluation (including its definitions, concepts, approaches, and procedures) in much the same way that engineering is the application of engineering science. This idea is consistent with a technically based view of practice that assumes a proven means can be used again and again to produce the same desired outcome. Hence, a set of rules, procedures, or checklists yielding a desired outcome can be passed on to others to follow.[4] The extreme case of practice as the application of scientifically validated theoretical knowledge is when a practice becomes manualized—that is, when "practicing" is a matter of applying a toolkit or following a pre-approved set of procedures or practice guidelines. There is, of course, nothing inherently wrong with providing models, tools, and procedures as resources useful for professional practice; the danger lies in *reducing* practice to the mere application of those things.[5]

However, Schön's studies of practitioners challenged the idea that practice is simply the site of the application of theoretical knowledge. He argued that the problems faced in practice are indeterminate, untidy, and not well formed; they are often referred to as "wicked" problems.[6] They are "wicked" because goals, means, and constraints are not particularly clear; there is the possibility of multiple solutions; there is uncertainty about which concepts, principles, or rules are necessary to address the problem; and the problems are continuous in the sense that they cannot be solved once and for all.[7] Schön claimed that practitioners engaged in reflection-in-action, a kind of ongoing experimentation, as a means to finding a viable solution to such problems. This experimentation yields a particular kind of craft knowledge (or the wisdom of practice). Schön explains:

> The practitioner allows himself to experience surprise, puzzlement, or confusion in a situation [that] he finds uncertain or unique. He reflects on the phenomenon before him, and on the prior understandings [that] have been implicit in his behavior. He carries out an experiment [that] serves to generate both a new understanding of the phenomenon and a change in the situation.[8]

This idea is consistent with a view of practice as comprising actions informed by situated judgments of practitioners. These judgments have the characteristic of being attentive to the particulars at hand, hence variable with situations, deliberative, and improvisational. Because this kind of reasoning is enacted anew in each situation—"What should I do now, in this situation, facing this particular set of circumstances?"—it cannot be captured in theoretical knowledge or general rules and procedures.[9] More recent studies of professional practice emphasize that a practitioner's reasoning is characterized by contextuality, acting that is continuous with knowing, and interaction with others. Taken together, these elements form an account of the kind of practical judgment required of a professional who works in an environment characterized by complexity, indeterminacy, and the necessity to act on the situation at hand.[10]

Practitioners experiment with ideas as sources of possible solutions to the practical problems they face in planning, implementing, and reporting an evaluation. They "theorize" for every case. Theorizing is a self-critical activity in which practitioners subject the beliefs, ideas, and the justifications they give for their ongoing practical activities to rational criticism. The activity of theorizing is thus a way in which they transform practice by transforming the ways in which practice is experienced and understood.[11]

Practice decisions can be enlightened by conceptual or theoretical knowledge that serves as an aid in thinking through options in a situation that a practitioner faces. It is helpful to think of this kind of knowledge as a repertoire of principles, concepts, insights, and explanations that professional practitioners can use as heuristics, tools "to think with." They are aids to the evaluation imagination as practitioners come to understand the problems before them and how those problems might be solved. The activity of problem solving in professional practices is routinized and unimaginative without these bodies of knowledge. Yet, it is also true that, without lessons learned from practice, these bodies of knowledge are abstract and empty of any concrete meaning. Thus theory and practice—or theoretical and practical knowledge, or thinking and doing—exist in a mutually informing relationship. To be sure, there are different knowledge interests at work here—those primarily concerned with developing and testing theory focus on general knowledge; those concerned primarily with practice focus on the specific case at hand and problem solving. Yet, this does not preclude productive interaction between the two. To paraphrase a famous saying from Kant, experience without theory is blind, but theory without experience is mere intellectual play.

Evaluation Theory

Perhaps the most widely discussed body of knowledge in evaluation is evaluation theory. However, it is generally accepted that the phrase *theory of evaluation* does not mean scientific theory, but rather refers to an organized set of ideas about what evaluation is—its goals, aims, methods, and so on. Thus, theory of evaluation is better understood as a body of knowledge composed of evaluation models and approaches (and these terms are used interchangeably in what follows). Michael Scriven's Goal-Free and Consumer-Based approach, Robert Stake's Responsive Evaluation, Stuart Donaldson's notion of Theory-Driven Evaluation Science, David Fetterman's Empowerment Evaluation model, Michael Patton's Utilization-Focused Evaluation, and Daniel Stufflebeam's Content-Input-Process-Product model are but a few examples of the more than two dozen evaluation approaches currently available.

Evaluation models are largely prescriptive because they offer a particular definition, set of principles, key concepts, and procedures for how evaluation *should* be done. These models do not explain how evaluation actually *is* done. In other words, they are not empirical theories that explain how evaluation unfolds in practice. Careful, systematic research on actual practice is needed to develop empirical, descriptive theories or *theories of practice* that "list the tasks that evaluators must do, the options for doing them, the resources required for each, the trade-offs among them, and the justifications for choosing one over another in particular situations."[12] There are few such studies of actual evaluation activities that aim at the development of a theory of practice, although research on evaluation practice is a topic of growing interest in the field in recent years.[13]

There are several ways in which prescriptive models for evaluation have been categorized and analyzed in order to provide an overview of the field. Common schemes differentiate models in terms of the way each

- Focuses an evaluation—for example, on

  Program goals and objectives

  Issues and concerns of those involved with the program

  Intended uses of the evaluation as expressed by intended users

  Causal efficacy—whether the program being evaluated actually caused the effects observed

  Improvement of practice and learning within an organization

  Understanding and appraising issues of power, discrimination, and oppression to enable the transformation of social circumstances

- Involves stakeholders in the evaluation as explained in Chapter 1

- Defines the evaluator's role and responsibilities.[14]

Roles tend to match the way a particular evaluation approach defines its purpose. Evaluators can define their primary role in any of the following ways (and roles can overlap): independent, objective external judge of quality; social researcher contributing to knowledge development and the study of policy; consultant for program improvement, program development, and/or organizational development; facilitator of (and perhaps advocate for) social action; auditor or inspector; and educator.[15]

A recent classification attempt uses an "evaluation theory tree" to identify the primary contributions of evaluation theorists. Theorists are differentiated in terms of whether the primary focus of their work is building our understanding of valuing (focusing on what it means to establish the value of some object of evaluation), use (focusing on what evaluation is used for, e.g., decision making, accountability, organizational learning), or methods (focusing specifically on the methodology and methods used in conducting an evaluation).[16]

There is merit in the in-depth and comparative study of evaluation models.[17] After all, we are indebted to our ancestors, and understanding the history of one's practice and those who helped establish it is important in developing a sense of sharing in a professional community of practice. Familiarity with and examination of evaluation theory as a specific body of knowledge is also important, because, as one prominent evaluator put it several years ago: "it is central to our professional identity. It is what we talk about more than anything else, it gives rise to our most trenchant debates, it gives us the language we use for talking to ourselves and others, and perhaps most important, it is what makes us different from other professions."[18]

Nonetheless, there are good reasons why introducing the study of evaluation via an examination of these models has significant drawbacks. First, although models provide frameworks for thinking about how to focus and organize an evaluation, a practitioner does not actually come across or encounter the task of doing evaluation at the level of theories or models of evaluation. Rather, the tasks of focusing and conducting an evaluation are encountered practically, not in terms of the specifications and features of any given evaluation model. Practical encounters involve dialogue and negotiation with commissioners, clients, and other stakeholders about evaluation objectives, time frames, organizational interests and needs, political issues, ethical concerns, costs, motivations, available means and procedures for data collection, data-gathering constraints, reporting requirements, and so on. Portraying the practice as if it were primarily a matter of making a choice from among a typology of models obscures the fact that every evaluation must confront a common set of issues and it impedes the development of flexible and responsive approaches to addressing those issues. Second, there simply is no one best way to design and conduct an evaluation. For example, a prominent evaluator argues that all evaluators must be skilled in "situational analysis":

> Every evaluation situation is unique. A successful evaluation (one that is useful, practical, ethical, and accurate) emerges from the special characteristics and conditions of a particular situation—a mixture of people, politics, history, context, resources, constraints, values, needs, interests, and chance.[19]

The capacity for situational analysis is a hallmark of competent professionals in every field, and it involves being intentional and reflective about decision making.[20] That capacity does not rest solely on evaluation practitioners' familiarity with the features of evaluation models (e.g., evaluation focus or purpose, methods preferences, stakeholder involvement, etc.). Rather, it is cultivated through being conversant in bodies of knowledge (repertoires of concepts, insights, explanations, and tools) bearing on the design, conduct, and use of evaluation.[21] The remainder of this chapter introduces several of these critically important bodies of knowledge.

Theories of How Programs "Work"

Every social or educational program is based on some set of often-implicit assumptions about how it is supposed to achieve its intended outcomes. This set of assumptions can be made explicit as a program theory and then modeled and portrayed in what is called a logic model (also referred to as a results chain, outcomes chain, causal chain, or social value chain). A very simple pipeline logic model is a linear depiction or description of program components in terms of

Inputs → Activities → Outputs → Outcomes →Impacts

Inputs are the human, material, and financial resources necessary to the production of a program. *Activities* refer to what is done with the resources (e.g., providing housing for the homeless, delivering a training program) to achieve desired ends. *Outputs* are measurable results from the activities undertaken (e.g., number of units of housing occupied, number of people placed into employment). *Outcomes* are changes that occur directly as a result of inputs, activities, and outputs, such as expected changes in attitudes, behaviors, knowledge, skills, status, or level of functioning (e.g., reduction in the number of homeless people, holding a job). Often outcomes are further divided into immediate and intermediate— the former usually referring to changes in attitudes, skills, knowledge, and the latter referring to actual behavioral changes that will lead to long-term *impacts* (reducing unemployment, creating a healthier population).

The theory of program process depicted in a logic model is derived from the conceptualization and design of a program and consideration of its context. It involves understanding and documenting how resources are secured, configured, and deployed, and how program activities are organized to develop and maintain the delivery of a service. It also involves understanding how the intended beneficiaries of a program (the "target population") are to gain access to the service in question and make use of it.[22] Some evaluators argue that the theory of how a program achieves its intended results ought to be informed by behavioral or social science theory and research. For example, in the field of public health, a variety of social-psychological theories (e.g., Social Cognitive Theory, Framing Theory, the Health Belief Model) have been used to design and evaluate health communication campaigns (e.g., campaigns related to safe sexual practices, stopping smoking, obesity prevention, and so on).

Program theory is an alternative to "black box" evaluation that documents the outcomes of a program without examining its internal operation and processes. Specifying program theory is, in other words, a way of getting inside the "black box" to understand not only whether a program achieves its intended effects, but how and why.[23] There is an extensive literature on how to develop program theories through the involvement of stakeholders and there are several methodologies available for developing program theory including the Logical Framework Approach (also called Log Frame and often used in international development evaluation).[24]

Despite the widespread interest in the use of program theory in evaluation, the idea is not without its strong critics.[25] A profound worry about the value of portraying program theory arises from the recognition that many of the interventions or programs that are evaluated are quite complex in that they involve systems of interacting agencies, organizations, and groups. Hence, they simply cannot be realistically portrayed in terms of a linear model where the hypothesized connections between the inputs, activities, outputs, and outcomes of the program are clearly specifiable and where outcomes are directly connected to the program activities in a short time frame.

Several different sets of circumstances can contribute to the complexity of a program.[26] First, intended outcomes are changeable and emergent as, for example, one might find in a community capacity development program that involves multiple projects aimed at increasing social and economic capital. Second, organizations making decisions about the program comprise an emerging list of partners and emerging relationships and responsibilities as, for example, in the Rockefeller Foundation's Disease Surveillance Networks (DSN) Initiative that involves cultivating robust transboundary, multisectoral, and cross-disciplinary collaborative networks that will lead to improved disease surveillance and response.[27] Third, the activities undertaken as part of the program or intervention are not standardized for a particular group of program participants but the intervention is adapted for each individual participant, as, for example, one might find in a health promotion program that uses different activities (brochures, web sites, information booths, public service announcements, workshops) targeted to different audiences and adapted over time to respond to new opportunities and information. Fourth, the relationship between the program or intervention and its outcomes and impacts cannot be readily predicted because (a) the impacts are often the product of a convergence of events; or (b) small differences in one outcome can have disproportionate effects on results as, for example, when an "advocacy program achieved a critical mass of active supporters and was able to produce information resources that went viral, growing exponentially;"[28] or (c) the intervention itself is about creating emerging initiatives such as developing self-organizing networks in the nonprofit sector, and hence the outcomes are not neatly tied to particular actions and are entirely unpredictable and emergent.[29]

In light of these circumstances, ideas from complexity science and systems theory are gaining a foothold in evaluation, planning, and policymaking.[30] Evaluators are examining both new tools of investigation (network analysis, outcome mapping, causal loop diagrams, scenario modeling, agent-based models)[31] and a different mental model or framework for thinking about interventions that is less given to assumptions of linearity, predictable effects, and simple cause-effect chains.[32] Writing about the applicability of this new way of thinking in the field of public health, John Sterman at the MIT Systems Dynamic group observes: "Systems thinking is an iterative learning process in which we replace a reductionist, narrow, short-run, static view of the world with a holistic, broad, long-term dynamic view, reinventing our policies and institutions accordingly."[33]

Theories of Change[34]

Some evaluators distinguish between program theory and program logic models and theories of change (ToC). They argue that the former are descriptive and begin with a particular program and then illustrate its components in a pipeline model, whereas the latter are explanatory, specifically linking outcomes and activities to reveal how and why desired outcomes are expected to come about in a given philanthropic, not-for-profit, or government agency or organization. ToC can be visibly portrayed in multiple ways, but every good theory of change answers the following six questions:

Who are you seeking to influence or benefit (target population)?

What benefits are you seeking to achieve (results)?

When will you achieve them (time period)?

How will you and others make this happen (activities, strategies, resources, etc.)?

Where and under what circumstances will you do your work (context)?
Why do you believe your theory will bear out (assumptions)?[35]

ToC are useful tools for developing solutions to complex social and educational problems because they begin not with a solution (i.e., a particular program) but with a desired outcome or long-term goal and then map backwards to depict a pathway of change that leads to that goal.[36] There are several uses of ToC, including strategic planning (mapping the change process and its expected outcomes facilitates project implementation), description (allows organizations to communicate their chosen change process to internal and external partners), and learning (a ToC helps members to clarify and develop the theory behind their organization or program).[37] ToC for a specific program context can be informed by research associated with more encompassing social-behavioral theories. The latter include theories of individual or behavioral change (e.g., theory of reasoned action, theory of planned behavior, self-efficacy theory) and theories of learning (e.g., behaviorism, social and situated cognition). Theories of organizational change can be helpful as well, particularly for evaluators concerned with using evaluation to build capacity for organizational learning.[38] Two central premises for the use of a ToC approach are that it is a catalyst for learning at the individual, group, and organizational levels and that an organization that links ToC and evaluation will be more effective.[39] Working with and within organizations on evaluation of this kind requires familiarity with the broad body of literature related to organizational dynamics (how an organization works), theories of administrative and organizational behavior and leadership, and theories of how change happens in organizations.[40]

Theories of Causality

Many (but not all) approaches to evaluation are particularly concerned with the outcomes (and longer-term impact) of a program, and specifically with the question of whether observed outcomes are actually attributable to the program in question. Consider, for example, a district that implements a new program in its elementary schools in which grade-level teams meet biweekly to review data on the performance of their students in mathematics to determine what changes must be made in instruction in order to improve student achievement. Two obvious evaluation questions are (1) whether student performance in mathematics increased and (2) whether any observed changes in performance are due to the new program. Or consider the complex circumstances of a multifaceted community-based health program in Sub-Saharan Africa intended to reduce the incidence of neonatal and maternal mortality. The intervention consists of bundled approaches of activities (community support groups, educational campaigns delivered by outreach workers, trained birth attendants working with individual women, rural health clinics). Critical questions include: Can intermediate and short-term outcomes (e.g., more mothers access neonatal and maternal care services) be attributed directly to the complicated intervention and can longer-term impacts (reduction in infant mortality) be attributed directly to the program as a whole?

To address these kinds of concerns, evaluators must know something about ways of understanding and assessing causality.[41] This includes being familiar with several issues. The first issue concerns the debate between evaluators who argue that the most important question to answer is "Does this program work?" versus those who argue that the more important questions are "What works, for whom in what circumstances, in what respects, and how?"[42] A second issue is evident in arguments and counterarguments for randomized, controlled experiments with their appeal to a counterfactual understanding of causality ("If the program had not occurred the outcomes would not have occurred") as the best designs for establishing causal inferences.[43] A third issue is about the difference between statements of causal *attribution* and causal *contribution*. Attribution is a matter of determining the direct relationship between a program or policy and its outcomes by investigating the question "Has the program caused the effects?" Contribution is a matter of determining ways in which the program might have made a difference by asking, "In view of the many factors that can influence an outcome, has the program made a noticeable contribution, and how?" Contribution analysis is emerging as a major methodology in evaluation.[44] Finally, a fourth issue has to do with the merits of approaches to establishing causation other than experimental and quasi-experimental methods including qualitative comparative analysis (QCA), process tracing, most significant change, success case method, outcome mapping, and the modus operandi approach.[45]

Political Theories

Evaluation practice is intimately connected to political goals, systems, and instruments of governance both nationally and internationally. Evaluation supports broad political goals such as accountability and transparency in decision making; it is intimately connected to policy instruments such as results-based management; it is used to strengthen and justify policy as is evident in the worldwide movement known as evidence-based policy; and it is seen as critical in the development of an informed citizenry. Evaluation practices support not only national but international political objectives. Governments throughout the world require that programs and policies be evaluated and these actions are tied to executive office and legislative mandates. In the arena of international development evaluation, much of the evaluation work of multilateral agencies such as the World Bank and the United Nations Development Programme as well as international donor agencies such as the Department for International Development in the United Kingdom (DFID), the Swedish International Development Cooperation Agency (SIDA), and the U.S. Agency for International Development (USAID) is built around measuring achievement of the global political Millennium Development Goals.[46] Moreover, evaluators themselves often adopt a political stance—that is, they assume or explicitly argue for ways in which evaluation best serves the public good. Explicit political stances in evaluation are most evident in the claims made for a deliberative democratic approach to evaluation, empowerment evaluation aimed at affirming participants' self-determination and political agenda, and a transformative approach to evaluation focused on ensuring human rights.[47]

These and other ways in which evaluation is implicated in matters of policy and politics require that evaluators have some understanding of the broad body of knowledge comprising the concerns of political science, including political theory, public administration, and comparative politics. Of course, this need not require becoming an expert on the views of major classical and contemporary political theorists such as Plato, Hobbes, Locke, Rawls, Habermas, and Sandel, but it does entail having some working knowledge of how evaluation as a social practice is wedded to conceptions of democratic accountability, public administration and practices of governing, and the goals of democratic societies. This includes the relationship between evaluation and (a) matters of public concern such as the purposes that governments serve (e.g., equality, justice, security), (b) political orientations such as liberalism, conservatism, and progressivism, and (c) political behavior (individuals' political views, ideology, and use of science in policymaking).

Theories of Knowledge Utilization

Numerous purposes are offered for why evaluation can (or should) be conducted, including to determine program effectiveness, demonstrate return on investment, guide resource allocation, improve ongoing program operations, assist in creating a climate of critical reflection with an organization, inform the citizenry (making decisions, programs, and policies more open to public scrutiny), demonstrate agency accountability and transparency, and provide information needed by decision makers for discrete decisions.

Yet actually achieving these purposes (or intended uses) of evaluation is not possible without some understanding of the phenomenon of using knowledge generated through research and evaluation in decision making. This, in turn, requires investigating possible answers to questions such as: What is the character of the knowledge that is used? Who is the user and what do we know or assume about that user? What is the purpose of use? What outcomes are intended? What would it be important to know about the situation and context of use? What should be the nature of interactions between the evaluator and the knowledge user? What do the answers to the above questions imply for improving knowledge transfer, communication, and utilization?[48] To answer these and similar questions, evaluators must be familiar with concepts, theories, and methods related both to the use of evaluation findings, specifically, and to research utilization more broadly. This includes awareness of the many ways in which use of scientific information has been defined, typologies of use, and factors affecting use. It involves an understanding of different theories linking knowledge to action including diffusion, dissemination, transfer, and translation.[49] It also incorporates understandings from the literature on how policymaking is accomplished (e.g., policy windows, agenda setting, coalition theory, and equilibrium theory from political science) as well as concepts and theories from social psychology related to group decision making and collective reasoning.

Conclusion

This chapter challenges the widely held view that theory and practice occupy different domains and that "theorists tend to see practice as a kind of muddling-through process that leans more on performance art than on science . . . [while]practitioners . . . tend to think of theorists as irretrievably divorced from reality."[50] The use of reason in deciding what to think (theoretical or speculative reason) and the use of reason in deciding how to act (practical reason) exist in a mutually informing relationship. The practice of evaluation is fluid, changeable, and dynamic and characterized by alterability, indeterminacy, and particularity with respect to aims and purposes. Evaluation practice is alterable or flexible because it changes over time in response to the demands of a given situation. Practice is indeterminate because choices of the appropriate and effective actions to take in dealing with others arise within specific circumstances and are thus contextually relative. Practice is concerned with the particular (rather than the general) precisely because it is about an evaluator taking the right action in consideration of *this* situation, with *these* people, at *this* time and place, in *this* set of conditions. Thus, the study of evaluation theory— better understood as evaluation models or approaches—should be viewed not as a prelude to picking a single approach to adhere to but as a means of exploring different conceptions of the practice that can inform the situated judgments that a practitioner must learn to make. Those judgments are informed and made more sensible, prudent, and thoughtful to the extent that the evaluator is familiar not only with evaluation theory but with other bodies of knowledge bearing on the conduct and use of evaluation. Subsequent chapters elaborate on this idea, beginning in the next chapter with knowledge about judging value.

3   Values and Valuing

Making real decisions depends on reaching conclusions about whether, for example, an educational program is *good*, is *better* than another, is *worth* the resources required or risks involved, or could be *improved* with specified changes. There is, however, little consensus in the evaluation community regarding how we best support these needed conclusions.[1]

As emphasized thus far in this book, the core purpose of evaluation is making decisions about the value (merit, worth, or significance) of programs and policies. But just *how* value is to be decided—that is, on the basis of what criteria for determining success or failure—*whether* claims about value can be defended as objective, and *who* should be involved in the act of judging (and *how*) are contested issues. Complicating matters is the fact that the term *value* has many referents in evaluation, and the practitioner needs to be clear about how the term is being used in conversations with other evaluators as well as with clients and stakeholders. For example, we might be concerned with how *scientific values* (e.g., objectivity, logical clarity, skepticism, consistency among claims, and reliance on evidence) characterize an evaluator's process of investigation; how *political values* (e.g., fostering democratic debate, accountability, social justice, inclusion, equity, or fairness) underlie the justification and conduct of evaluation as an important social practice; and how *professional values* such as honesty, integrity, and responsibility govern the behavior of an evaluator. However, in this chapter we are concerned with better understanding values as *the basis of criteria* that inform the judgment of the merit, worth, or significance of a program or policy.

The present chapter begins with a short introduction to the importance of understanding the nature of value judgments. That is followed by a discussion of several issues involved in viewing evaluation as a judgment-oriented practice, grasping the relationship between values and criteria, using criteria as the basis for evaluative judgment, judging value when using multiple criteria, and deciding on the evaluator's role in making judgments.

The Nature of Value Judgments

This book is based on the objectivist premise that judgments of policy or program value can be and should be made on the basis of evidence and argument. Those judgments can serve as a guide for decision making on the part of program beneficiaries, program funders, program managers, and policymakers. To understand this claim, we begin with a primer on the nature of value judgments.[2] In brief, there are two major points of view—an objectivist and a subjectivist perspective. The *objectivist* holds that value judgments "can be based on reason, properly understood, and that they can be objective in a straightforward sense of that word."[3] "Objective" here means these judgments can be empirically warranted and that this can be determined by "working toward unbiased statements through the procedures of the discipline, observing the canons of proper argument and methodology, maintaining a healthy skepticism [toward all claims of value], and being vigilant to eradicate sources of bias."[4] The *subjectivist*, to the contrary, argues that value judgments are nothing more than expressions of personal opinion, preferences, emotions, and tastes. Thus, they are radically different than statements of fact that can be determined to be true or false. Because they have this subjective character, there will always be disagreement about value judgments, and they can never be decided and justified (warranted) by reason and evidence; they can only be chosen or accepted.

A subjectivist view of value judgments is often associated with what is called a *descriptive view of valuing* in evaluation. In this case, evaluators avoid making judgments of value and instead argue that their responsibility is to describe the views held by different stakeholders and at best to offer statements of the following kind: "If X is what you value, then this program is good (or not so good) for the following reasons; if Y is what you value, then this program is good (or not so good) for the following reasons, etc." On the other hand, an objectivist view of value judgments is often associated with what is called a *prescriptive view of valuing* in which the evaluator conducts evaluation from some explicitly justified value framework (e.g., social justice, empowerment, or enhancing the self-determination of native peoples). However, an evaluator can be an objectivist with respect to the nature of value claims and yet not adopt any particular prescriptive approach to evaluating. How subjectivist and objectivist understandings of value judgments and how descriptive and prescriptive approaches to valuing in evaluation are manifest in evaluators' decisions are discussed later in this chapter.

Evaluation as Judgment of Value

The distinguishing feature of evaluation as a practice is that it directly engages questions of the value of programs and policies. Evaluation is a judgment-oriented practice—it does not aim simply to describe some state of affairs but to offer a considered and reasoned judgment about the value of that state of affairs. There is some confusion about this statement because of the way formative and summative purposes for evaluation are often distinguished. A common argument is that formative evaluation is "improvement-oriented"—it is about gathering data on a program's strengths and weaknesses, assessing progress toward desired outcomes and gathering data useful in solving problems of implementation. On the other hand, summative evaluation is said to be "judgment-oriented"—it is about applying specific criteria to determine whether a program achieved its intended outcomes (i.e., was effective) and whether it provided value for money (i.e., was efficient).[5]

This way of distinguishing between the formative and summative purposes of evaluation is misleading because both involve judgment. As a program is underway, an evaluator charged with examining its implementation and progress toward stated goals makes judgments about whether implementation is going as planned, whether the program is reaching its targeted audience (the program beneficiaries), whether problems in the delivery of the program are severe enough to require attention, whether progress toward goals is reasonable and timely, and so on. These decisions are made on the basis of evidence and on appraising the quality, strength, and relevance of that evidence for each kind of decision. In short, judgment is required in doing "improvement-oriented" evaluation.

Judgment is also involved in making a summative evaluation of the overall value of a program. Questions of overall value have to do with program quality understood as its *merit and worth*. Merit is an assessment of the intrinsic value of a program or how effective it is in meeting the needs of its intended audience, whether benefits (outcomes) are in proportion to costs involved in achieving them, and, sometimes, how the program compares to alternatives. Worth is an assessment of the extrinsic value of the program to those outside the program such as the larger community or society.[6] (To imagine the difference between merit and worth, consider (a) evaluating the merit of a faculty member in terms of what her profession considers to be standards for research knowledge and skills as well as the originality and productivity of a research program, or (b) evaluating her worth to the institution that employs her in terms of the income her research program generates for the institution, the number of graduate students and postdoctoral researchers she is able to support, her ability to attract other faculty and students, her contributions to the well-being of the academic community of which she is a part, and so on. Decisions regarding promotion and tenure of a faculty member involve judgments of both kinds of value.)

Values and Criteria as the Basis for Judgment

Whether an evaluation is being conducted for formative or summative purposes, the key question is, "What is the basis for making evaluative judgments?" Judgments are made on the basis of some criteria—aspects, qualities, or dimensions that make it possible to determine that a program or policy is "good," "poor," "successful," "unsuccessful," "better (or worse) than some alternative," "effective," "ineffective," "worth its costs," "morally defensible," and so on. These criteria rest (often rather implicitly) on values held by stakeholders and evaluators—normative beliefs about how things should be, strong preferences for particular outcomes or principles that individuals and groups hold to be desirable, good, or worthy. These beliefs, preferences, and principles include social-political values such as accountability, equity, effectiveness, and security as well as moral values such as respect for persons, dignity, and freedom of self-determination. It is on the basis of such values that individuals and groups judge the success or failure of a program or policy. In other words, what we value surfaces in the kinds of criteria we think are important. In the field of evaluation, inquiry into values addresses the question, "What are the criteria by which the success of a policy or program should be judged"?[7] These criteria must be made explicit if an evaluator is to offer a reasoned, defensible judgment of the merit or worth of a program or policy.[8]

A commonsense perspective is that social and educational programs and policies ought to be judged on the basis of widely shared values such as effectiveness (achievement of intended objectives), efficiency (value for money), and equality (of opportunity and social outcome for intended beneficiaries). But the matter is not so simple as is this; not least because liberals, conservatives, and libertarians differ on the value of equality as represented in social programs (e.g., affirmative action, universal health care, and progressive income taxes)[9] but also because the determination of what constitutes adequate measures of effectiveness and efficiency is contested, not only among evaluators but by various stakeholders to an evaluation as well. There are at least three major issues involved in inquiry into evaluative criteria: (1) identifying and determining criteria, (2) dealing with multiple criteria, and (3) deciding who should do the "valuing" based on the criteria and how it should be done.

Identifying and Determining Criteria

There are multiple sources and types of criteria that evaluators rely on in making judgments of the value of a program or policy, including stated program objectives; established requirements; expert opinion, benchmarking, or professional standards; needs assessment; stakeholder surveys and group interviews; and indices of well-being. The overwhelming consensus in the evaluation literature is that choices of criteria used in judging program value are contextually determined—that is, they depend on (a) stakeholders' perspectives on the importance of a given social problem in a particular arena (e.g., the environment, education, health care, social welfare, criminal justice) to be addressed by a program or policy; (b) stakeholders' vested interests in solutions to those problems; (c) the norms and values of the organizational and political system in which a program or policy is developed, located, and administered; (d) cultural understandings; and (e) evaluators' own values and perspectives on criteria they believe are important. Thus, there are no decision rules to guide the systematic and responsive determination of appropriate criteria to be used in all evaluations. Evaluators must learn the "contextual pragmatics of valuing," that is, a form of practice that is contextually sensitive and matches the selection of criteria and methods for determining them to the conditions and needs of the specific evaluation in question.[10] The following sections offer a view of the range of criteria relevant for almost all program evaluations. Criteria are not presented in any particular order of importance.

STATED PROGRAM OBJECTIVES

Program goals and objectives are typically found in documents related to program planning or the program proposal. Using program objectives or intended outcomes—what a program was supposed to accomplish—as the basis for an evaluative judgment makes intuitive sense. However, often program goals are either very broadly stated or ill specified by program management and staff. Even when they are precisely defined and accompanied by measurable targets, it is possible that relying only on objectives as criteria for determining the value of a program or policy can be problematic.[11] Consider for, example, a program that has three specific, measurable objectives. On Objective 1, the program fails to reach its target; on Objective 2, the program reached its target; and on Objective 3, it dramatically exceeded its target. Is the program a failure because it did not reach one of its objectives? Or is it a success because even though it failed on one objective it met a second and exceeded its target on a third? Suppose that Objective 1 was a particularly difficult one to meet while Objective 3 was comparatively easy to attain. What if there were other unanticipated and unintended positive effects not specified in the original objectives—should they be included? Does the attainment of those effects somehow compensate for the fact that a stated objective was not met? Suppose there were unintended negative effects—how are these to be weighed in light of program objectives? How is the value of a program to be determined if in fact it is discovered that to meet Objective 2, program staff had to work overtime and suffered considerable stress and eventually quit the program? Program goals and objectives can be used as the criteria on which to base an evaluative judgment, but usually only in the following circumstances: first, when there are clear, measurable standards of desired program performance; second, when there is no interest in unintended effects of a program; third, when objectives are not simply those stated by program or policy developers and administrators but include objectives as understood by other stakeholders as well; and, fourth, when it is possible to prioritize or weight the relative importance of multiple objectives.

EFFECTIVENESS

This criterion is a close cousin of the former. A dictionary definition of program effectiveness indicates it is the degree to which a program is successful in producing desired (intended) results, and this suggests that effectiveness is a matter of determining whether a program achieved its objectives. This is in fact the way that effectiveness is defined in the widely cited Organisation for Economic Co-operation and Development/ Development Assistance Committee (OECD/DAC) criteria for evaluating development interventions. That definition also includes examining the major factors influencing the achievement or nonachievement of the objectives as part of determining effectiveness.[12]

However, effectiveness is given its own listing here because challenging and rigorous definitions of effectiveness, as a particular kind of scientific appraisal of social and educational interventions, often follow from the way the term is understood in medical research. These definitions typically emphasize the role that experimental designs (particularly, randomized controlled trials or RCTs) play in determining program effects. For example, the Society for Prevention Research (SPR) in the U.S. distinguishes between *efficacy*—the extent to which an intervention (technology, treatment, procedure, service, or program) does more good than harm when delivered under optimal conditions—and *effectiveness*—which refers to program effects when delivered under more real-world conditions and may be concerned with establishing for whom, and under what conditions of delivery, the intervention is effective.[13] Furthermore, SPR sets standards for evidence of each criterion.[14] A view of program effectiveness similar to that offered by the SPR is common in many approaches to impact evaluation that use causal methods for comparing outcomes or results attained by a program to some equivalent group that did not receive the program.[15]

RELEVANCE

In the field of international development evaluation especially, the relevance of a program or policy is often considered an important criterion. Relevance is generally understood as the extent to which program or policy objectives are consistent with beneficiaries' requirements, country needs, global priorities, and partners' as well as donors' policies.[16] But it can also include other dimensions of significance. For example, the United Nations Development Programme (UNDP) argues that relevance involves assessing the congruency between the perception of what is needed as envisioned by the initiative planners and the reality of what is needed from the perspective of intended beneficiaries; the extent to which the program or policy is responsive to UNDP human development

priorities of empowerment and gender equality; and the extent to which
UNDP was able to respond successfully to changing and emerging development priorities and needs.[17]

EQUITY FOCUS

Programs and policies, again particularly but not exclusively those in
development aid, are often designed to be equity-focused. This might be
considered a special case of the "relevance" criterion. Pro-equity interventions target or prioritize groups of beneficiaries typically regarded as
"worst off," and these include the disadvantaged, the vulnerable, and the
marginalized. The criterion here is whether equitable development results
were achieved. It is common that an evaluation approach that employs
this criterion in judging the success of an intervention is itself evaluated
for being equity-focused—that is, whether the evaluation design involved
the use of participatory and empowerment-oriented processes to ensure
that worst-off groups were directly involved in the design and execution
of the evaluation.[18]

EFFICIENCY

The extent to which monetary costs, time, and effort are well used
in achieving specific outcomes is a criterion that is widely accepted (although perhaps not always well researched) in everyday life. The phrase
"value for money" is a common expression of this idea. In the field of program evaluation generally (with the possible exception of some practices
of policy analysis), the criterion of efficiency (understood as a quantitative
measure of the ratio between outcomes and the types and amounts of
resources required to produce those outcomes) is not widely employed.
This is due largely to the lack of evaluators' understanding of issues in
economic reasoning and the quantitative skills needed to employ tools
such as cost-effectiveness and cost-benefit analysis.[19] However, an interest
in efficiency criteria using cost data as a means of judging program value
is becoming increasingly important in the field of evaluation in view of
the growing interest in the criterion of social impact.

SOCIAL IMPACT

For the past decade or two, in both the philanthropic sector that funds
social and educational programs and in the international development

community (e.g., multilateral organizations such as the UNDP and the World Bank) there has been a growing interest in what is broadly referred to as social impact assessment and social return on investment.[20] A 2003 report summarizing discussions held at a meeting of fifty funding agencies sponsored by the Goldman Sachs Foundation and the Rockefeller Foundation noted two trends: (1) a shift in the philanthropic sector from thinking only in terms of grantmaking to thinking more like venture-type investors and (2) a concomitant emphasis on measurement and evaluation to determine whether investments are yielding desired results.[21] As defined on the Internet portal SIAhub for Social Impact Assessment (SIA) practitioners, SIA covers the entire set of processes involved in monitoring, analyzing, and managing both positive and negative, intended and unintended social consequences of a planned intervention as well as any social change processes set in motion by that intervention.[22]

Social impact assessment is often used as a label for measuring "social, public, or civic value—that is, the value that nongovernmental organizations (NGOs), social enterprises, social ventures, and social programs create."[23] That measurement is undertaken with a diverse set of tools drawn from fields of social science research, evaluation, and business practices that experts have judged to be useful. Among these tools are cost-benefit and cost-effectiveness analysis, the Balanced Score Card, Theory of Change models, Value-Added Assessment, and Social Return on Investment (SROI) analyses.[24] The latter are performed in different ways by various organizations including The World Bank, the William and Flora Hewlett Foundation, the Edna McConnell Clark Foundation, and the SROI Network International.[25]

A review of eight approaches (including cost-effectiveness analysis and cost-benefit analysis) to integrating cost data in measuring and/or estimating social value creation noted that these approaches are (a) still in the emerging stages of development; (b) plagued by many unresolved technical issues that affect utilization; and (c) must deal with a lack of a common language, common measures, quality data, and incentives for transparency on the part of organizations who seek to use them. The report concluded by warning of the following three dangers in such approaches:

1. The lure of false precision—given the detailed and often quite complicated methodologies, it can be easy to be convinced of the certainty of the results of these seemingly precise calculations.

2. The desire for a silver bullet—it is tempting to focus on a single number to indicate whether an investment is successful or not. However, social value metrics should be interpreted in a broader context of organizational performance.

3. The risk of cherry picking—cost-benefit metrics may overwhelmingly indicate that one intervention should be favored over another; yet sometimes the problems that are the most cost-effective to solve do not end up focusing on the most needy or hardest-to-serve populations.[26]

SUSTAINABILITY

Program sustainability is a criterion concerned with determining whether a beneficial program can continue to exist beyond the termination of initial support or investment and whether the benefits of a program continue after a program has run its course. Sustainability is a critical issue in the evaluation of many development assistance projects, and it often involves gathering evidence on factors such as organizational capacity, political support, funding stability, and capacity for program adaptation.[27]

CULTURAL RELEVANCE AND RESPONSIVENESS

Programs and policies in education, health care, and social services are designed on often largely unexamined assumptions about the behaviors, beliefs, attitudes, and ways of thinking of program beneficiaries. Or perhaps it is more accurate to say they are often designed on the basis of an understanding of these matters that reflects the cultural understandings of the program designers and planners. The criterion of cultural relevance is based on the assumption that culture influences how individuals perceive the benefits of a program, how and why they participate (or do not participate) in a program, and whether they view the program as consonant with their ways of thinking and acting. The notion of *culture* here is not limited to race and ethnicity, but also includes language, gender, age, religion, sexual orientation, and social class; it encompasses the values, norms, and beliefs of any group involved in the evaluation. Assessing whether a policy or program is both culturally relevant and responsive involves determining whether the design and implementation of the program in question, as well as the definition of its effectiveness (and the choice of measures to determine effectiveness), take into account the lifestyle behaviors of program recipients, their beliefs and attitudes regarding the intervention (e.g., health, education, the value of social services, and so on), their cultural understandings of program objectives (e.g., how they understand what it means to be "educated" or "healthy" or "safe and secure"), their understanding of valued outcomes of participation, and their modes and patterns of communication. In short, cultural relevance and responsiveness is a criterion that aims to assess what might be called program-community alignment.[28]

ESTABLISHED REQUIREMENTS

Requirements for programs and policies can be found in legislation that authorizes them as well as in policies and procedures that govern actions of members of an organization or agency in which a program is located and implemented. They might include statutory requirements regarding selection of eligible program participants, accounting and financial management standards, legal rules governing the conduct of staff (e.g., prohibitions against sexual harassment or requirements for disclosure of conflict of interest), as well as ethical requirements involving fair and equitable dealings with program participants.

EXPERT OPINION

Expert judgment by itself is not a criterion but a source of criteria. Experts with specific subject-matter expertise may have developed agreed-upon norms, procedures, or standards in a specific field that can serve as criteria. For example, experts in the field of health care management have benchmarked best practices in business process redesign. The Department of Health and Human Services in the U.S. supports a project called Healthy People 2020 that provides a resource of scientifically (expert) validated evidence-based practices related to a wide variety of public health concerns that can be used as standards against which to evaluate programs.[29] The U.S. Government Accountability Office (GAO) used evaluation experts and a review of the evaluation literature to develop a framework of ten evaluation criteria that the U.S. Congress can use to compare the value of a variety of federal programs serving children and families: program need, including problem magnitude, problem seriousness, and duplication of programming; program implementation, including interrelationships among program elements, program fidelity, and administrative fidelity; and program effects, including targeting success, achievement of intended outcomes, cost-effectiveness, and other effects.[30]

NEEDS ASSESSMENT

Again, strictly speaking, needs assessment is not a criterion but a tool for identifying and defining criteria. It is important to distinguish two ways in which the term is used in evaluation. Evaluators might be called upon in the early stages of program planning to determine whether or not a particular program should be developed, that is, whether there is enough need to justify proceeding with program design and implementation. This kind of assessment is a systematic study involving identification of the social problem(s) to be solved, the extent of the problem, the target population to be served by the program addressing the problem, and the specific service needs that the program is to provide. It includes collecting information identifying the gap between the current state of affairs (what is) and the desired state of affairs (what should be) with respect to a given social, health, or educational condition to be addressed. That gap is the identified need and that in turn can serve as the basis for determining priorities and comparing possible alternatives for addressing the gap.[31] This kind of comprehensive study describing and diagnosing social needs is referred to as a "needs assessment," and it is "fundamental [in planning and decision making] because a program cannot be effective at ameliorating a social problem if there is no problem to begin with or if the program services do not actually relate to the problem."[32]

Sometimes, particularly in needs assessments conducted as part of policy analysis and planning in international development, broad measures of social well-being based on indicators are used to determine needs. These often include output measures of well-being such as health, happiness, and basic liberties as well as measures of inputs to achieve well-being (e.g., food, shelter, potable water, resources devoted to education). The indicators reported in the World Bank's annual *World Development Report* and the United Nations Development Programme's annual *Human Development Report* are examples.[33] Indicators can be used to identify gaps to be addressed by development programs. Broad, comprehensive needs assessment is often associated with other kinds of organizational processes including front-end analysis, root cause analysis, and performance analysis and is typically viewed as the first step in a process of

$$\text{Assess} \rightarrow \text{Plan} \rightarrow \text{Act} \rightarrow \text{Monitor} \rightarrow \text{Evaluate}$$

However, "needs assessment" can also refer to a more restricted, yet still systematic, effort to identify what stakeholders (funders, service providers, program beneficiaries) consider to be the desired outcomes of a program at the planning stage or even after a decision has been made to proceed with a program. In this situation, "needs" are understood as value-driven perspectives on what a program should accomplish. Often, stakeholders prematurely jump to solutions or "wants" (e.g., "We need a training program," "We need to hire more staff to serve our clients," "We need better educational materials directed at explaining the health effects of smoking") without fully understanding the nature of the problem (or the need) to be addressed by a program and how that program is supposed to address or solve that problem.[34]

Surveys of members of stakeholder groups (e.g., program beneficiaries, funders, program managers and staff, community members who have a vested interest in a program that uses tax dollars) as well as focus group interviews can be useful tools for surfacing needs.[35] Likewise, working with stakeholders to develop a theory of change model that illustrates the cause-and-effect links through which a program is to achieve its intermediate and long-term outcomes can be an effective way of identifying various perspectives. None of these tools is simple to use (there are decisions to be made about sampling, instrument and protocol design and administration, and so on), nor do they necessarily provide unambiguous evidence of stakeholders' value-driven perspectives. This is so for at least three reasons.

First, it is not at all uncommon that different stakeholders with vested interests in a particular program will value different outcomes. In the example noted above, where evaluation experts identified ten criteria for evaluating federal policies serving children and families in the U.S., the GAO noted that Congressional policymakers are likely to prioritize these criteria in different ways, thus leading to potentially different overall assessments of a program's merit and complicating the effort to use uniform criteria or standards as the basis for evaluation. Or consider a relatively more simple case of a job-training program for unemployed youth—some stakeholders might value the outcome of obtaining a job and staying on the job for at least six months; others might value attitudinal changes such as youth accepting authority on the job and having a positive attitude toward work, or behavioral changes such as youth performing their work well and getting along with co-workers. Each of these valued outcomes typically reflects what a stakeholder regards as the most important need for the program.

Second, stakeholders (including the public) who share a genuine concern for a social problem will value different solutions to that problem, and thus be focused on different kinds of outcomes. Consider, for example, addressing matters of violence and other criminal behavior in a community. All stakeholders might agree this is a serious issue. However, those stakeholders committed to a restorative justice perspective will emphasize healing, social well-being, and repairing the harm to individuals and communities caused by criminal behavior as opposed to punishing the offender. Other stakeholders will value treating crime through various measures of crime control such as targeting repeat gang offenders and community policing.

Third, stakeholders' perspectives on what a program or policy is intended to accomplish (the needs it is intended to meet) often rest on a tenuous understanding and often not very clear empirical evidence of the current state of affairs (what is) regarding the problem to be addressed by a program or policy and the desired state of affairs or outcomes (what should be). Consider, for example, the case of evaluating the performance of a community shelter for women who are victims of domestic violence. The shelter is likely to include several kinds of services: community awareness and other prevention initiatives directed at families and organizations, protection services (e.g., emergency shelter, crisis line), and direct assistance (e.g., temporary housing, child care, job placement). Despite a general shared sense among stakeholders of the overall objectives of the shelter—that it serves as an advocate for these women, helps to empower them, and to make them self-sufficient—it is very likely that various stakeholders such as criminal justice agencies working with the shelter (police, the courts, the district attorney's office), program staff involved in protective services and direct service delivery, funders (community donors, federal agency funders), and the general public (the local community) will differ in (a) their understanding of the needs that the shelter should be addressing and how those needs are to be measured in terms of a gap between what is and what should be, and (b) their understanding of the kinds of indicators that should be used to assess key variables such as what counts as an "instance of domestic violence," "use of the crisis line," "becoming self-sufficient," and so on.

Dealing with Multiple Criteria

Recall from Chapter 1 that the final step in the logic of evaluation is synthesis—integrating results into an overall judgment of value. This is a particularly difficult task because the processes by which synthesis judgments are made is not well understood, and there is little consensus in the field of evaluation about how to aggregate findings across multiple criteria or across stakeholders' differing perspectives on important criteria.[36] Somewhat ironically for a practice concerned with making warranted judgments of value, the lack of explicit justification for a synthesis procedure continues to be regarded as the Achilles' heel of the practice.[37] As one observer of evaluation practice noted,

> [E]valuative synthesis [is] arguably the most important of the methodologies that are distinctive to our discipline. Simply defined, evaluative synthesis is the systematic combination of evidence with definitions of "quality" and "value" to draw well-reasoned and defensible conclusions about performance. . . . It's shocking but true . . . the vast majority of those who identify as evaluators don't even have it in their toolkit.[38]

Despite this depressing news, evaluators have four possible approaches to consider.

RULE-GOVERNED, ALGORITHMIC, AND RUBRIC-BASED APPROACHES

These are empirically based, systematic procedures for reaching a synthesis judgment and can be either qualitative or quantitative in nature.[39] Rubrics are used to determine levels of performance or what quality looks like, so to speak, on each criterion. A rubric might specify, for example, what "excellent," "good," "adequate," and "inadequate" performance looks like. Quantitative approaches (often referred to as Numerical Weight and Sum) require assigning numerical importance weights and a numerical performance score to each criterion, multiplying weights by performance scores, and then calculating the sum of these products. Table 3 displays this general approach.

Table 3. Illustration of Numerical Weight and Sum

Criterion	Weight*	Score**	Weighted Score
A	5	4	20
B	5	3	15
C	3	3	9
D	3	2	6
E	1	5	5
TOTAL			55

* Weight is determined on a five-point scale where 1 = minimally important;
3 = moderately important; 5 = maximum importance.

** Each criterion is rated on a five-point scale where 1 = poor performance;
3 = average performance; 5 = exceptional performance.

In qualitative approaches (called Qualitative Weight and Sum) each criterion receives a qualitative weight using ratings in the form of symbols (e.g., Δ stands for high importance; Θ stands for moderate importance; π stands for low importance), and performance on each criterion is also rated qualitatively.

NON-ALGORITHMIC, INTUITIVE-BASED
HOLISTIC JUDGMENT APPROACHES

To synthesize in this way is to assume that the overall merit and worth of a program cannot be adequately captured using the analytic, objective heuristics that characterize rubric-based approaches. A leading proponent of this approach, Robert Stake, expresses the antipathy toward rule-governed judgments characteristic of those who think more holistically:

> I am one evaluator who does not find it necessary to be highly explicit as to the quality I am looking for. Some evaluators try hard to be explicit. But I am wary of using a single or even just a few criteria, wanting to become experientially acquainted with the collection of aspects of the program. . . . One can squeeze the summary of program quality into a single rating or descriptor, such as A– or Barely Acceptable or Smashing, but to ignore the complexity of the evaluand's activity and merit is to misrepresent the truth and to short-change the audiences.[40]

Intuitive-based approaches to judgment assume that the value of a program is "almost entirely constructed by people through their perceptions, choices, and judgments."[41] It is therefore the task of the evaluator to capture those ways of perceiving quality and to offer a holistic portrayal of this complex understanding of overall value in such a way that it is accessible to the immediate stakeholders in a program.[42] Stake explains, "As I see it, the task for the evaluator is not to have the last word, but to describe effectively and usefully the diverse aspects of quality in the program."[43] This holistic approach is unique in that it is a narrative construction—the evaluator tells a story of what happened and what it means (and why it is important) to both the evaluator and the participants. All other approaches to synthesis (including the algorithmic approach and the ones discussed below) are arguments structured around premises that logically lead to conclusions.

ALL-THINGS-CONSIDERED APPROACHES

Although in the discipline of philosophy what constitutes an all-things-considered judgment is a matter of some dispute, it is a common way in which many of us make judgments and it involves taking into simultaneous consideration facts, values, criteria, and interests in some specific decision-making context. To state it formally, a program (X) is considered valuable when every way in which X could be valuable is weighed one against the other. The general form of this approach is that a decision maker compares and weighs reasons for and against a particular choice, conclusion, or course of action and in so doing reaches an "all-things-considered" judgment. This is the kind of judgment one makes when preparing a list of pros and cons about buying a particular house, for example, and then making a decision based on having considered all those factors. This idea has been explained in evaluation as follows: "Evaluators work within a specific context to produce an all-things-considered synthesis that provides the most coherence possible from the information available from various sources."[44]

DELIBERATIVE APPROACHES

Deliberative approaches are one means of reaching an all-things-considered judgment. Deliberation broadly defined as a process for achieving democracy means "discussion that involves judicious argument, critical listening, and earnest decision making."[45] It also requires the establishment or endorsement of evaluative criteria and the use of these criteria in reaching a judgment.

Deliberative approaches to an overall assessment of the value of a program or policy assume (a) that synthesis judgments are best reached through a process of public reasoning in which people's informed and considered judgments and underlying values in relation to the program or policy in question are brought together, (b) that the process of public reasoning involves encounters with contrasting points of view and a requirement to justify perspectives through arguments that make sense to others, and there is an expectation that the beliefs and values of participants may be transformed by involvement in the process, and (c) that the evaluator provides information on the value of the program or policy based on empirical investigation.[46]

Ernest House and Kenneth Howe have developed a framework for deliberative democratic evaluation. They argue that the primary responsibilities of an evaluator in this framework include (a) bringing the interests of program or policy beneficiaries to the table if they are neglected, (b) including and sufficiently representing major views and values of stakeholder groups, (c) ensuring sufficient procedures for dialogue and deliberation, and (d) providing assistance in resolving competing claims by sorting out good from bad data and information.[47]

The synthesis judgment in a deliberative approach takes on a political character, in the following sense of that word: "Political judgment [is] a function of a commonality that can be exercised only by citizens interacting with one another in the context of mutual deliberation and decision."[48] A political judgment is always "we-judgment" or public judgment in that it assumes a view of citizens in a deliberative democracy as mutually engaged, not as individual agents pursuing private interests in the marketplace of ideas.[49]

The House and Howe framework for democratic deliberation (particularly their insistence that an evaluator has a special responsibility to ensure that the views of program beneficiaries are included in deliberations) is grounded in their view of how evaluation ought to serve social justice. This is a prescriptive approach to valuing.

ALTERNATIVES TO SYNTHESIS

In some evaluation circumstances (perhaps too many in the view of some evaluators), little or no synthesis is ever attempted. Instead a descriptivist approach to valuing is used that involves documenting program performance on several criteria without reaching an overall judgment across those criteria. This is often referred to as "interest group depiction"—making summaries of performance matched to the preferred criteria (values) of different interest groups.[50]

In some forms of policy analysis and evaluation, synthesis judgments are avoided because of the complexity of the political decision-making process where ideology, interest group pressure, and political concerns can weigh more heavily in policy decisions than empirical evidence from evaluations. For example, some policymakers may argue that the government has an obligation to foster the healthy development of young children even in the absence of significant evidence revealing that an investment in preschool programs is yielding expected outcomes. Or decisions over the value of programs of school choice may be made not on the basis of evidence of whether charter schools yield positive effects but on the basis of ideological stances pitting those in favor of market solutions to education against those who support the government's responsibility for public education. In such circumstances, the evaluator, like the policy analyst, may be content to simply make plain the empirical and normative (value) arguments involved in the debate over the merits of a program or policy in order to facilitate assessment, comparison, and debate among policymakers.[51]

The assistant director of the Center for Evaluation Methods and Issues at the U.S. Government Accountability Office (GAO) has argued that GAO does not make aggregate judgments of a program's value. She explains that the GAO takes this position because a synthesis requires a political decision to prioritize some criteria of performance over others, and most program evaluations are designed for a particular policy purpose and thus the choice of criteria applies to the specific situation: "The weighing or prioritization of criteria or values is in essence a political decision, assigning priority to some values over others. GAO, as an audit agency, is charged with providing objective, nonpartisan, nonideological analyses, which precludes it from making these political choices."[52]

Deciding Who Does the "Valuing"

A distinctive feature of all approaches to making a synthesis judgment as noted above is that the evaluator has the primary (or even sole) responsibility for making such a judgment. In other words, overall judgments of value rest on the expertise of evaluators who may employ different means to exercise that expertise. Yet there are at least two other options.

One option, as described above in the case of evaluations conducted by the GAO, is to leave the judgment of value to stakeholders. In some evaluations, the stakeholders are the immediate audience for an evaluation (e.g., funders, program managers, program staff, program participants). For others, particularly policy-level evaluations, stakeholders are a broader, more general audience that has been referred to as the "policy-shaping community" and includes decision makers as well as advocacy groups, the media, and interested citizens.[53] Evaluators who focus on the latter tend to see the primary purpose of evaluation as educating that policy-shaping community about the nature of social problems and how best to address them.[54]

A second option is to make the judgment of program value the joint responsibility of evaluators and stakeholders. However, what "joint responsibility" entails is subject to multiple interpretations. In some instances, the evaluator, during the planning stages of an evaluation, guides stakeholders in establishing a framework (criteria and standards) that the stakeholders will later use for judging overall program value.[55] In other circumstances—for example, in forms of evaluation that aim to empower program participants—evaluators facilitate the process of stakeholders themselves conducting the evaluation, interpreting the findings, and putting them to use. Other forms of participatory and collaborative evaluation vary in the extent to which control of both the process of evaluation and responsibility for judging overall program value is shared between the evaluator and stakeholders.

Implications

Although there is broad acceptance of the idea that evaluation is a judgment-based practice, the grounds for making judgments, the means of constructing those judgments, and the extent to which the evaluator is solely responsible for those judgments are all contested issues in the field.

Determination of the grounds and means for judgments of program value depend a great deal on the capacity of an evaluator to understand context—where context minimally includes (a) the kinds of decision needs that might be driving the evaluation (e.g., mid-course corrections to improve ongoing programs; continuing the program, expanding the program, eliminating the program, testing a new idea), (b) stakeholders' beliefs about a program, (c) program intentions, (d) the organizational context in which a program was developed and will be operated, and (e) the political context in which the evaluation takes place and in which evaluation judgments are likely to be used. These understandings are entwined with the evaluator's own views and perspectives on the value and importance of evaluation.[56] The situation regarding the proper role for the evaluator in making judgments of value can be characterized as a choice among four alternatives:

1. Evaluators can be engaged in valuing *by guiding stakeholders* in the process of reaching conclusions about value.

2. Evaluators can be engaged in valuing *by acting as a social conscience* in reflecting on the meaning of findings.

3. Evaluators can assist in valuing *by providing stakeholders with the opportunity to actively engage in evaluation* and, in that process, themselves determine the worth of the enterprise.

4. Evaluators can perceive their role *as personally making a decision* of merit or worth.[57]

How evaluators decide among these options is, in part, based on their own sense of moral-political commitments that inform their understanding of the public purpose of the practice as well as their obligations and responsibilities as professional practitioners.

4   Reasoning, Evidence, and Argument

> [M]uch of our thinking, left to itself, is biased, distorted, partial, uninformed or downright prejudiced. . . . Excellence in thought . . . must be systematically cultivated.[1]

The previous chapter emphasized that evaluation is a judgment-oriented practice, specifically concerned with rendering decisions about the value of programs and policies. This chapter is concerned with the anatomy of judgment making in evaluation, especially with those significant parts of its composition known as critical thinking, credible evidence, and persuasive argument. The chapter first considers judgment making as a cognitive process[2]—a process of critical thinking that is guided by principles of scientific reasoning, method, and evidence as well as ethical principles. It then turns to a discussion of evidence—its definition, sources, and properties—which forms the basis of judgments of value. That is followed by a brief examination of salient issues surrounding the use of evidence in evaluation. The chapter concludes with a discussion of key considerations involved in making evaluative arguments.[3]

Evaluative Thinking Requires Critical Thinking

Although it may seem tautological to state it in this way, the kind of thinking required in evaluation is evaluative thinking or how one arrives at judgments of value. That capability, in turn, rests on skills of critical thinking or what John Dewey called "reflective thought" and what some evaluators have identified as "reflective practice."[4] Critical thinking has many applications, but in evaluation it is used in service of assessing and making claims of value, specifically seeking the ground or basis for those claims and examining the adequacy of that ground to support those claims.

67

Critical thinking is distinct from everyday thinking. It is reflective in that it involves appraisal of an issue or situation before deciding and acting. A synonym for critical thinking is clear, reasoned judgment. Critical thinking is related to other forms of higher-order thinking including metacognition, creativity, and problem solving; it requires a specific set of skills, including those show in Table 4.

Although critical thinking is a cognitive process, it also requires a set of virtues or dispositions.[5] These include being habitually inquisitive, self-informed, trustful of reason, open- and fair-minded, flexible, honest in facing personal biases, willingness to reconsider, diligent in pursuing relevant information, and persistent in seeking results that are as precise as the subject and the circumstances of inquiry permit. Critical thinking is also opposed to what is commonly called sociocentric thinking—the tendency to see the world from a narrow, group-centered perspective that

Table 4. Skills of Critical Thinking

Skill	Subskill
Interpretation	• Categorization • Decoding significance • Clarifying meaning
Analysis	• Examining ideas • Identifying arguments • Analyzing arguments
Evaluation	• Assessing claims • Assessing arguments
Inference	• Querying evidence • Conjecturing alternatives • Drawing conclusions
Explanation	• Stating results • Justifying procedures • Presenting arguments
Self-Regulation	• Self-examination • Self-correction

Source: Adapted from Peter Facione. 1990. "Critical Thinking: A Statement of Expert Consensus for Purposes of Educational Assessment and Instruction." Millbrae, CA: The California Academic Press, p. 6. Available at http://assessment.aas.duke.edu/documents/Delphi_Report.pdf

reflects the prejudices of the group or culture, also seen as the failure to study the insights of other cultures (thus restricting the breadth and depth of one's thinking) and the failure to think historically and anthropologically (thus being trapped in current ways of thinking).[6]

Because critical thinking is related to other higher-order thinking skills[7] and because the relationships between these forms of thinking are not easily sorted out (either philosophically or psychologically),[8] critical thinking is often used as a generic term that covers a variety of intellectual tasks; for example, clarifying goals, examining assumptions, uncovering hidden values, formulating workable solutions to complex problems, deliberating what courses of action to take, as well as analyzing the assumptions and quality of the methods and evidence used in arriving logically at a reasonable level of confidence about a hypothesis. Similarly, critical thinking can be a placeholder for desirable personal attributes such as being systematic, methodical, introspective, and disciplined.

To be sure, understood in this broad way, careful, critical thinking is required in most all decisions one faces in evaluation practice, including determining clear objectives for an evaluation, judging whether a particular evaluation question is answerable given the circumstances, appraising stakeholder needs and values, explaining key concepts that shape an evaluation design, judging the veracity of statements that stakeholders and participants make about programs, and so on. However, the most important and consequential application of critical thinking lies at the heart of the evaluative enterprise in the ability to *analyze and weigh up evidence and present arguments for the value of what is being evaluated*. In other words, critical thinking means being clear about the criteria that form the basis for valuing; gathering appropriate evidence; appraising the quality and sufficiency of evidence as well as its probative importance (the capacity to demonstrate or support a claim about value); and offering a coherent and persuasive explanation for the value of a program or policy that is warranted by means of the "evidential, conceptual, methodological, criteriological, or contextual considerations upon which that judgment is based."[9]

Critical thinking involves the use of norms or standards in making judgments. Some of those norms are general, while others are specific to a particular kind of practice. For example, two general standards that matter in judgments made in several applied fields including evaluation might be "conflict of interest detracts from the credibility of a source," and "the most valid judgment is based on independent, multiple sources of evidence." On the other hand, norms or standards for making judgments can be specific to particular practices. For example, in mathematics the standard for a good judgment is deductive proof; in clinical medicine the standard is more like "all things considered" (i.e., taking into account simultaneously the patient's history, clinical evaluation, pathophysiological examination, laboratory tests, and so on); in most empirical work in the social-behavioral sciences the standard for a judgment on whether or not to reject a hypothesis is statistical significance; in the practice of criminal law, the standard for appraising an argument of guilt or innocence is "beyond a reasonable doubt," while in civil law, the standard is "the preponderance of evidence."

In evaluation, gathering and analyzing evidence and making arguments for the merit and worth of a program or policy requires knowledge of several kinds of norms, including scientific principles governing the gathering of evidence and its interpretation as well as ethical guidelines for the practice (e.g., cultural competence in interpretation; valuing as reflective of an interest in the public good). The next section discusses scientific principles involved in generating and using evidence.

Evidence in Evaluation

Evaluative judgments require evidence. Thus, the professional evaluator needs to be familiar with the nature, types, and properties of evidence as well as several controversies surrounding what constitutes the best evidence for evaluative judgments. This is no small task for, as a recent examination of the nature and use of evidence in evaluation noted, "we are a long way from consensus and a universal answer to the question of what counts as credible evidence in contemporary applied research and evaluation."[10] First, it is helpful to recognize that evidence is a logical feature of all forms of empirical inquiry. *All* inquirers, whether they are detectives, historians, archaeologists, investigative journalists, scientists, or evaluators, display a respect for evidence, persistence in seeking it out, and care in weighing it.[11] Second, evidence is correctly viewed as a critical part of an argument structure, as displayed in Figure 1.

In this argument structure, the term *evidence* generally refers to information helpful in forming a conclusion or judgment (these terms are used interchangeably in what follows). Framed in a more rigorous

Figure 1. Argument Structure for an Evaluative Judgment

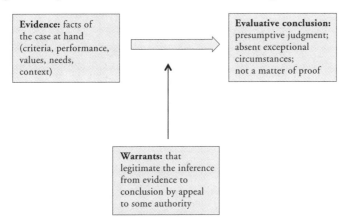

Source: Adapted from Albert R. Jonsen and Stephen Toulmin. 1998. *The Abuse of Casuistry*. Berkeley: University of California Press.

epistemological perspective, evidence means factual information bearing on whether a statement such as a hypothesis or conclusion is true or false, valid or invalid, warranted or unsupported. *Warrants* legitimate the inference drawn between evidence and a conclusion. They are support for the use of evidence of a particular kind. These warrants vary from one practice to another. For example, what warrants the use of DNA evidence in the determination of the guilt or innocence of someone accused of a crime is what is considerable acceptable in the criminal justice system. What warrants the causal inference of a program's impact based on a randomized, controlled field experiment is an appeal to sampling theory accepted with the community of applied social researchers. *Conclusions* or judgments reached in evaluation are considered presumptive, which means the conclusion is not a matter of proof but what is considered plausible, reasonable, and acceptable within a given set of circumstances.

SOURCES AND TYPES OF EVIDENCE

There are multiple types of evidence useful in evaluation including implementation evidence, descriptive and analytical evidence, attitudinal evidence, economic and econometric evidence, ethical evidence, and evidence of outcomes and impact. One way to grasp the array of sources of evidence is to consider the types of questions an evaluator must address and the evidence required in each case.[12]

There are *descriptive questions* such as "How many?" "How much?" and "In what proportion?" Sources of evidence here include administrative data, survey data, as well as index numbers often used by economists to measure inequality, well-being, poverty, and the like. Descriptive questions also include "What happened?" or "What does this program look like?" Evidence here includes data on program purposes drawn from program documents as well as staff descriptions, data from observations of program operations and procedures, data on relevant demographic and personal characteristics of program clients or beneficiaries, program staffing patterns, management structure, and so on. There are *explanatory questions*, inquiries into whether observed outcomes are attributable to a program or policy. Sources of evidence useful in answering these questions include causal modeling, process tracing, and qualitative comparative analysis, as well as experiments and quasi- experiments. Evaluators may also address *normative questions* that invite comparison of what is actually being done in a program to an agreed-upon or required way of doing things; for example, "Are insurance exchanges established in the states throughout the U.S. complying with the regulations specified in the Affordable Health Care Act?" "Are regional training centers delivering the full array of employment services that they were to provide as specified in the proposal that funded them?" Sources of evidence for validating or establishing the standard involved in each case might be surveys or case studies that are based on established criteria for performance.[13] Admittedly, some normative questions relevant to an evaluation may be more complicated to answer. These typically are questions that have to do with the ethical, fair, and just treatment of program participants or beneficiaries. Consider, for example, the evaluation of a housing-first intervention for homeless individuals.[14] A key question in evaluating the value of such an intervention may well be, "Are program participants treated with respect and dignity during intake and in the assessment of their needs?" Determining the evidential base on which an evaluator judges that a participant is (or is not) being "treated with respect and dignity" will require that standards for such action on the part of program staff be carefully articulated.

MULTIPLE PROPERTIES OF EVIDENCE

Credibility, probative force, and relevance are three interrelated properties of evidence. *Credibility* is a matter of whether the evidence is true, and that judgment is subject to interpretation by the relevant reference group charged with making that judgment. The reference group might be a particular, disciplined-based community of inquirers—for example, historians who judge the credibility of evidence drawn from documents— or the reference group might be some other body convened to make the determination such as a jury, for example. Credibility of evidence is commonly justified by warrants (which are often unstated or implicit). In evaluation and applied research, judging whether the evidence gathered is credible will depend, in large part, on whether agreed-upon methodological guidelines for generating the evidence were followed. These guidelines cover matters such as the design or selection of instruments used to generate evidence; for example, the selection of a valid indicator to measure some social circumstance (e.g., individual welfare as measured by family income and individual health), or an indicator to measure learning outcomes (are participants' ratings of their own skill and knowledge an adequate measure?), or a measure of a behavioral state such as healthy lifestyle (are self-reports about eating and exercise adequate here; should there be some actual observation of meals consumed?). Of course, because they are guidelines for practice, not rules, whether guidelines have been followed is always a matter of interpretation.[15] Assessing whether the evidence is credible will be a matter of argument and rational consensus because it is widely accepted that there is no foundation of unquestionable evidence in terms of which the validity of any judgment can be adjudicated.

Probative force of evidence is closely related to the question of credibility. It has to do with how strongly the evidence in question points to the conclusion under consideration. Probative force can be understood in this way: some evidence literally clinches or all but guarantees a conclusion; other evidence vouches for a conclusion, that is, it makes it more likely.[16]

The strength of evidence in the assessment of program impact (did the program actually cause the observed outcomes?) in the socio-behavioral, psychological, and medical sciences is often determined by grading schemes, such as a hierarchy of evidence. These schemes are qualitative rankings of different types of evidential support for judgments of the effectiveness of one intervention over another. A simplified hierarchy of methods that yield strongest to weakest evidence of policy or program effectiveness might look like this:

1. Randomized controlled trials (RCTs) with definitive results
2. Non-randomized quasi-experiments and econometric methods
3. Case control studies[17]
4. Observational studies
5. Expert opinion

The philosopher Nancy Cartwright has pointed out two major problems with this view of evidential strength.[18] First, grading schemes that rank types of evidence generated by different methods offer no guidance on combining evidence. Yet the judgments made by evaluators as well as the decisions faced by policymakers almost always demand multiple kinds of evidence generated from a variety of methods (e.g., evidence of whether a practice or policy is morally, socially, or politically acceptable; evidence of cost; evidence of deleterious side effects; evidence of "will it work here?"). In the field of public health, for example, political decisions about programs dealing with improvements in population health, reductions in avoidable morbidity and mortality, and decreases in health inequalities rely on much more than evidence of the effectiveness of a particular intervention. Evidence is also needed to speak to concerns about economic impact, fairness and quality, social justice, and human rights.[19]

The second problem with the emphasis on grading schemes for determining the strength of evidence is that it has led to the unproductive debate about whether a given method, particularly an RCT, is the so-called gold standard for generating evidence. Cartwright has argued that gold standard methods are "whatever methods will provide (a) the information you need, (b) reliably, and (c) from what you can do and from what you can know on that occasion."[20] RCTs sometimes, but not always, meet these criteria.

Evidential *relevance* is concerned with what to do with credible evidence once we have it. It is a matter of determining whether one empirical claim is relevant to the truth of another.[21] For example, suppose we have in hand the credible, empirical claim (E) that Mr. P's fingerprints were found on the murder weapon at the scene of the crime. Given a number of other auxiliary assumptions (A) about the circumstances (e.g.,

Mr. P had motive and opportunity, there is other evidence placing him at the scene or evidence casting doubt on his alibi for where he was at the time the murder was committed, etc.), we might then say that this empirical claim provides a reason to believe (or is relevant to) the hypothesis (H) that Mr. P is guilty of the crime. Put simply, E is evidence for H given the argument A for H.[22]

A concern for relevance shifts the focus from the method used to generate evidence to the issue of the role evidence plays in establishing a warranted conclusion that is part of an argument involving many premises and assumptions. Relevance of evidence reminds us that evidence that is pertinent to one kind of question or hypothesis may not provide support for another. Thus, for example, evidence of the efficacy of intervention— that is, program X caused outcome Y in circumstances C—may not at all be relevant to the question of "If program X were to be implemented with a new population and new methods of implementation, will it produce outcome Y?" In both policy and practice, we are concerned about a range of questions or hypotheses, only one of which concerns whether a particular intervention achieved its intended effects in the circumstances in which it was studied. Other important questions concern beneficial and damaging side or unintended effects; what represents successful implementation; whether a policy or decision is morally, politically, and culturally acceptable; and whether effects of an intervention are sustainable. All of these claims are subject to empirical investigation, and all are claims for which relevant evidence is needed.

ASSESSING A BODY OF EVIDENCE

Evaluators may be engaged not simply to evaluate a single program but to offer an opinion on a body of evidence bearing on a policy decision; for example, what do we know about the effectiveness of early childhood programs from multiple studies? In these circumstances an evaluator must be able to systematically assess the evidence, both in terms of the quality of evidence produced by any single study and in terms of the whole corpus or body of evidence that is available. Guidance on conducting evaluations of this kind emphasize attending to four additional characteristics or properties of evidence, including:[23]

1. Technical quality (similar to credibility as discussed above) of the studies comprising the body of evidence. This includes the concep-

tual framing of a study, the use of an appropriate design and methods, issues of validity and reliability, and whether there is a clear, warranted argument linking the conceptual framing to the data, the analysis, and the conclusions of the study.

2. Size. For example, a large, medium, or small number of studies.

3. Context in which the evidence is set. This relates to the issue of generalizability: Are the findings of the study context-specific or more global?

4. Consistency. Does the range of studies point to identical or similar conclusions, or do some studies refute or contest the findings of others?

Based on the combined appraisal of these characteristics, an evaluator uses a rubric to determine whether the body of evidence is very strong, strong, medium, or limited, as partially illustrated Table 5. Notice that this is a variant on an evidence-grading scheme as discussed above.

Table 5. Rating Scheme for Determining the Overall Strength
   of a Body of Evidence

Strength of Evidence	Combination of Quality + Size + Consistency + Context	Features of the Body of Evidence	Significance
Very strong ↕ Limited	High quality, large number of studies, consistent, closely matched to a single context	Studies based on systematic reviews, meta-analyses, and experimental designs	High confidence in overall findings as stable; few deficiencies in the body of evidence
	Moderate- to low-quality studies, small body of studies, inconsistent findings, context varies	Studies based on varied designs and methodologies that do not meet minimum standards for technical quality	Very limited confidence in findings; major deficiencies in the body of evidence

Source: Adapted from Department for International Development (DFID). 2013. "How to Note: Assessing the Strength of Evidence." London: Department for International Development. Available at https://www.gov.uk/government/publications/how-to-note-assessing-the-strength-of-evidence

Issues Surrounding Evidence in Evaluation

The field of evaluation grapples with several issues surrounding the nature of evidence and its use. As noted previously in Chapter 3, one issue is how evidence of program performance on multiple criteria is to be combined in a synthesis judgment of program value. Three other salient concerns include the controversy surrounding evidence-based policy and practice (EBPP), debates about establishing evidence of the causal effect of programs and policies, and ensuring the use of adequate measures (i.e., sources of evidence) for determining program processes and outcomes.

EVIDENCE-BASED POLICY AND PRACTICE

Beginning roughly at the turn of this century, the notion of evidence-based policy and practice or evidence-based decision-making (EBDM) had become practically de rigueur when discussing governance in nation states, the effective actions of nongovernmental organizations, decisions made by philanthropic institutions, and the management and delivery of education, health, and social service practices via government agencies. All kinds of social practices from providing mental health services, to parenting, to sex education, to policing, to management, to teaching reading are thought to be better if they are based on what the evidence shows about the relative efficacy of different means of achieving the aims of those practices. In the arena of public policymaking, the case for EBDM has been succinctly put as follows:

> [W]hile scientific evidence cannot help solve every problem or fix every program, it can illuminate the path to more effective public policy. . . . [T]he costs and lost opportunities of running public programs without rigorous monitoring and disinterested evaluation are high. . . . [W]ithout objective measurements of reach, impact, cost effectiveness, and unplanned side effects, how can government know when it's time to pull the plug, regroup, or, in business lingo, "ramp up?"[24]

Whether the concern is policymaking or the decisions faced by teachers, social workers, counselors, and health care practitioners in their daily practice, basing decisions about the direction, adoption, continuation, modification, or termination of policies and practices on what the evidence shows is thought to be the key to actions that are more wise, unassailable, effective, fair, and robust.[25]

On the face of things, using social scientific and evaluative evidence as the basis for decisions hardly seems controversial. After all, to substantiate one's claims or actions on the basis of evidence is surely more dependable and defensible than appealing to habit, ideology, and personal preference. We routinely praise the accomplishments of inquirers of all sorts, from scientists to historians, health care practitioners to investigative journalists, when it is obvious that they have systematically pursued evidence, carefully weighed it, and judiciously used it to form a conclusion. However, as patently obvious the claim might be that using evidence in decision making is both a social and intellectual good, relations between the generation of social scientific evidence and its use in decisions about policy and practice are challenging in several important ways.

First, the idea that evidence literally forms a *base* or *foundation* for policy or practice decisions is problematic. We know that whether evidence is so strong as to rule out *all* possibility for error is always a matter of interpretation. The long-standing tradition of epistemological skepticism reminds us that we lack conclusive evidence for most every topic we can think of. Second, over time evidence becomes obsolete—that is, it is "provisional, and always capable of being overturned, modified, refuted or superseded by better evidence."[26] These characteristics of evidence are consonant with our understanding of the fallible, imperfect character of knowledge. Third, even if we were to accept the idea that evidence forms a secure basis for decision making, we must address the fact that evidence per se cannot be wrong or right in some absolute sense. Our interpretations of it, however, can be flawed. We may choose to ignore the evidence—recall, for example, the Bush administration's claims that there were weapons of mass destruction in Iraq. We may make an incorrect inference based on the evidence— as that sage columnist Ann Landers once said, "Don't accept your dog's admiration as conclusive evidence that you are wonderful." We may leap too quickly to a conclusion absent sufficient corroborating evidence. This is the worry addressed by such methodological moves as data source triangulation and the use of multiple methods, and it is why a good physician always integrates evidence from the clinical examination, the patient's history, pathophysiological rationale (reasoning from principles of physiology to presumed clinical effect), knowledge of previous cases, and results of empirical studies in reaching a diagnosis and recommended treatment.

Thus, the phrase *evidence base* must be interpreted with caution: to claim that evidence ought to figure importantly in our decisions is one thing; to claim it is the foundation for our actions is another. We would be well advised to talk about *evidence-informed* decision making instead. The latter phrase implies that there is more to decision making than a straightforward appeal to scientific (or evaluative) evidence. A case for this way of thinking has been made in a National Research Council report that examined the role that scientific evidence (including evidence from evaluations) plays in public policymaking. The authors of the report reasoned that policymaking is a process best modeled as a form of policy argument that includes appeals to scientific evidence as well as "generalizations, extrapolations, assumptions, analogies, metaphors, anecdotes, and other elements of reasoning that differ from and can contradict scientific reasons." Scientific evidence is interpreted, made sense of, and used in persuasive ways in policy arguments. Hence, they concluded, "evidence-influenced politics is . . . a more informative metaphor, descriptively and prescriptively, than evidence-based policy."[27]

A similar argument has been made in examining the use of evidence in informing practitioners' decision making: *what* information is noticed in a particular decision-making environment, *whether* it is understood as evidence pertaining to some problem, and *how* it is eventually used all depend on the cognitions of the individuals operating in that environment. Furthermore, what these actors notice and make sense of is determined in part by the circumstances of their practice environment.[28]

EVIDENCE OF EFFECT

A significant amount of the discussion about EBDM centers on program and policy effectiveness—that is, whether intended outcomes and impacts were achieved and are directly attributable to the program or policy in question. The focus is thus on providing credible evidence of causal claims, claims of "what works." Establishing those claims is the purpose of impact evaluation.[29] Considerable controversy surrounds the best methods for impact evaluation and how causal claims are to be warranted.[30, 31] However, the prevailing view is that the most credible evidence of a claim that a program caused a particular outcome comes from the application of experimental methods (specifically, randomized controlled field trials).

At the heart of the controversy lies a set of beliefs and empirical observations about the character of social interventions, how they work to achieve their effects, and whether a given intervention alone is responsible for observed effects. As noted in Chapter 2, evaluators are increasingly recognizing that they are dealing with policies and programs that unfold in complex environments with multiple interacting actors (both individual and institutional), inter- and intra-program and policy interactions, and emergent effects.[32] This is the case domestically in evaluating comprehensive community change initiatives as well as internationally in country- or sector-led development aid initiatives. This set of circumstances not only produces variations in outcomes but also frequently leads to the development of unpredicted (and unpredictable), unplanned emergent outcomes that arise from the feedback processes involved between the different individual and institutional actors.

This awareness is challenging assumptions of simple theories of change that often underlie thinking about policies and programs as social interventions. These assumptions include that change is the direct result of a well-defined intervention; it is proportional to effort involved, additive, and predictable; and that a causal chain leading from inputs to outcomes can be fairly clearly specified.[33]

These ideas are also challenging evaluators' views of how best to determine whether observed outcomes are actually attributable to a given policy or program. The past decade has seen a significant shift toward evaluating program and policy impact using statistical methods, particularly randomized controlled field trials.[34] The promotion of this approach to evaluation has been an especially significant development in the field of international aid, where critics label development economists committed to the use of this methodology the "randomistas."[35] The argument underlying the use of these methods is that addressing causal questions is most important when either policy decisions or knowledge development is the objective of the evaluation, and that randomized designs provide the most solid assurance that it was the intervention in question (the particular program) that caused the outcomes, and not some other factor.[36] To convincingly rule out these other factors (often called rival hypotheses), impact evaluation studies use the methodology of random assignment to create an equivalent comparison group. The experimental group receives the intervention; the comparison group does not. After the intervention has been put in place and is determined to be working well, each group is measured on outcomes of interest. Assuming that there are no systematic differences between the two groups other than the intervention in question, any differences seen in outcomes are attributed to the intervention.

Randomized experiments to determine program or policy impact are clearly valuable under a specific set of conditions—where cause and effect are predictable, linear, and sequential; where circumstances can be held constant; and where experimental sites are isolated. Yet critics claim that the kinds of social problems we face and the interventions proposed to address those problems are rarely amenable to studies based on these conditions. Problems such as racial disparities in health, high rates of academic failure and school dropout, teen births, asthma, substance abuse, obesity, family and neighborhood violence, and child neglect have neither a single, straightforward causal mechanism nor are they solvable by means of a single, standardized intervention.[37]

The controversy has occasioned a broad examination of methods other than randomized experiments to generate evidence of impact. It has also led to a vigorous discussion about the causal logic of attribution versus contribution. The attribution question—is the observed effect attributable to the program in question (often called the study of the effects of a known cause)—is the kind of question addressed by experimental designs. These designs are based on counterfactual reasoning—i.e., "What would have happened without the intervention?" Hence, experimental designs are used to test the hypothesis that without the intervention there would be no impact or a different impact.[38]

In contrast, contribution analysis focuses on multiple causes and requires a well-developed theory of change for the intervention in question:

> A theory of change sets out why it is believed that the intervention's activities will lead to a contribution to the intended results. . . . The analysis tests this theory against logic and the evidence available on the results observed and the various assumptions behind the theory of change, and examines other influencing factors. The analysis either confirms—verifies—the postulated theory of change or suggests revisions in theory where the reality appears otherwise.[39]

This analysis often employs a "causal pie" model in which no single "slice" of the pie is a sufficient cause, but taken together all of the "slices" act in concert to produce an effect.[40]

The controversy over the best methods to produce evidence of program and policy impact is not likely to be resolved any time soon. One prominent observer claims that the debate has polarized into two camps:[41] the Experimentalists insist that trustworthy evidence is to be found only through the use of experimental designs. The Inclusionists acknowledge that under particular circumstances experimental designs can be valuable, but argue that any knowledge base that is limited to results of experiments is too narrow to be useful. The latter group advocates for the use of evidence that comes from other research and from practice and community experience.

ADEQUATE MEASURES FOR GENERATING EVIDENCE

Evaluators rely on documentable or measurable data on program characteristics, processes, and outcomes in order to develop evidence for judgments of program value. Some of these data are rather direct and straightforward, such as number of clients served, training sessions offered, numbers of high-risk families and children reached with relevant information about immunizations, and the like. Other data are more difficult to obtain because they require the use of proxy or indirect indicators and choices in measurement. For example, suppose one is evaluating an educational program that claims it offers culturally competent training—what would be an adequate measure of such training? What would an evaluator observe in order to provide evidence that culturally competent training was indeed delivered? Or imagine an evaluation of a preschool program designed to enhance school readiness. There is no direct measure of school readiness; thus an evaluator faces measurement issues about the choice of a indicator or a set of composite indicators that will serve as a proxy for the outcome of school readiness, such as family literacy level or developmental and intellectual gains in children enrolled in the program (which in turn require a baseline measure). How both program processes and outcomes are measured will largely determine the degree to which a program is determined to be effective.

A critical part of planning an evaluation involves the choice of measures, and this may require involving primary stakeholders including program funders and program staff in a process of negotiation, particularly about measures of program outcome. Stakeholders often express their interest in desired program outcomes in very broad and imprecise terms—e.g., reducing obesity, increasing students' interest in STEM careers, or promoting safe sexual practices. These general interests must be interpreted and turned into documentable and measurable outcomes. In this negotiation process, the evaluator must consider a number of interrelated issues including the time available to collect data from program participants, the feasibility of using particular measures, and what is known as participant burden—that is, time and effort required from participants in data collection (e.g., filling out questionnaires, competing logs, participating in interviews).[42] An evaluator is always involved in balancing a need for rigor and precision in measurement against what is feasible and practical in the situation in question.[43]

The issue of adequate measures is not, however, only a matter of an evaluator negotiating the choice of measures with stakeholders in a given set of circumstances. Often evaluators rely on available databases of indicators from federal and state programs as well as administrative data from school districts, municipal agencies, and health and social service agencies. A common concern is that "high-quality, widely accepted, readily understood, user-friendly measures and indicators are not available where they are most needed" in cities and neighborhoods where social service and public health programs are directed at children, families, and communities.[44] A variety of problems plague efforts here to develop adequate measures—the difficulty of making data-sharing agreements across agencies, the costs of collecting new data, the absence of quality (valid and reliable) survey instruments that can be used across multiple communities, and the lack of uniform or standardized definitions of such matters as child abuse and neglect, positive youth development, school readiness, recidivism, and so on.[45]

Evaluative Arguments

In its completed form, an evaluation is an argument for the value (or lack of value) of some particular program or policy. An argument is an attempt to persuade some particular audience of the conclusion about program value by giving reasons for accepting that conclusion as evident. The use of evidence in an argument demonstrates that evidence is not synonymous with data or information. Rather, evidence is data or information introduced at a specific point in an argument in order to persuade a particular audience of the veracity of the conclusion about program value.[46] An evaluation argument has several distinguishing features.

First, an evaluative argument is not a matter of demonstrative proof of the value (or lack of value) of a program. Proof is possible only in a formalized system of axioms such as geometry or with established rules of inference, as in deductive logic: "Argumentation does not start from axioms but from opinions, values, or contestable viewpoints; it makes use of logical inferences but is not exhausted in deductive systems of formal statements."[47] Moreover, a proof is designed to convince a general audience, while an argument is aimed at "gaining the adherence and increasing the understanding of *particular* audiences. . . . The evaluator does not aim at convincing a universal audience of all rational men with the necessity of his conclusion" (emphasis added).[48]

Second, such an argument is *contextual*. As should be readily apparent from previous chapters, context determines, in part, what comprises reasonable data, criteria, and evidence. Evaluators do not deal with abstract (theoretical) questions of value; rather, they deal with concrete (pragmatic) instances of value. For example, an evaluator does not investigate whether intervention *A* is timelessly of greater importance or value than intervention *B*. Instead, the value of intervention *A* compared to *B* is studied in a particular context of debate, conflict of opinion, value preferences, criticism, and questioning about the relative merits of each. Furthermore, it is with reference to a context composed of some particular client(s) and stakeholders and their circumstances and concerns that the evaluator aims to make a persuasive case for her or his judgment.

Third, an evaluation argument is *dialectical*. In other words, the argument is understood as part of a real or possible exchange between parties who differ over the value of the program. The argument that the evaluator constructs is designed to respond to particular doubts about the credibility, plausibility, and probability that clients and other stakeholders might raise about the judgment of the value of the program. In addition, evaluators also have an imagined or real meta-evaluator or peer group in mind in constructing their arguments. They develop their argument while thinking, "Would this stand up to the scrutiny of my peers?"[49]

Fourth, an argument for the value (or lack thereof) of a program or policy involves both *persuasion and inquiry*.[50] The argument is grounded in empirical inquiry; it is a knowledge-based or evidentiary argument. At the same time, argumentation is a purposeful activity in which the evaluator aims to persuade clients and other stakeholders of her or his conclusion or point of view on the value of the program in question. Thus, the rhetoric of the written (or oral) argument matters (clarity, thoroughness, organization), for the evaluator always asks, "How can I put my case so that others will not misunderstand?" Because persuasion matters in making an evaluation argument, we are well advised to be cautious about dismissing persuasion as a rhetorical art that has no place in the world of presenting evaluative findings based on the use of scientific methods (i.e., the idea that "facts speak for themselves"). There is much to be learned from key findings in the literature on the science of communication that is relevant to evaluation arguments. For example, the political scientist Arthur Lupia explains how social science research on two communication-related concepts—attention and source credibility—helps us better understand how audiences react to the presentation of scientific information,[51] and the psychologist Robert Cialdini has studied the notion of influence and explains how we can understand and defend against pervasive nonrational influences on our decision making.[52]

Finally, arguments themselves can be evaluated. There is a considerable body of literature in informal logic examining the kinds of fallacies that arguments are subject to. Some of the more familiar are the ad hominem fallacy, the argument from ignorance (where "ignorance" stands for lack of evidence to the contrary; thus someone argues that a conclusion is true because it has not been proven false), and the post hoc fallacy (i.e., taking correlation as evidence of causation, or assuming that "after that, therefore because of that").[53] A study of arguments made by intelligence analysts indicated that the rigor of an argument could be evaluated in terms of several kinds of risk that are captured in the following questions:

- Is it structured centrally around an inaccurate, incomplete, or otherwise weak primary hypothesis (which is sometimes described as favoring a "pet hypothesis")?
- Is it based on an unrepresentative sample of source material?
- Does it rely on inaccurate source material—as a result of "poor vetting," for example—or treat information stemming from the same original source as if it stems from independent sources?
- Does it rely heavily on sources that have only a partial or, in the extreme, an intentionally deceptive stance toward an issue or recommended action?
- Does it depend critically on a small number of individual pieces of often highly uncertain supporting evidence proving accurate, that is, a "house of cards" analysis?
- Does it contain portions that contradict or are otherwise incompatible with other portions?
- Does it incorporate relevant specialized expertise?
- Does it contain weaknesses or logical fallacies in reasoning from data to conclusion, alternatively described as having a "thin argument," a "poor logic chain," or as involving "cherry picking" of evidence?[54]

Conclusion

A hallmark of all professional practices is that they require the exercise of judgment—in the face of alternative options, reaching a well-reasoned decision to act in a responsible way based on the facts and circumstances available at the time the decision is demanded. Professional practice encompasses countless deliberations involved in decisions regarding the general question, "What should I do now under these circumstances?" These everyday professional judgments involve ethical, political, and methodological matters that cannot be resolved by an appeal to established procedures or rules: How many people should I interview? What is the best means to gather data on this aspect of the program? Have I respected this informant's right to privacy? How and when should I present preliminary findings to a client? What do I do about the fact that stakeholders radically disagree about important outcome measures? Making wise and considered judgments in these situations requires an ability to "read" the situation correctly, identify its salient features, and engage in an open-textured process of deliberating an appropriate and effective course of action.

While evaluators make many such everyday judgments, the distinguishing feature of evaluation as a practice is that it involves making a particular kind of decision or finding, namely, judgments of the value of a program or policy. To make such judgments, an evaluator must be skilled in more than methods for generating and analyzing data. An evaluator must know something about the types of value claims (see Chapter 1); the nature, properties, and sources of empirical evidence; controversies surrounding the notion of evidence in evaluation; and how to construct and appraise an evaluation argument. Evaluators must be aware of the fact that evidence is always generated within some kind of bounded institutional context (e.g., an organization, a particular site such as a school or hospital, a profession, a political culture) with its own logic of what counts as persuasive evidence. Further complicating matters is that the generation and use of evidence in evaluation is intimately connected to matters of the politics of evaluation and our understandings of what "use" of evaluation actually means—topics that are explored in the two chapters to follow.

5   Politics and Policymaking

A theory of evaluation must be as much a theory of political interaction as it is a theory of how to determine facts.[1]

It stands to reason that the evaluation of public programs and policies targeted at improving social conditions is ineradicably implicated in matters of politics and policymaking. Politics and policymaking are not one and the same, although they are related.[2] In democratic governments, politics is the process of bargaining, negotiating, and compromising necessary for decision making in situations marked by competing interests, conflicts over the desirability of different outcomes, and disagreements about social values. Policymaking is a process that results in a course of action—a policy decision or, simply, a policy—chosen from among alternatives. Ideally, that process is informed by scientific knowledge, including evaluation studies of the value of programs and policies.[3] However, policymaking in representative democracies under the rule of law inevitably involves political considerations as well. For example, there is a well-documented link between policy choices and gaining and maintaining majority political support; the policymaking process is clearly influenced by the lobbying efforts of organized interest groups; and arguments for why a policy is (or is not desirable) can be made on the basis of the value orientations and preferences of politicians (e.g., libertarianism, neoconservatism, neoliberalism, social democracy) irrespective of what the evaluative evidence may indicate.[4]

Of course, in forms of government lacking a strong democratic tradition, politics may also signify coercion, corruption, threat, and various forms of oppression of the weak by the powerful or elites. In these circumstances, building a country's evaluation capacity becomes a means to foster a democratic process of policymaking, as well as to promote equity and social justice in policy decisions. The international initiative known as EvalPartners is especially relevant in this respect. Launched in 2012 by the International Organization for Cooperation in Evaluation (IOCE) and UNICEF in conjunction with donor agencies and national and regional evaluation associations, EvalPartners aims to enhance the capacities of civil society organizations (CSOs) to engage in national evaluation processes that will, in turn, influence policymakers and the public to adopt policies that are based on evidence and that incorporate considerations of equity and effectiveness.[5]

This chapter expands on these initial observations, examining several distinct, but interrelated, ways of understanding the political character of evaluation. All significant matters in the politics-policymaking-evaluation nexus are often entangled in daily practice, but for analytic purposes I have disaggregated them here. The discussion is organized from micro- to macro-level considerations, beginning with an "interior" look at politics in the conduct of evaluation planning and execution, then to assumptions evaluators hold about the politics of policymaking or the "politics of interaction," from there to considering evaluation as a means of governance, and finally to exploring the political point of view of evaluation itself.

The "Interior" Politics of Evaluation

The day-to-day decisions that evaluators make in their myriad interactions with clients and other stakeholders in planning, designing, conducting, and reporting an evaluation are often characterized by the process of micro-politics. The term refers to the use of formal and informal, covert and overt processes through which individuals and groups exercise power to promote or protect their interests and to achieve their goals.[6] A focus on micro-politics reminds us that not every interaction between groups or individuals who disagree about an issue is characterized by reasoned and reasonable arguments but often reflect partisan interests, self-serving objectives, or ideologies. Micro-political concerns are often associated with the idea that politics is a menace to evaluation (or science more generally), endangering evaluation as an objective undertaking and threatening evaluator integrity and independence.

Micro-politics are involved in negotiating the terms of evaluation contracts with clients, particularly around matters of critical evaluation questions as well as ownership of data and release of evaluation findings.[7] This can be a particularly complicated and challenging task in evaluations that require collaborations and consensus among several community agencies to deliver community-based initiatives around, for example, programs to reduce substance abuse, or to lower risks for HIV/AIDS, or to promote economic development or access to decent housing. Micro-political considerations are also often involved in negotiations surrounding the choice of particular outcome measures, as discussed in Chapter 4. Political issues are clearly involved, for example, in a medical establishment's choice of outcome measures for determining quality of life or a criminal justice agency deciding what counts as juvenile delinquency or what a university decides is the best measure of the learning outcomes of its graduates (e.g., a direct measure such as the Collegiate Assessment of Academic Proficiency, an indirect measure such as the National Survey of Student Engagement, or performance-based measures).

Micro-political issues are manifest in somewhat different ways in collaborative and participatory approaches to evaluation that involve working closely with stakeholders in all phases of an evaluation—from planning to use.[8] Participative decision making involves processes of power sharing and, thus, means of negotiation and conflict resolution. Evaluators must learn who the key players are in participatory processes and understand their sources, forms, and degrees of power as well as their interests and incentives. And they must be able to design and orchestrate processes for addressing and resolving competing interests and perspectives among these key players. Participatory processes involving groups with diverse perspectives cannot be based on the naive assumption that discussion about important evaluation questions will be underpinned by a common interest and that all parties will agree about what counts as evidence of program outcomes. Good communication skills, a capacity for cultural sensitivity, and *Fingerspitzengefühl* (which literally means "finger tips feeling" and signifies keen situational awareness and tact in responding to controversies) are essential to navigating the micro-political dimensions of these forms of evaluation. Finally, we might note that the term *political* receives a particularly positive interpretation in participatory approaches to evaluation. Being "political" refers to a legitimate, preferred means of reaching a decision, specifically, resolving conflict through bringing disputed points of view together, compromising, and negotiating, as compared to resolving conflict through force, threats, coercion, or the exercise of raw power.

An emerging issue in micro-politics of evaluation, particularly in evaluation of development efforts, relates to the challenges of thinking and working politically, not just technically. That is, learning how to design monitoring and evaluation processes that are compatible with the dynamics of working with local leaders, elites, and coalitions to achieve sustainable developmental change through local political processes.[9] It involves relationship building, networking, and coalition building as well as acute awareness of the complexity and nonlinearity of development interventions.

The Politics of Policymaking I

Evaluation is intended to support decision making by those responsible for conceptualizing and funding programs and policies. Examining the ideas that evaluators hold about how policy decisions are made provides a different perspective on the politics that lie in the "interior" of evaluation. Evaluators have long recognized that "policies and programs . . . are the creatures of political decisions. They were proposed, defined, debated, enacted, and funded through political processes, and in implementation they remain subject to pressures—both supportive and hostile—that arise out of the play of politics."[10] Borrowing Harold Lasswell's oft-cited definition of politics as the process of determining who gets what, when, and how, we can focus on how evaluators envision the political process of policymaking.

Although it has been accompanied by considerable skepticism since it was first introduced, a rational-linear model of the policymaking process dominates much of our thinking.[11] Policymaking is said to proceed through a series of steps involving the careful, conscious formulation of goals and objectives; the enumeration of alternative ways of achieving those goals; gathering information about each alternative and evaluating whether it is the best means of achieving the goal; then choosing the optimal alternative.[12] The role of the evaluator is to provide the evidence necessary to make the best choice among alternatives. This model is also known as "decisionism"—"a limited number of political actors engaged in making calculated choices among clearly conceived alternatives."[13]

In this model of how policymaking happens, evaluation focuses on empirical questions that can be answered through disciplined, scientific inquiry and avoids normative questions surrounding social values and goals routinely debated by policymakers and the public at large. In this way, and somewhat paradoxically, the evaluator stays out of political disputes while at the same time aiming to be useful to the political policymaking process. To the extent that the separation of evaluation science and politics is successful, this model assumes that scientific knowledge can actually rescue policymaking from the "political" problems that plague it, namely, power politics, influence peddling, logrolling (exchanging favors, e.g., "I'll vote for your legislation if you vote for mine"), and the like. This view has been summarized as the "rational ideal":

> Inspired by a vague sense that reason is clean and politics is dirty, Americans yearn to replace politics with rational decision-making. Contemporary writings about politics, even those by political scientists, characterize it as "chaotic," "the ultimate maze," or "organized anarchy." Politics is "messy," "unpredictable," an "obstacle course" for policy and a "hostile environment" for policy analysis. . . . Policy is potentially a sphere of rational analysis, objectivity, allegiance to truth, and the pursuit of the well being of society as a whole. Politics is the sphere of emotion and passion, irrationality, self-interest, shortsightedness, and raw power.[14]

A wide variety of criticisms have been directed at this picture of how policymaking takes place including that it fails as both a descriptive and normative account of how political decision making unfolds; that it ignores the important role that value judgments and nonscientific considerations play in decisions about programs and policies; and that decisions made are rarely optimal.[15] Yet the model persists. It persists because we believe that grounding policy decisions in an appeal to reason coupled with "the facts of the matter" produced through unbiased techniques is preferable to decisions made on the basis of emotion, momentary passion, unconscious biases, political allegiances, or blind loyalty.[16] It persists because we want to keep the kind of reasoned analysis characteristic of evaluation (and scientific inquiry, more generally) distinct and separate from politics and in so doing improve the rationality of the policymaking process.

There is, however, an alternative view that holds that the rational ideal "misses the point of politics" and that it is misguided to assume that politics is fundamentally a "bad idea" and a departure from the best (i.e., rational) way of making policy. On the contrary, this view holds that "politics is a creative and valuable feature of social existence."[17] In contrast to the rational model which holds that decisions are made by systematic evaluation of alternative options to achieve clear goals, this view is based on a model of political reason in which goals are almost always relatively undefined and changeable, metaphor and analogy are employed to try to get others to see a situation as one thing rather than another, and the end output is persuasion rather than certainty.[18] The theory of political interaction at work here holds that the policymaking process does not parallel the linear process of reasoning characteristic of the rational model of decision making. Rather, the process is a struggle among multiple actors over ideas, classifications, labels, and boundaries. Argumentation, dialogue, and multiple perspectives are all involved in interpreting differences and contradictions and allowing participants to clarify underlying value conflicts.

Evaluators are mindful of two kinds of dangers in the policymaking process, regardless of which of the two models discussed above they might endorse. On the one hand, while it is clear that policymaking is a politicized process, evaluators are wary of the politicalization of evaluation itself. This is evident when evaluation is treated by policymakers as little more than ammunition in an adversarial process of decision making or where it is used in a tactical way. Tactical moves can include funding evaluation as a means to avoid making a policy decision, using evaluation to justify an existing course of action rather than to critically examine it, and using evaluation to give legitimacy to an agency or its policies.[19] The other danger is the scientization of politics through the use of evaluation. This is the idea that political debate can be resolved through the use of evaluation and scientific research, in effect replacing politics with science and turning a democracy into a technocracy. The assumption here is that increases in scientific certainty about the merits of a particular course of action or intervention will necessarily lead to a reduction in political uncertainty.[20]

The Politics of Policymaking II

The previous section described two frameworks for viewing the political process of policymaking within the institutions of government and argued that evaluation practices are often aligned with one or the other view. The relevance of the politics of policymaking for evaluation can also be examined from a different perspective. Evaluators often work with foundations and nongovernmental organizations that are both formally and informally connected to policy networks that aim to shape public policy around major issues in education, health care, and the environment. Increasingly, foundations are involved in grant-making not simply for purposes of funding discrete programs and direct services but for advocating for the achievement of specific policy goals such as expanding children's health insurance coverage (the David and Lucile Packard Foundation) or eliminating the use of institutional foster care for young children (the Annie E. Casey Foundation).[21] Likewise, agencies engaged in direct service delivery such as reproductive health services (e.g., PSI, Pathfinder International) often find that they must combine service delivery with advocacy for policy change that affects access to such services.

Evaluators are called upon to assess these advocacy and policy change efforts, and that work often requires the development of a theory of change for how advocacy efforts achieve outcomes related to policy change (see Chapter 2).[22] That theory, in turn, can be informed by social scientific theories of how policy change happens and what advocacy tactics can achieve. In other words, evaluators that work in these circumstances need to understand the politics of policymaking, as they are captured, for example, in the theory of policy windows, coalition theory, regime theory, or punctuated equilibrium theory.[23] This kind of knowledge of the politics of policymaking is essential in working with these types of evaluation clients who build networks with other agencies and engage in a variety of communication efforts to shape public policy agendas.

Evaluation as a Component of Governance

The politics of policymaking focuses on the processes by which policymakers, typically holding divergent views, reach decisions that are enacted as policies. Public sector governance, on the other hand, refers to the administrative and process-oriented aspects of governing and to how economic, political, and administrative authority is exercised. It is concerned with who has power, who makes decisions, how other players make their voices heard, and how accountability is decided.[24] Broadly accepted principles of democratic governance as promoted by the United Nations Development Program are shown in Table 6.[25]

Table 6. United Nations Principles of Good Governance

Participation
All men and women should have a voice in decision making, either directly or through legitimate intermediate institutions that represent their intention. Such broad participation is built on freedom of association and speech, as well as capacities to participate constructively.

Consensus orientation
Good governance mediates differing interests to reach a broad consensus on what is in the best interest of the group and, where possible, on policies and procedures.

Accountability
Decision makers are accountable to the public, as well as to institutional stakeholders. This accountability differs depending on the organizations and whether the decision is internal or external.

Transparency
Transparency is built on the free flow of information. Processes, institutions, and information are directly accessible to those concerned with them. Enough information is provided to understand and monitor institutions and their decision-making processes.

Responsiveness
Institutions and processes try to serve all stakeholders.

Effectiveness and efficiency
Processes and institutions produce results that meet needs while making the best use of resources.

Equity
All men and women have opportunities to improve or maintain their well-being.

Rule of law
Legal frameworks are fair and enforced impartially, particularly the laws on human rights.

Source: Adapted from "Governance for Sustainable Human Development—A UNDP Policy Document." Available at http://gis.emro.who.int/HealthSystemObservatory/Workshops/Workshop Documents/Reference%20reading%20material/Literature%20on%20Governance/GOVERN-2.PDF

Evaluation is traditionally linked to these principles of governance in democratic societies in at least three ways. First, the importance of evaluation arises in the context of the principles of democratic governance:

> Evaluators derive their legitimacy, and also their role and mandate, their need for technical competence and credibility, along with their right to independence, from the political notion of accountability in government: that is, the idea that governments are responsible to the people for their actions.[26]

Second, evaluation is considered necessary to the effective functioning of democratic societies because it supports legislative oversight; contributes to a knowledge base for decision making; helps agencies develop improved capabilities for policy and program planning, implementation and analysis of results, as well as greater openness and a more learning-oriented direction in their practice; and strengthens public information about government activities through dissemination of evaluation findings.[27] Third, as is readily evident in the world of international aid, evaluation is a means of examining whether reforms undertaken in the public and private sector contribute to good governance—that is, to a strong civil society, to the creation and maintenance of a professional bureaucracy, and to an executive arm of government that is accountable for its actions.[28]

However, in addition to this often-recited view of the relationship between evaluation and governance in democratic societies, evaluation occupies other roles in changing forms of governance; roles that may be viewed by some practitioners as more disturbing than reassuring of the commonsense understanding of the relationship.

Perhaps the most prominent idea is that evaluation, as it is wedded to New Public Management (NPM), becomes a tool for institutional control.[29] Briefly, NPM refers to an approach to reform in western governments that has been taking place since the early 1980s. The general thrust of the reform is to improve the efficiency and performance of public sector organizations by making services more responsive to users or consumers, applying private sector management techniques with a strong focus on benchmarking and measured performance, and creating a performance-oriented culture in the public sector.[30] Some advocates for reforming public administration even argue, "public sector management must become synonymous with performance management."[31]

This requirement for accountability in terms of public agency performance and results has, in turn, become the prime driver of the development of evaluative systems that function as a technology of control in public sector governance. Within NPM, evaluation plays a central role because assessment of performance compared to targets is central to its philosophy, so much so that some critics argue we are living in an "evaluative state."[32] The notion of an "evaluative state" refers to the fact that performance of public agencies is scrutinized and controlled at different levels through a variety of means including tracking outputs through performance measurement systems and indicators, using managerial

M&E processes, and conducting quality audits.[33] In other words, evaluation functions less like a critical voice weighing in on the value (or lack thereof) of public programs and policies and more like a technology that operates with well-defined procedures and indicators in a "society engaged in constant checking and verification, an audit society in which a particular style of formalized accountability is the ruling principle."[34] Procedures for performance monitoring, results-based management, audit, and inspection are increasingly installed in organizations, linked to decision-making routines and budgeting processes and used as management tools.[35] In such a scenario, we are increasingly confronted with evaluation as an autonomous, and seemingly agentless, system within organizations.

Other perspectives on how evaluation is wedded to governance focus on evidence-based practice (see Chapter 4). The argument here is that evidence-based practice, as supported by evaluation, is something more than simply a vehicle for improving decision making by practitioners in education, public health, and social services. Evidence-based practice is viewed as an instrument of politics because it shifts responsibility for decision making away from professionals toward consumers, who will use evidence to make informed service choices—a phenomenon readily evident in the publication in local newspapers of tables reporting the performance of public schools, and more recently seen in the Obama administration's efforts in 2013 to develop a college-rating system based on access, affordability, and student outcomes.[36] In the field of clinical medicine, evidence-based practice that forms the basis of managed care organizations (MCOs) functions politically by shifting power away from physicians to payers. The development of MCOs has been accompanied by the appearance of a new class of professional managers who rationalize the provision of medical services and who evaluate, oversee, and control medical practice, particularly the conduct of physicians.[37]

Thus, far from simply being a means to improve practice, the introduction of evidence-based practice into medicine has political consequences—it not only reduces the discretion and autonomy of physicians, it also redefines standards for appropriate medical practice by making it possible for payees and purchasers to deny payment for medical services that they deem medically unnecessary or ineffective.[38] A similar phenomenon is evident in the field of education, where evaluation as a form of data-driven governance secured through quality assurance and assessment-information systems reduces the professional discretion of teachers in the classroom to make instructional decisions.[39]

In sum, the relationships between evaluation and the process of public sector governance are complicated and manifold. On the one hand, evaluation is seen as both reflective of and promoting principles of democratic governance. This is readily evident in the work of EvalPartners, mentioned earlier. The practice of evaluation can also be influential in shaping what governments can gain from evaluation, what policies they have with respect to evaluation, how they manage evaluation, and how they use evaluation.[40] A clear example is the work of the American Evaluation Association's Evaluation Policy Task Force that developed a vision for the role of evaluation in all three branches of the federal government in the U.S.[41] On the other hand, rather than being practiced as informed critical analysis that might help in the resolution of social problems and thus enhance democratic governance, evaluation can be seen as fostering a particular type of social and political relations, and assuming a pivotal role as part of a governing process by which compliance with program goals and policy targets can be assured.[42]

Evaluation's Political Point of View

As suggested in the discussion of the evaluator role in valuing in Chapter 3, evaluators themselves have political stances. They may have sympathies with liberal, conservative, social democratic, or pragmatic political ideologies, for example. More apparent might be the fact that evaluators advocate for particular interests—some advocate for the judging of the value (or lack thereof) of a program strictly on the basis of the "scientific merits of the case." Others advocate for evaluation as a means of improving the rationality of political debate; for representing the points of view and needs of program participants or beneficiaries; for the inclusion of key stakeholders in the design and conduct of an evaluation; for addressing the specific interests of the immediate stakeholders in a program or policy (versus the broader public interest); for the importance of determining whether the design, delivery, and outcomes of a social intervention literally empowered its beneficiaries, and so on. Finally, and perhaps less obviously, there are political values implicit in the way evaluators (as well as legislators, the general public, program stakeholders, and others) view a given social issue. For example, values implicit in many evaluation studies in the field of corrections are that "the offender, not society, needs correcting; that we know how to, and should, change a person's behavior (for the better); that problem amelioration will lead directly and immediately to reduced recidivism; and that measuring failure is appropriate in correctional studies."[43] In short, the evaluator qua evaluator has a sense of what is politically appropriate, best, right, just, and fair. Viewed as a collective social practice (versus the action of individual evaluators), we can also say that the enterprise of evaluation itself has a political stance.[44]

Nearly thirty years ago, two prominent evaluators surveying the state of affairs of evaluation practice noted that it was widely acknowledged that evaluation is intrinsically concerned with values and value judgment. They added, however, "What we find missing from such discussions is that all valuing derives from some broader framework of values . . . about which ends the profession should serve. . . . Implicitly, evaluators work with some set of humanitarian and democratic values but careful explication of these values is rare."[45] In the intervening years, the field has become more explicit about those values. When discussing the political stance of evaluation as a social practice, two broad professional orientations seem most relevant as directional aids. They have been labeled either as rationalistic compared to argumentative[46] or as public interest compared to populist,[47] reflecting their respective authors' appeals to somewhat different literatures. Each stance embraces a different understanding of how democratic values, multiple stakeholders' interests, the public's interests, power, and the expert authority of the evaluator should be dealt with in evaluation.

Rationalistic and public interest approaches to evaluation are characterized by several key assumptions and beliefs. First, they are predicated on a separation of the production of evaluation knowledge by expert evaluators from the use of that knowledge by practitioners, policymakers, citizens, and program beneficiaries. Evaluators may involve clients and other stakeholders in evaluation planning (deciding what is to be evaluated, on the basis of which criteria, when, etc.) but the evaluator is solely responsible for the design, data collection and analysis, and reporting of the evaluation.[48]

Second, these approaches tend to endorse instrumental rationality as the norm for the behavior of evaluators and the conduct of public policy (see the earlier discussion of the rational ideal).[49] Instrumental rationality is concerned with discovering appropriate and effective means to given ends. Accordingly, the role of evaluation is to appraise the merits of different social interventions designed to ameliorate social problems. In restricting what it means to be rational to choosing the best means to a given end, instrumental rationality relegates matters of social and cultural values, opinions, and interests to the domain of the irrational or the political, and hence outside the immediate concerns of the evaluator.[50] (Of course, rationalistic evaluators *are* concerned with how those matters might unduly influence or bias the evaluation, and thus they take steps to prevent that from happening.)

Third, there is a strong emphasis in these approaches on value-neutrality and rendering objective, impartial assessments in as even-handed a manner as is possible. Value-neutrality here does not mean that rationalistic approaches reflect no values whatsoever. In fact, these approaches are premised on several well-understood and accepted *epistemic* values including logical clarity, empirical adequacy, and transparency of procedures. Value-neutrality in rationalistic approaches means striving to produce evaluation knowledge unaffected by *nonepistemic* values—in other words, knowledge that is objective and empirically warranted but unbiased by any particular set of social, cultural, or personal values and independent of any special interests or partisan perspectives.

Fourth, the central beliefs animating this perspective are that (a) thoughtful democratic societies seeking to realize values of equity, equality, fairness, social justice, public disclosure, and so on can best accomplish this through a rational process of decision making, and (b) that process is best served by an evaluation practice that produces valid, reliable, empirical evaluative knowledge that is rigorously independent of any agenda or particular special interests.

This species of evaluation claims that evaluation should be uninterested in politics. Of course, that itself is a political stance because it promotes a particular kind of political relevance for evaluation. This family of approaches has been labeled the "public interest family" because it reflects the political belief in the importance of evaluation serving the public interest or common good as opposed to addressing the diversity of interests that characterize a democracy.[51]

Argumentative and populist approaches to evaluation are somewhat more difficult to characterize because they embrace a wider variety of ideas. Recall that in Chapter 3 we pointed out that a *prescriptive* view of valuing occurs when an evaluator conducts evaluation from some explicitly justified value framework. Argumentative and populist approaches are prescriptive. They have been labeled "populist" in the field of evaluation because they reflect a deep concern for the populace by attending in specific ways to the multiplicity and diversity of interests in a democracy and often advocating for those most disenfranchised in society.[52] They are also populist in that they broadly share the political doctrine of populism, which means supporting the rights and power of "the people" versus social elites. In the field of policy analysis, these approaches are referred to as "argumentative" because they begin with the view that "in politics, politicians and policy decision-makers advance proposals about what to do based on normative arguments. Empirical questions come into play where there are reasons to doubt factual aspects of the argument. In this view, normative-based analysis can be facilitated by an organized dialogue among competing normative positions."[53]

These approaches have also been called "democratically oriented" for several reasons: some (e.g., participatory and collaborative models) advocate for democratic participation via stakeholder involvement in evaluation design, implementation, and decision making; others endorse variants of deliberative processes in which the evaluator facilitates public argument around stakeholder and citizen interests, values, and evaluative findings; others aim to democratize evaluation by practicing it in culturally responsive ways; and still others hold that truly democratically oriented evaluation means evaluation by and for indigenous peoples.[54]

One salient aspect of politics for many evaluators committed to argumentative and populist approaches is whether the political and civil rights of program recipients are being respected and fostered as a result of a social or environmental intervention. The concern, particularly in the evaluation of international aid, is often with how the political power of donors and aid agencies impacts local control, ownership, and sustainability of outcomes and program beneficiaries' rights to self-determination. A strong example of attending to the interplay between politics and evaluation in this way is evident in the UNICEF publication *Evaluation for Equitable Development Results*. The volume explores a variety of perspectives on "equity-focused evaluations"—evaluations that focus specifically on the equity dimensions of social interventions, particularly whether such interventions support the poor and marginalized to be agents of their own development.[55]

It is a mistake to claim that argumentative and populist approaches such as this are "democratically oriented" while those characterized as rationalistic and public interest-oriented are somehow not. What distinguishes the two is not that one endorses democratic values of equity, equality, and social justice and the other does not. Rather, the approaches disagree on the way evaluation can best serve those democratic ideals. Rationalistic and public interest approaches argue that evaluation best fosters goals of democracy by providing fair, balanced, impartial scientific information to both the public and to decision makers while remaining above or outside of the political process characterized by arguments over appropriate social directions. The tasks of rational analysis and objective judgment on the part of the evaluator should remain distinct from the choices of the political community.

On the other hand, argumentative and populist approaches generally hold that evaluation is a form of practical argumentation that unfolds in complex, often highly political environments in which normative concerns and political choices cannot be neatly separated from the analytic, scientific process involved in determining the value of a program or policy. This does not necessarily mean that evaluation is "all political" or that evaluators face a dichotomous choice between evaluations that are scientifically credible or politically viable. The empirical orientation of the evaluation matters, and the concern for rendering warranted claims about program outcomes and value (or lack thereof) does not disappear. However, the evaluation process involves integrating this kind of analysis (or technical-analytical discourse) with additional kinds of considerations (or other discourses) related to (1) relevance of the program to local context, (2) fit of the program with societal arrangements, and (3) compatibility of the program with broad social goals.[56]

To illustrate how evaluation would involve an argumentative process incorporating these multiple considerations, consider a hypothetical example of a comprehensive social intervention operating across many geographically dispersed and culturally different sites with the aim of improving educational opportunities for preschool-aged children.[57] One consideration is whether the intervention achieved one of its primary stated objectives of improving the reading ability of the children. Another consideration, raised by some stakeholders, is that the program was designed for middle-class children and thus poorly suited for the circumstances that children living in poverty find themselves in. Yet another group of stakeholders argue that this kind of program is essential for a society committed to equal educational opportunity for all children. But a particularly radical African American organization in the community argued that they did not want to prepare their children for achievement in a white middle-class American society.

Argumentative and populist approaches to evaluation would engage all these multiple discourses or considerations. However, each approach might do so differently. For example, one might see the evaluator offering "humble support" to citizens who are charged with the responsibility of reasoning about what is good and right in this situation; another might argue that the evaluator must advocate for the views of stakeholders and program beneficiaries who are traditionally least represented or disenfranchised in these kinds of processes.[58] Yet a third approach might find the evaluator serving as a broker between groups with differing interests and concerns who attempts to negotiate a consensus view.

Conclusion

This chapter provided an overview of some of the more significant practical and intellectual issues and controversies that constitute the evaluation-politics-policymaking nexus. An essentially important idea emphasized in this chapter is that being politically aware means more than being on the lookout for the way pressures stemming from ideological perspectives, the pursuit of special interests, the raw exercise of power, and so forth impact one's practice. Of course, these are important considerations. Yet an awareness of politics in evaluation is not simply a matter of evaluation "encountering" the political; it is also about realizing that evaluation is both practiced within and promotes some kind of political framework. To come to this realization is to accept the fact that although logically we may distinguish matters in evaluation practice that are scientific and nonpolitical from those that are normative and value-laden, practically, this is virtually impossible to do. The political framework of evaluation practice has two significant components. One is concerned with how the practice envisions the politics of policymaking. The other has to do with how the practice adopts a political stance with respect to its understanding of the public good or public interest, how different interests are represented and addressed, and what role evaluation plays or ought to play.[59] One of the major issues is the alignment of evaluation with two different conceptions of democracy, often referred to as thin versus thick or weak versus strong.[60] A thin version of democracy is an electoral-based liberal democracy in which individuals are relatively passive and exert democratic control primarily through voting. Politics is a matter of the struggle among competing interests. A strong version of democracy holds that individuals are citizens and ought to be able to participate in at least some aspects of self-government at least some of the time. Politics is participatory and a search for the common good.[61] The political framework of evaluation also has much to do with how the use of evaluation is envisioned, and that is the topic of the next chapter.

6 Use

No doubt every evaluator has had moments of glorious dreams in which a grateful world receives with adulation the findings of his or her evaluation and puts the results immediately and directly to use. Most of our dreams must remain dreams.[1]

The objective, purpose, and use of evaluation are intertwined and often not readily distinguishable. (This is attributable, in part, to the fact that those three terms are often treated as synonyms in everyday English language usage.) The objective or goal of evaluation is to determine the merit, worth, value, or significance of a program or policy. That is considered a purpose worthy of pursuit because knowledge forthcoming from an evaluation is clearly intended for particular uses including supporting decision making about a program (i.e., improve it, discontinue it, modify it), building a knowledge base about effective interventions, enhancing the accountability of agencies that fund and operate programs, or informing the public. In other words, there is something inherent in the objective and purpose of evaluation that has to do with its use; evaluation is undertaken to be useful.

However, we know that no expert knowledge—whether forthcoming from evaluation or any other form of disciplined, scientific inquiry—compels action. If that were so, we would see few, if any, patients not complying with their doctor's directives to lose weight, exercise regularly, and stop smoking; few, if any, legislators supporting funding for social programs for which there is no empirical evidence of effectiveness; and few, if any, members of the general public claiming that global warming and climate change are little more than a political agenda. In short, use of scientific or evaluation knowledge does not just naturally happen.

Thus, dating approximately to the mid- to late 1970s, a sizable body of conceptual and empirical scholarship in the social sciences has arisen around what is often referred to as the knowledge-action gap or, more

specifically, the use of scientific knowledge in decisions made in both policymaking and practice arenas.[2] This literature aims to define knowledge
use, explain how it happens and why it doesn't, how it can be enhanced,
and how it can be assessed. This chapter draws on this considerable literature to identify prominent issues surrounding how use might be explained, the factors and circumstances that affect use, and the way in
which different evaluation approaches position the idea of use in practice.
This chapter focuses broadly on the use of knowledge forthcoming from
scientific research, where the latter is understood to mean systematic, disciplined, empirical inquiry that includes the form of inquiry known as
evaluation. The phrases *research use, use of scientific knowledge,* and *use of
evaluation* are employed fairly interchangeably in what follows. Where
there is a noticeable difference in the use of scientific knowledge more
generally versus evaluation more specifically, that is explained.

Defining Use

The current body of knowledge on use of evaluation and scientific
knowledge comprises multiple literatures including examinations of data-
driven decision making initiated in business management and now firmly
part of the discussion of education reform and improvement;[3] evidence-
based practice originating in clinical medicine and now spread through
virtually all sectors of social services and education;[4] knowledge utilization
as studied in sociology, organizational theory, and political science focused
not only on the use of scientific knowledge but also on the use of program-
matic interventions and policies and covering diffusion and implementation theory;[5] and the literature specifically concerned with evaluation use.[6]
Given these varied sources, it is not particularly surprising that the study
of use is plagued by lack of common terminology. Across the literature,
we find the terms *knowledge translation, knowledge exchange, knowledge
transfer, knowledge utilization, research uptake, data use,* and in the field of
evaluation, *evaluation use* (and *misuse*) and *evaluation influence.*[7]

Almost from the inception of research on the topic, debates arose
over the proper terminology. In the early 1980s, Carol Weiss, one of the
leading scholars of the use of science and evaluation in policymaking,
argued that the term "use" should replace "knowledge utilization." She
claimed that the latter had overtones of tools and instruments and suggested imagery of instrumental, episodic application of knowledge, when

in fact her research revealed that knowledge was used in far more diffuse and subtle ways in decision making.[8] Several decades later, Karen Kirkhart, a prominent evaluator, contended that the broader term "influence" is more appropriate than "use" because it signifies the "capacity or power of persons or things to produce effects on others by intangible or indirect means."[9] Her argument was that if we think in terms of evaluation influence, we are better able to consider a range of effects of evaluation beyond unidirectional, intended use of evaluation results, and to attend to multidirectional, incremental, unintentional, noninstrumental influences that can unfold over time.

Regardless of whether it is called use or influence, there are three aspects of the phenomenon that require further careful consideration: (1) What is the locus of use? (2) What kind of object is use? (3) What types of use are there? These aspects are interrelated but differentiated here for analytic purposes.

WHAT IS THE LOCUS OF USE?

Locus is a matter of determining where "use" actually occurs. Scholars and practitioners disagree about whether the study of the use of evaluation and other types of scientific knowledge should focus on what happens at the collective or organizational level (for example, the policymaking arena in national governments or the deliberations of a board of directors at a nonprofit organization) or at the level of changes in behavior, knowledge, or attitude of the individual. Both are legitimate concerns. In the literature on evidence-based practice and data-driven decision making, the focus is on how and why the autonomous professional social worker, nurse, classroom teacher, school administrator, or physician takes specific actions or makes specific decisions as a result of making sense of evidence or data. Some examples are how the classroom teacher uses data from interim student assessments to make adjustments in instructional practices or how the clinician adjusts treatment recommendations in view of evidence of the efficacy of different therapies. Evaluators may find themselves in circumstances where this concern with individual behavior change is the primary locus of "use" of findings from evaluation studies. However, more often, they are likely to be in situations where the use of evaluation is more a matter of what happens at a collective or systems level. These circumstances are characterized by high levels of interdependency and interconnectedness among decision makers, reliance on multiple sources of information and evidence, and processes of collective sense making and coalition building that involve the rhetorical and persuasive powers of various actors in the situation.[10]

The issue here is whether use is best understood as a process, outcome, or practice. Or perhaps we might ask, "If one were to study use from one of these three perspectives, what would one learn?" Treating the use of evidence arising from evaluation or other forms of scientific inquiry as a process or activity is evident in views such as the following in political science: "Collective-level knowledge use is the process by which users incorporate specific information into action proposals to influence others' thought and practices."[11] This process is characterized in part by the rhetorical capabilities of the multiple users to influence one another's thoughts and actions, as well as by the interaction of evaluation and scientific evidence with other forms of evidence, information, and beliefs in the process of agenda setting (how issues are problematized, conceptualized, and prioritized).[12] A similar concern with use as a process is evident in a National Research Council study that argued scientific and evaluative knowledge—data, findings, concepts, and theories—becomes evidence when it is used in a policy argument, understood as a bundle of considerations backed by reasons presented to persuade a particular audience of the validity and need for a given action.[13] The focus on use as a process of "making an argument," "engaging in agenda setting," or "developing an action proposal" disassociates the phenomenon of use from any particular outcome. Use is an *activity or event* that individuals participate in.

However, use can also be studied as an *outcome*.[14] Some prominent evaluators have argued that to understand use, we need to identify mechanisms or change processes and outcomes at three levels—interpersonal, intrapersonal, and collective. In addition, we ought to consider the ways in which one process and outcome can trigger another, for example, evaluation findings leading to new knowledge which in turn changes one's attitude toward a program, which in turn leads one to advocate for change within an organization, and so on.

Finally, use might profitably be examined as a *practice*, where a practice is understood as the "coordinated activity of individuals and groups in doing their 'real work' as it is informed by a particular organizational or group context."[15] Employing practice as an analytical tool for studying use has gained significant traction in the field of data-driven decision making.[16] The use of data is characterized as an interactive endeavor and a situated phenomenon that unfolds in the "natural habitat" of a particular workplace.[17] Thus, for example, the practice of data use in a legislative committee in the federal government would differ from the practice of data use by a principal in a local school. Both data use practices involve sense making, that is, determining *what* data or information will be attended to in a given decision-making environment, *whether* that data or information is considered evidence pertaining to some problem or issue at hand, and *how* it will eventually be used. But how sense making happens and what it signifies will differ in each practice because the cognitive process of sense making is distributed across a web of actors in the particular circumstances of each situation and constituted as well, in part by key features of the situation including organizational norms and routines.[18]

WHAT TYPES OF USE?

There have been multiple attempts to develop typologies of use. The most common typology includes instrumental, conceptual, symbolic, and process use. *Instrumental use* means the direct application of an evaluation or piece of research to a specific decision or in defining a solution to a particular problem.[19] As noted in the previous chapter, this kind of use rests on what many believe is an unrealistic, rational, problem-solving model of decision making where one assumes that the decision to be made drives the application of research knowledge.[20] In addition, even when instrumental use occurs, it is rare and most likely to happen only under the following conditions: where research findings are noncontroversial and there is low scientific uncertainty about findings, where the decision context is characterized by high value consensus, where only a limited change in a policy or practice is required, and where that change will be implemented in a low-conflict environment in which current thinking or the present state of affairs is not likely to be altered.[21]

Conceptual use refers to more subtle and involved ways in which scientific knowledge gradually enters into the perspectives, understandings, attitudes, and actions of decision makers. Use is not the direct application to solving problems, but rather a matter of setting the terms of a discussion around significant concepts, propositions, empirical generalizations, and the like.[22] Over time, scientific findings shape both problem defini- tion and decisions about how best to address those problems. Conceptual use often is spoken of as a way in which scientific research and evalua- tion serve to "enlighten" policymakers and practitioners. However, it is equally possible that just the opposite may be the case. Because the indi- rect process of influencing decision making is subject to oversimplifica- tion and distortion, "it may come to resemble 'endarkenment' as much as enlightenment."[23]

Symbolic use of evaluation and research is variously interpreted as both a bad thing and an inevitable occurrence in organizations. On the shady side indicating misuse, symbolic use refers to perfunctory support for evaluation and research but no real intent to take the findings or evidence seriously. It might include shrewd political maneuvering by individuals or groups in support of evaluation or research in order to give the appearance of endorsing evidence-based decision making or using findings of evalua- tion and scientific studies selectively to support a political position.[24]

From another perspective, symbolic use of evaluation (particularly in governments) is an aspect of impression management, that is, the forma- tion of a public image: "Evaluation can be seen as a ritual whose function is to calm the anxieties of the citizenry and to perpetuate an image of gov- ernment rationality, efficacy and accountability. The very act of requiring and commissioning evaluations may create the impression that govern- ment is seriously committed to the pursuit of publicly espoused goals, such as increasing student achievement or reducing malnutrition. Evalua- tions lend credence to this image."[25] This view is consistent with the idea that organizations use evaluation and other forms of scientific knowledge symbolically as a source of legitimation. For example, an organization can draw on expert knowledge to bolster its claim to jurisdiction over a par- ticular policy area; in that way, expert knowledge endows the organization with "epistemic authority."[26] This view of symbolic use is associated with institutional organizational theory.[27] Rational models emphasize that or- ganizations draw on knowledge instrumentally to realize their mandated goals, maximize performance, expand their power, or adjust their poli- cies. In contrast, institutional theory emphasizes that organizations are primarily concerned with securing legitimacy both from their members and from their external environment. Legitimacy is understood in the sense of how an organization meets societal expectations about appropriate structures, practices, rhetoric, or output.[28] Evaluation comes to be seen as a necessary organizational procedure, "expected by societies that furnish resources and legitimacy to organizations."[29] The sociological phenomenon of symbolic use of evaluation and other forms of knowledge is not necessarily a conniving and calculating move, so to speak, on the part of organizations. Rather, it is a taken-for-granted action that aligns with the way an organization sees itself conforming to expectations of its members and its external audiences.[30]

A type of use apparently unique to evaluation practice is *process use*, understood as individual or organizational outcomes attributable to having *participated* in an evaluation. The central idea is that the experience of participating in the evaluation process provides a kind of direct and indirect instruction in learning to think evaluatively that, in turn, may lead to changes in individual cognitive processes, attitudes, and behavior, as well as in organizational culture.[31] Recall that in Chapter 4 we explored the idea that evaluative thinking is critical thinking. Process use of evaluation might be viewed as a way of instilling and cultivating critical thinking skills in evaluation participants. No other form of professional knowledge generation, for example in law, medicine, or accounting, is said to have such a "use." Process use calls attention to the fact that what it is literally being "consumed" or "used" is not necessarily the typical knowledge product—the report of the evaluation results or findings. Process use shares something in common with the idea of use as an activity or event in which one participates. Yet it also focuses on an outcome (and a particularly positive one at that) of participation in the event of use.

Via their focus on stakeholder engagement in and ownership of the process, participatory, empowerment, and collaborative evaluation approaches are specifically designed to accomplish process use of evaluation.[32] The utility of these evaluations is to be judged in part by the degree to which stakeholders identify individual or collective value added as a consequence of their involvement with the evaluation.[33] Value added at the organizational level is discussed in terms of evaluation capacity building (ECB) that is concerned with developing and implementing teaching and learning strategies, leadership support, resources, and processes and policies that will lead to sustainable evaluation practice within an organization.[34] Current interest in ECB focuses specifically on both the capacity to do evaluation and the capacity to use it. In this framework, evaluation use can be regarded as planned and intentional decision support, process use, or even "serendipitous influence on organizational and program thinking and decision making."[35]

Typologies of the kind sketched above can be heuristically useful (no pun intended) in examining different ways in which decision makers encounter and make sense of the product and process of evaluation as well as other forms of scientific knowledge. However, as a means of moving forward the development of a theory of knowledge use, typological analysis is of questionable value because the categories in these typologies are neither mutually exclusive (types overlap, e.g., the line separating instrumental from conceptual use is rather thin) nor collectively exhaustive (taken together, all the types of use do not necessarily cover all options). Moreover, it is very doubtful that these types can be neatly distinguished: "Empirically, making the distinction would require perfect access to users' cognitive processes, and it remains debatable whether users would be able to make the distinction."[36]

Factors Affecting Use

After almost four decades of research there are a substantial number of fundamental questions about the use of scientific research and evaluation in policymaking that remain unanswered. This was made quite clear in the outcome of a collaborative exercise undertaken in 2012 involving 52 participants with a wide range of experience in both science and policy, including individuals from government, nongovernmental organizations, academia, and industry. Participants initially identified 239 unanswered questions, and via a workshop procedure narrowed the list to the 40 most important. Table 7 displays several of these questions across six critical areas.[37]

Equally troublesome is the fact that a theory of use remains frustratingly elusive. There are dozens of definitions and models of use, as well as multiple measures of utilization, no single one of which dominates the literature.[38] There is a widely shared sentiment in the literature that the phenomenon of use is so contextually embedded in organizational, policy, and institutional contexts that it probably will never be explained by any particular theory.[39] However, the context-dependency of use does not necessarily simply mean "it all depends." In much the same way that typologies have value for investigating what use might mean in practice, there are several heuristics for examining factors that influence the use of evaluation and other forms of scientific knowledge.

Table 7. A Sample of Key Unanswered Questions about the Use of Science
in Policymaking

Topic: Understanding the role of scientific evidence in policymaking
- How do different political cultures and institutions affect the acquisition and treatment of scientific evidence in policy formulation, implementation, and evaluation?

Topic: Framing questions, sourcing evidence and advice, shaping research
- What are the most effective mechanisms for identifying the evidence required to inform policymaking on new and emerging problems?

Topic: Policymaking under conditions of uncertainty and disagreement
- How is agreement reached on what counts as sufficient evidence to inform particular policy decisions?
- How is scientific evidence incorporated into representations of, and decision-making about, so-called "wicked" problems, which lack clear definition and cannot be solved definitively?

Topic: Democratic governance of scientific advice
- What factors (for example, openness, accountability, credibility) influence the degree to which the public accepts as trustworthy an expert providing advice?
- What governance processes and enabling conditions are needed to ensure that policymaking is scientifically credible, while addressing a perceived societal preference for policy processes that are more democratic than technocratic?

Topic: Advisory systems and networks
- How are national science advisory systems constructed and to what extent do different systems result in different outcomes?
- How and why does the role of scientific advice in policymaking differ among local, regional, national, and international levels of governance?

Topic: How do scientists and policymakers understand expert advisory processes?
- What factors shape the ways in which scientific advisors and policymakers make sense of their own and each other's roles in the policy process?

Source: William J. Sutherland et al. 2012. "A Collaboratively-Derived Science-Policy Research Agenda." *PLoS ONE* 7(3): 1–5.

The most common heuristic arises from the two communities framework.[40] The framework posits that, on the one hand, there are scientists concerned with the norms and cognitive values of the scientific enterprise and, on the other hand, action-oriented and practically oriented policymakers. Each community has a different language, values, reward system, and social and professional affiliations. One deals in rational analysis and disciplined research, the other in politics and undisciplined problems. The two spheres or communities are thought to be separate, with evaluators, scientists, and policy analysts concentrating on specific issues, technical detail, gathering data, and conducting defensible studies, while the political people are involved in many more issue areas than the former group, and concentrate on winning elections, promoting party platforms, and mobilizing support for issues.[41] The scientific community supplies the knowledge; the political community demands and consumes it.

In this framework, use is affected by problems on both the supply and demand side. The list of potential supply problems is long and generally is concerned with whether the knowledge produced is relevant, credible, and accessible to decision makers. Other supply-side problems can include inadequate production of policy-relevant research possibly due to lack of capacity, inability to relate findings from a specific study to the social and political history of a policy idea, ineffective communication or packaging of existing research and evaluation, lack of sufficiently robust and cumulative findings, methodologically weak research, failure to deliver findings in a timely manner, and so on. Demand-side problems can include an inability of policymakers to spell out objectives in researchable terms, lack of incentives for policymakers to use evidence and data, ignorance of existing research on the part of policymakers, incapacity of policymakers to absorb or make sense of research, a tendency toward anti-intellectualism on the part of policymakers, and so on. Calls for educating policymakers to be proficient in the use of indicator data is one example of a demand-side problem and remedy; another is the broad plea to better educate practitioners and the citizenry more generally in quantitative literacy. In the current climate surrounding the evaluation of international aid, we see both supply-side and demand-side problems at work. A common compliant is that, on the one hand, evaluators produce highly technical and statistically sophisticated impact evaluations that are difficult for policymakers to make sense of. On the other hand, many organizations lack internal structures for decision making and incentive systems that encourage managers and decision makers to use such evaluations and reward them for doing so.[42]

Another approach to understanding factors affecting use was suggested earlier when discussing whether use can be viewed as a practice of sense making. Here, to study factors that affect use, we need to understand how the practice of sense making unfolds in the interactions among decision makers and how those interactions are mediated by aspects of their specific situation (e.g., plans, policy directives, formal and informal organizational norms and routines, and tools such as decision-making protocols and monitoring and evaluation systems).[43] For example, to understand what the use of behavioral data as well as data from student assessments means as practiced by a team of grade-level teachers in an elementary school, we would have to study factors related to teachers' own knowledge about how to interpret such data and how that knowledge is "situated" within not only the interactions of the team but also within the policies, climate of concerns, and regular practices of the school in which they teach. A focus on practice draws attention to how those engaged in "use" make sense of the decision-making environment in which they find themselves.

One additional approach to studying factors that affect use argues that three contextual factors are most important: politics (the degree of issue polarization), economics (cost-sharing equilibrium), and social structuring (channels of communication).[44] Issue polarization, also often spoken of as the degree of values consensus and uncertainty,[45] can be understood in the following way:

> Contexts are said to be characterized by low issue polarization when potential users share similar opinions and preferences regarding (1) the problematization of the issue (consensus on the perception that a given situation is a problem and not the normal or desirable state of affairs), (2) the prioritization and salience of the issue (compared with other potential issues), and (3) the criteria against which potential solutions should be assessed. Conversely, as the level of consensus on those aspects diminishes, issue polarization grows.[46]

When polarization is low, use more closely resembles the instrumental, problem-solving model of decision making noted earlier. Conversely, when issue polarization is high, use more or less resembles a political model where evaluation or research is used to support a particular stance. Much of the political science literature takes for granted that the normal state of affairs in policymaking is highly polarized.

The economic issue centers on the assumption that producers and users of evaluation and scientific research will invest in use to the extent that they perceive their investment to be profitable:

> Any operational system of knowledge exchange and use will be characterized by a given cost-sharing equilibrium between users, on one hand, and producers or intermediaries, on the other. For example, one well known user-centered equilibrium is consultancy, in which users assume most of the costs,

as they hire and pay the consultant and usually devote attention to the results. At the other end of the continuum, another well-known equilibrium is the push model, in which the results of research funded by a third party are more or less actively brought to the attention of potential users. In this model, it is either the producers or interested intermediaries who will devote time and resources to catch users' attention.[47]

To understand use, one must understand this cost-sharing equilibrium and who is bearing the costs. This will vary, in part, depending on the kind of evaluation model employed and the circumstances under which evaluation is funded and commissioned.

Finally, the social aspect of context has to do with the nature of and channels for communication between producers and users. Research on use reveals that use is enhanced when there are open and natural channels of communication between producers and users of knowledge.[48] The focus on social context has to with the nature of interactions between these two groups including formal linkages and means for frequent exchange.[49] Use is, in part, a consequence of whether the form and nature of existing communication networks can be deliberately modified to enhance collaboration or whether new networks must be designed to achieve this goal. More on this idea is provided in the following section.

Frameworks for Supporting Use

In the previous chapter we saw that evaluation does not simply encounter or interact with politics, but is practiced within and promotes some kind of political orientation. Similarly, the ways in which evaluation is practiced are wedded to one of two broad political frameworks of use: one originates from the perspective of the producers of scientific knowledge, a second stems from the perspective of the users of that knowledge.

PRODUCER-CENTERED FRAMEWORKS

Also called source-based and supply-centered, these frameworks are about bringing research and evaluation to practice.[50] There are two variants. One variant assumes a climate of rationality; that is, a culture of decision making that values rational behavior (as described in Chapter 5).[51] It is firmly grounded in the two communities hypothesis described above and regards use as largely unidirectional and linear—knowledge moves from producer to user. The most commonly recognized form of this effort to link scientific knowledge to practice is the Research-Development-Diffusion Model.[52] A more contemporary version is evidence-based practice that is largely a technical exercise linking research to action via the development of clinical guidelines and model practices.[53]

A second variant of producer-centered frameworks also accepts the basic idea of two communities but embraces more bidirectional approaches to the use of research and evaluation knowledge. These frameworks are often spoken of as interactive, knowledge translation models, and they display three common characteristics: (1) they do not assume that research and evaluation findings will be necessarily used in rational ways; (2) they emphasize the role that a range of interrelated cultural, organizational, personal, and political factors shape whether and how research is used; and (3) they reject the notion that research is disseminated and then adopted, arguing instead that it is adapted and blended with other forms of knowledge depending on the contexts of its use.[54]

The Canadian Institutes of Health Research (CIHR) has pioneered thinking about an interactive, knowledge translation model. The CIHR defines knowledge exchange as "collaborative problem-solving . . . [that] involves interaction between decision-makers and researchers and results in mutual learning through the process of planning, producing, disseminating, and applying existing or new research in decision-making."[55] Unlike unidirectional models of research-to-practice, interactive frameworks emphasize that use is a dynamic, iterative, and social process. They may attend to an important role for individuals or agencies that serve as knowledge brokers or policy entrepreneurs (who have one foot in the world of research and evaluation and another in the policy world) in bridging the two communities.[56] These frameworks also stress the significance of institutional arrangements that promote closer, longer-term working relationships between researchers, funders, practitioners, and policymakers. One example is an interactive systems framework in prevention science that links three interrelated systems—one dealing with the distillation of research on interventions and its translation into user-friendly formats; another providing practitioners training and support for general capacity building (enhancing the infrastructure, skills, and motivation of an organization to use research) as well as support tailored to adopting specific interventions; and a third devoted to support for implementation.[57]

USER-CENTERED FRAMEWORKS

Awareness that use is highly contingent on some means of collaborative problem solving does not come as news to those evaluators who have long been committed to participatory and empowerment forms of evaluation in which the evaluator supports program participants and staff as they engage in their own evaluation.[58] These forms of evaluation are examples of a broader class of approaches known as "utilization-focused evaluation" (UFE), defined by its founder as "evaluation done for and with specific intended primary users for specific, intended uses."[59] UFE is a philosophy of evaluation more than a particular model or method. It requires that an evaluator first act as a facilitator, building working relationships with primary intended users to help them determine the kind of evaluation they need.[60]

Community-centered models are another variant of a user-centered approach. They focus on improving the quality of life in communities by improving the quality of the practices of treatment, prevention, health promotion, and education. They emphasize the involvement of community agencies (public health, education, criminal justice, etc.), researchers, evaluators, practitioners, and service recipients in collaborative learning aimed at improving outcomes of social practices. Key features of this kind of framework, as described by one of its strongest advocates, include (a) viewing best practices not as off-the-shelf packages but as a process of matching practitioner capacity with appropriate processes for implementing interventions that fit community needs; (b) regarding practitioners, clients, and community not as passive recipients of scientific information but contributors of knowledge and evidence; (c) engaging in local evaluation and self-monitoring (as is consistent with principles of empowerment evaluation);[61] and (d) tailoring research information to fit particular community circumstances.[62]

Community-centered frameworks are also focused on building local capacity for continuous, real-time learning integrated across community agencies that deal with issues surrounding the health of mothers and children, school readiness, school achievement, physical and mental health, and safe neighborhoods. It is widely acknowledged, however, that to achieve this perspective on the use of research data and evaluation requires particular kinds of human resources including skilled individuals to lead the process in which multiple agency partners review data and experience, learn from it, and chart their future course as well as neighborhood residents who can serve as influential leaders in this process.[63]

Another variant of user-centered frameworks is particularly focused on policymaking rather than on evaluation per se but shares the user-focused intent of participatory and collaborative forms of evaluation. There is no convenient label for these frameworks that are broadly concerned with democratizing scientific expertise. The rationale is summarized in a report from the United Nations Educational, Scientific, and Cultural Organization (UNESCO):

> The growing importance of science and technology in daily life is demanding a less linear, less authoritarian and more complex way of organizing the interplay of science, decisionmaking and society. . . . It would seem that we are moving towards more complex patterns of governance, regulated by a demand for public proof. . . . This public proof requirement means that those involved in any scientific or technical issue (governments, the scientific community, the private sector, civil society and the public in general) are obliged to argue their case not only according to the evidence and proofs that belong to the world of science, but also within the framework of civic debate and public deliberation, where political and ethical principles come into play.[64]

These frameworks employ different means of bringing citizens and scientific experts and scientific and local knowledge together in forms of cooperative inquiry known as participatory policymaking, participatory policy analysis, participatory technology assessment, and consensus conferences.[65]

Conclusion: Responsibility for Ensuring Use

What do we know about the "use" of knowledge arising from evaluative studies and how it is best facilitated? Quite frankly, the actual explanatory value of the current literature is frustratingly meager. There simply is no single theory that explains use. At best, we can draw some very broad empirical generalizations.

It seems undeniable that whether understood as knowledge transfer, knowledge exchange, or influence of research and evaluation, the phenomenon is something that unfolds in systems of collective action. These systems are composed of multiple human actors (and often multiple agencies as well) with cognitive and normative frames of reference that are shaped, in part, by their participation in practices located in particular organizational circumstances (e.g., as school administrator, legislator, foundation director) that, in turn, are formed by the culture, norms, routines, and tools available within that organization. This is the practical, political, and intellectual context of use.

Equally undisputed is the claim that across fields of research that have a bearing on the definition of and solutions to problems in health care, the well-being of families and children, education, the environment, and so on there is widespread concern about the knowledge-action or knowledge-practice gap. This may be somewhat less the case in the field of evaluation that assumes it is by definition undertaken to be useful (why else would one do it?), yet the gap is worrisome in evaluation as well, for why else would there be an extensive evaluation literature related to understanding and facilitating use?

There may also be little disagreement around the proposition that legislators, program managers, agency directors, and the like at local, state, and national levels as well as practitioners in education, health care, and social services may not be adequately prepared to interpret and employ findings from research and evaluation. One test of whether use is itself effective is whether we have wiser "clinicians," so to speak, working in the fields of education, social services, and health care. At the same time, there appears to be a broad concern shared across social science research and evaluation as to whether our notions of use have been too narrowly conceived in terms of serving the decision-making needs of the manager, administrator, practitioner, or policymaker, thereby ignoring how the public or civil society deals with expert knowledge.

Finally, it seems quite likely that most all researchers and evaluators would share the assumptions that (a) engagement, interaction, and communication between evaluators/researchers, and policymakers, practitioners, and in some cases, program recipients as well is critical for use to occur,[66] and (b) use is more likely to happen if there are procedures, systems, established practices, technologies, and norms in an agency or organization that encourage and facilitate use as well as incentive structures that reward it.[67]

While these may be views fairly widely shared, there is less agreement on the question of what it means for evaluation and research to actually be of use, because evaluators and researchers have different ways of interpreting stakeholder involvement and different ideas about the extent of their responsibility for assisting in the development of organizational and procedural structures that are likely to enable use. As noted, what stakeholder involvement means and how it is to be accomplished varies considerably across producer-centered versus user-centered frameworks. Moreover, even within user-centered approaches to evaluation there is disagreement as to the evaluator's responsibility for ensuring use. Evaluators committed to practicing evaluation capacity building, for example, or those who conduct evaluation with a framework of community science, will likely do more than simply ensure that evaluation and research findings are accessible. They will help ensure that evidence-informed discussions among stakeholders and between evaluators (and researchers) and stakeholders are appropriately resourced and facilitated. Whether all researchers and evaluators ought to be engaged in developing and fostering mechanisms for linkage and exchange with stakeholders is a question that concerns the professional responsibilities of an evaluator, and that is the broad topic of the next chapter.

7   Professionalism and Professionalization

> Society will obtain the assistance that evaluations can give only when there is a strong evaluation profession, clear about its social role and the nature of its work.[1]

Signs of efforts to professionalize the field of evaluation are evident as early as the mid- to late 1970s in the U.S. with the formation of the Evaluation Network and the Evaluation Research Society. In 1986 the American Evaluation Association was formed from the merger of those two associations.[2] Through the early and late 1990s other societies began to form around the world including the United Kingdom Evaluation Society, the European Evaluation Society, and the African Evaluation Association. The early years of the twenty-first century saw additional growth (e.g., the International Development Evaluation Association, Swedish Evaluation Society, the International Organization for Cooperation in Evaluation), and at present there are approximately 140 national and regional societies or associations and international networks. The existence of these societies can be regarded as necessary but not sufficient for the establishment of evaluation as a profession.[3]

While there are multiple and not necessarily compatible theories of how professions form and what characteristics define them, one common sociological understanding is that professions exhibit the following traits:

- Prestige and status—apparent in high and rising demand for services; respectability and a recognized place among other professions

- Ethical dispositions—evident in orientation toward the public interest, loyalty to the occupational group; commitment to a lifelong career; collegial behavior; occupational solidarity; responsibility for the quality of one's work

- Expertise—demonstrated through acquiring high-quality education; exposure to practice; theoretical knowledge; specialized skills; sound judgment; mastery of techniques
- Professional autonomy—observed in the way the profession controls recruitment and training and promotes and enforces professional guidelines, ethical standards, and quality assurance
- Credentials—as seen in the fact that a professional is identified by means of a degree from accredited tertiary education establishment, carries a professional designation; holds a license or equivalent; and maintains membership in professional associations.[4]

Debates over whether evaluation is best defined as a knowledge occupation rather than a profession center on the extent to which the field of practice exhibits all of these characteristics. The general consensus is that it does not, particularly with respect to professional autonomy and credentials. While many evaluators claim that evaluation is an emerging profession evident, for example, in the rapid growth of professional associations and the development of ethical codes of conduct and guidelines for practice, for others these characteristics alone do not make evaluation a profession. The authors of a widely used textbook in the field argue: "The labels 'evaluators' and 'evaluation researchers' conceal the heterogeneity, diversity, and amorphousness of the field. Evaluators are not licensed or certified, so the identification of a person as an evaluator provides no assurance that he or she shares any core knowledge with any other person so identified. . . . In brief, evaluation is not a "profession," at least in terms of the formal criteria that sociologists generally use to characterize such groups."[5]

As is discussed in earlier chapters of this book, there is disagreement about the very nature of evaluation—that is, whether it is distinct from applied social research, for example—as well as whether it offers a unique contribution to society, as is characteristic of other professions. And we might add there is no uniform definition of who is an "evaluator." That matter is typically decided based on a process of credentialing, certification, or licensure for entry into the profession. The issue of whether the practice of evaluation can be legitimately called a profession and whether admission to it should be controlled in some manner has gained increasing attention. This development is the outcome of three forces: the maturation and growth in membership of evaluation societies and associations, rising demand for evaluation across the globe, and mounting concerns about what constitutes "quality" evaluation and who is qualified to conduct it.

Whether or not evaluation is a profession—and that matter is not likely to be resolved any time soon—those who practice evaluation routinely face two important, interrelated issues. The first is what the trend toward professionalization of evaluation might mean for the practice in a global or international perspective. The second is what characterizes professionalism or professional conduct in evaluation. This chapter engages these two broad issues in the following way: it first explores the characteristics that comprise the "good evaluator" by discussing efforts to define competencies and what might be involved in providing evidence that one who self-identifies as an evaluator possesses them. It then examines criteria for determining what counts as a "good evaluation" and what it might mean for evaluation as a profession to offer some assurance that it engages in quality assurance, so to speak. The chapter ends with a discussion of the ethics of professional conduct; an especially complicated matter related to being a "good evaluator."

The Good Evaluator

We begin by distinguishing between the terms *competence* and *competencies*.[6] The latter are single skills, functions, abilities, or dispositions that reflect underlying knowledge. The former is a broader term encompassing the totality of knowledge, skills, attributes, behaviors, and attitudes demanded in a particular undertaking and the ability to orchestrate these in addressing the problems one faces. The following definition of competence is found in medical practice: "The habitual and judicious use of communication, knowledge, technical skills, clinical reasoning, emotions, values, and reflection in daily practice for the benefit of the individual and community being served."[7] If we interpret "clinical reasoning" in a generic sense of critical thinking involved in the appraisal of information and evidence in reaching a warranted decision, and "individual and community" to refer to the evaluation client and other stakeholders, then this definition works well for understanding what competency in evaluation looks like.

Donald Schön argued that professional competence was more than a matter of having factual knowledge and skills in solving problems with clear-cut solutions; rather, it was an ability to manage ambiguous problems, tolerate uncertainty, and make decisions with limited information.[8] Competence exhibits two other important characteristics: it is context-dependent and it is developmental.[9] Competence is not defined by mastery of a list of competencies but by the interaction among a person's ability, the task or problem at hand, and the particular context in which that problem or task arises. Competence is developmental in that it changes as one moves from amateur to craftsman to specialist and professional or from novice to expert.[10]

To be sure, competence—understood as a successful or worthy performance—is tied to the possession of competencies. Thus, it is not surprising that identifying core or essential competencies for evaluators has arisen across the globe as a major concern for evaluation societies and associations as well as for several major development aid organizations that conduct and commission evaluations. A comparison of the broad categories of competencies endorsed by several evaluation associations is shown in Table 8.

There is some convergence of competencies across these organizations and associations. For example, the United Kingdom Evaluation Society (UKES)[11] and the European Evaluation Society (EES)[12] display commonality in their approaches that are referred to as capabilities frameworks.[13] The Canadian Evaluation Society (CES) Competencies for Canadian Evaluation Practice[14] are based in part on a set of essential competencies for evaluators developed over several years by Jean King and Laurie Stevahn and colleagues, who are members of the American Evaluation Association (AEA).[15] The AEA has neither adopted nor endorsed those competencies, although it does have two official positions on the issue of competencies, broadly construed, endorsed by its membership. One is the Guiding Principles for Evaluators that is primarily a set of guidelines for ethical conduct, not an enumeration of competencies.[16] The other is the Statement on Cultural Competence in Evaluation.[17] The latter emphasizes several essential practices required for an evaluator to demonstrate cultural competence including acknowledging the complexity of cultural identity; recognizing the dynamics of power in play in an evaluation; recognizing and eliminating bias in social relations; employing culturally congruent epistemologies, theories, and methods; and engaging in continued self-assessment of one's ethical and epistemological standpoint. A strong concern with cultural competence in evaluation is also evident in the Aotearoa New Zealand Evaluation Association's (ANZEA) project

Table 8. Comparison of Categories of Evaluator Competencies

Stevahn et al. Essential Competencies for Evaluators	CES Competencies for Canadian Evaluation Practice	UKES Evaluation Capabilities Framework	IDEAS Competencies for International Development Evaluators
Professional Practice: Fundamental norms and values, evaluation standards, and ethics	*Reflective Practice*: Fundamental norms and values; awareness of evaluation expertise and needs for growth	*Evaluation Knowledge*: Evaluation designs and approaches; effective use of evaluation methodologies	*Professional Foundations:* Concepts, terms, approaches, methods, cultural competence, ethics, international standards
Systematic Inquiry: Technical aspects of evaluation including design, data collection, analysis, reporting	*Technical Practice*: Evaluation design, data collection, analysis, interpretation, reporting	*Professional Practice*: Project management skills, contextual awareness, fair reporting, interpersonal skills	*Monitoring Systems*: Developing and using monitoring systems and data
Situational Analysis: Attending to unique interests, issues, and contextual circumstances	*Situational Practice*: Application of evaluative thinking to unique issues and contextual circumstances	*Qualities and Dispositions*: Sound and fair judgment, independence of mind and integrity, etc.	*Evaluation Planning and Design*
Project Management: Nuts and bolts of conducting an evaluation, e.g., budgeting, use of resources	*Management Practice*: Managing a project or evaluation; budgeting, coordinating resources, and supervising		*Managing the Evaluation*
Reflective Practice: Awareness of needs for growth and professional development	*Interpersonal Practice*: People skills, such as communication, negotiation, conflict resolution, collaboration, and diversity		*Conducting the Evaluation*
Interpersonal Competence: People skills, e.g., communication, negotiation			*Communicating Evaluation Findings*
			Promoting Cultural Learning from Evaluation

to develop competencies. ANZEA holds that evaluators are responsible for providing leadership in ensuring the inclusion and participation of indigenous perspectives and worldviews. It also argues that cultural competency is demonstrated in the process of conducting an evaluation in a culturally appropriate and responsive manner and in establishing the credibility and validity of evaluative conclusions:

> It . . . means drawing on the values, needs, strengths and aspirations of the culture of those a policy or programme is intended to benefit to define what is meant by "good program content and design," "high quality implementation and delivery," and "outcomes of value."[18]

The development of evaluator competencies or capabilities is thought to be useful in several respects including providing a basis for developing education and training programs; setting a common ground for moving toward certification, licensure, or credentialing; and providing some assurance to those who hire evaluators that they are getting evaluators who know what they are doing.[19] There is widespread concern in the field that many who take on the job of conducting or managing an evaluation lack formal training or experience, resulting in evaluations that are poorly conceived, poorly executed, and poorly managed.[20] In 2012 the International Development Evaluation Association (IDEAS) adopted a set of competencies for both evaluators and evaluation managers. It claimed these competencies would be particularly useful for evaluator self-assessment, for encouraging professional development by setting up individual capacity-building plans around the competencies, and for promoting training.[21] The competencies developed by the German Evaluation Society (DeGEval), entitled Recommendations on Education and Training in Evaluation: Requirement Profiles for Evaluators, as well as the Australasian Evaluation Society's (AES) Evaluators Professional Learning Competency Framework are specifically aimed at influencing the type of content that should be offered in evaluation training programs.[22]

A different use is envisioned for the Technical Competency Framework of the Department for International Development (DFID) of the United Kingdom. DFID claims that its competencies "provide a standard of what is expected of people performing a particular evaluation role. They are set at a level that someone who has been carrying out the post, role, or function for 6–12 months should be able to demonstrate that they are meeting."[23] Unique to its approach is the fact that for each of five broad competencies—using best practice evaluation approaches and methods; gathering and using evidence for evaluation; communicating and sharing evaluation findings, knowledge, and expertise; upholding evaluation independence, quality, and standards; and leading, managing, and delivering evaluations—indicators of expected performance are specified for four levels of proficiency labeled "foundation," "competent," "skilled," and "expert."

Only two professional evaluation associations, the Japan Evaluation Society (JES) and CES, use competencies as the basis for credentialing evaluators.[24] However, in 2014 the EES announced it intended to pilot-test a Voluntary Evaluator Peer Review System (VEPR) in which members of the society would apply to the society to undergo a structured professional practice review (guided by the EES capabilities framework) with the assistance of two accredited peer reviewers drawn from a voluntary pool of reviewers established by the EES Board of Directors.[25] For the CES, the process of applying for an evaluation credential involves three sets of qualifications including an appropriate graduate-level degree, two years of evaluation-related work experience, and a combination of education and experience directly related to 70 percent of the competencies stated in the Competencies for Canadian Evaluation Practice. In addition, to keep the credential current, one must complete 40 hours of continuing education over three years. The CES maintains a public registry of credentialed evaluators.

These efforts by various evaluation associations and societies to develop sets of competencies are involved and time-consuming. The IDEAS project evolved over four years before the list of competencies was put to the membership for a vote; similar time was devoted to the creation of the UKES capabilities framework; ANZEA's project took two years. From the time initial discussions got underway in CES about competencies and credentialing until the official credential process was agreed to and put into a place, ten years elapsed. The consultation process involved in the development of an association's policy such as this is extensive, particularly in an organization like IDEAS, whose approximately 1,300 members are drawn from over 100 countries, or in the AEA, whose membership is now nearing 8,000.

Although these developments around the establishment of evaluator competencies are evidence of the growing professionalization of the field, the issue remains whether, after such considerable work on the part of members of these various organizations, there will be tangible effects of such efforts. For example, whether education and training programs in evaluation will align their curriculum with some set of competencies is surely a complicated matter. For while training and professional development offered through evaluation associations and societies might be designed to directly align with competencies, requiring university programs to align their curricula toward such competencies is far more difficult. Alignment of curriculum with standards and competencies and uniformity in professional education curriculum (in, for example, nursing, business, or public administration programs) across universities generally only follow from a process of accreditation of professional schools, and there is no such mechanism in the field of evaluation. Will other associations follow the lead of CES in using a competency or capability framework as the basis of some means of credentialing or certifying evaluators? If so, how will the credentials issued by several different evaluation societies and associations be harmonized or equated? The lack of agreement on competencies and the absence (with the exception of CES and JES) of a system for certification or credentialing make it difficult not only for those who call themselves evaluators to claim some kind of homogeneity in a knowledge base, experience, and qualifications but also for those who commission and fund evaluation to know whether they are purchasing genuine, authentic competence when they hire an evaluator. Yet, absent a credentialing or certification process, is it possible to provide the kind of assurance that funders and clients of evaluation seek while preserving the diversity in evaluation approaches, aims, and methods that currently characterize the field?

What Makes for Good Evaluations?

The interest in developing evaluator competencies was preceded by efforts to develop standards and guidelines for what constitutes good evaluation or best practice. In all evaluation associations and societies that have developed such standards, they are regarded as voluntary, aspirational, consensus statements endorsed by the organization's membership and not rules that are mandatory or carry a penalty if violated. The oldest effort in this regard is the work of the Joint Committee on Standards for Educational Evaluation in the U.S. that began in 1975 and resulted in the first version of the Program Evaluation Standards in 1981 that has subsequently been revised twice, in 1994 and 2011.[26] Although it is an independent body not affiliated with any evaluation association, the Joint Committee and its standard-setting efforts have been foundational for the establishment of evaluation standards in many associations and organizations including those in Germany, Switzerland, and Africa, all of which have adopted, with modifications, the general framework of the Joint Committee standards shown in Table 9.[27]

Other agencies directly involved with evaluation have also adopted evaluation standards consonant with the particular circumstances of the evaluations they fund, conduct, or commission. The OECD/DAC Quality Standards for Development Evaluation reflect the fact that evaluations take place in the context of shared development goals such as the 2005 Paris Declaration on Aid Effectiveness. Its standards are intended to "improve the quality of development evaluation processes and products, facilitate the comparison of evaluations across countries, support partnerships and collaboration on joint evaluations, and increase development partners' use of each others' evaluation findings."[28] In the U.S., the Council of the Inspectors General on Integrity and Efficiency is charged with detecting and preventing fraud, waste, abuse, and violations of law

Table 9. Summary of the 2011 Program Evaluation Standards

Standard Category	Definition
Utility	The extent to which evaluations are aligned with stakeholders' needs such that process uses, findings uses, and other appropriate influences are possible (8 standards)
Feasibility	The extent to which resources and other factors allow an evaluation to be conducted in an efficient and effective manner (4 standards)
Propriety	The extent to which the evaluation has been conducted in a manner that evidences uncompromising adherence to the highest principles and ideals (including professional ethics, civil law, moral code, and contractual agreements) (7 standards)
Accuracy	The extent to which an evaluation is truthful or valid in the scope and detail of what it communicates about a context, program, project, or any of their components (8 standards)
Evaluation Accountability	The extent to which an evaluation demonstrates responsible use of resources to produce value; requires a meta-evaluation (3 standards)

Source: Donald B. Yarbrough, Lyn M. Shulha, Rodney K. Hopson, and F. A. Caruthers. 2011. *The Program Evaluation Standards: A Guide for Evaluators and Evaluation Users* 3rd ed. Thousand Oaks, CA: Sage.

as well as promoting efficiency and effectiveness in federal government operations. Accordingly, its Quality Standards for Inspection and Evaluation include several standards unique to its work with departments and agencies of the federal government including this standard for fraud, illegal acts, and abuse: "In conducting inspection work, inspectors should be alert to possible fraud, other illegal acts, and abuse and should appropriately follow up on any indicators of such activity and promptly present associated information to their supervisors for review and possible referral to the appropriate investigative office."[29] Inspections and evaluations conducted by Offices of Inspector General often yield recommendations, hence this standard for "follow up": "Appropriate follow up will be performed to ensure that any inspection recommendations made to Department/Agency officials are adequately considered and appropriately addressed."[30] Finally, the United Nations Evaluation Group—a network that brings together units responsible for evaluation across the nearly 45 special agencies, funds, and programs of the United Nations (UN)—includes in its standards for evaluation four directly aimed at the institutionalization and professionalization of evaluation practice within the UN: (1) an adequate institutional framework for the effective management of their evaluation function, (2) development of an evaluation policy that is regularly updated, (3) UN assurance that evaluation plans are submitted to their Governing Bodies and/or Heads of organizations for review and/or approval, (4) assurance of appropriate evaluation follow-up mechanisms and an explicit disclosure policy.[31]

One of the most important potential uses for evaluation standards that in effect spell out the criteria on which evaluations should be judged is meta-evaluation. This is a systematic review of an evaluation, often conducted upon its completion, to determine the quality of its process and findings. It is a particular kind of peer review that can be used for purposes of quality control or quality assurance as well as to demonstrate accountability (i.e., the evaluator or evaluation team delivered a high-quality product).[32] According to the Joint Committee's Program Evaluation Standards, assessments of evaluation accountability examine "how evaluations are implemented; how evaluations could be improved; how worthwhile, significant or important evaluations are to their stakeholders; and how evaluation costs, including opportunity costs, compare to benefits."[33] Meta-evaluation differs from meta-analysis (also called systematic or synthetic reviews) focused on aggregating findings across evaluations of similar interventions. This is the kind of evaluation synthesis work undertaken, for example, by the Campbell Collaboration (www.campbellcollaboration.org).

There are a number of ways in which meta-evaluations can be undertaken. Evaluators or evaluation teams can use the Program Evaluation Standards or any other set of standards discussed earlier to check on their plans and activities in the early stages of developing an evaluation. In these circumstances, standards can be used as a checklist. There is a variety of different kinds of checklists already developed for various evaluation approaches as well as for aspects of evaluation design, management, and reporting.[34] Peers can be engaged to examine draft evaluation reports to determine whether evidence supporting findings, conclusions, and recommendations is sufficient and relevant. External evaluators can be contracted to evaluate an evaluation upon its completion. Providing that kind of quality assurance, for example, is one of the functions of the Evaluation Advisory Panel for the Independent Evaluation Office (IEO) of the United Nations Development Programme (UNDP). The UNDP IEO was also the first to participate in 2005 in a process of peer assessment of its evaluation function.[35]

Few organizations actually require meta-evaluations; they remain voluntary exercises for the most part. However, they are a significant aspect of some of the evaluation work undertaken in the field of international development by agencies such as UNICEF, DFID, and the sector-wide network of international humanitarian aid organizations known as the Active Learning Network for Accountability and Performance (ALNAP). USAID, for example, conducted a meta-evaluation of the quality and coverage of evaluations it funded between 2009–2012 to answer three key questions: To what extent has the quality of evaluation practices and reports changed over time? On what aspects of evaluation quality do USAID evaluation reports excel and where are they falling short? Where do the greatest opportunities lie for improvement in the quality of reports?[36] An extensive meta-evaluation was undertaken of the Phase 2 evaluation of the Paris Declaration on Aid Effectiveness. The original evaluation that was being examined included more than 50 studies conducted in 22 partner countries.[37]

Meta-evaluation has been called an imperative for the field in that its utility lies in guiding both the planning and implementation of evaluation as well as in publicly reporting the strengths and weaknesses of that endeavor.[38] Commitment to meta-evaluation demonstrates the fact that evaluators practice what they preach; it is a responsible answer to the query "Who evaluates the evaluator?"[39]

On Being Appropriate, Fair, and Just: Evaluation Ethics

The previous section primarily addressed the question of "is it good"— is an evaluation of high quality as judged by some set of meta-evaluative standards or guidelines? Obviously, assessments of evaluation quality as well as any determination of whether an evaluator is competent also involve questions of whether the actions of an evaluator are appropriate, fair, and just; in short, whether an evaluator is doing the right thing. These are questions about moral behavior, some of which have to do with the law—e.g., rules governing conflict of interest, fraudulent acts, or privacy of data as, for example, required under the Family Educational Rights and Privacy Act—but many more of which have to do with ethics.

Ethics is about making tough choices when faced with a dilemma about what to do. Such dilemmas come in two forms.[40] Some have to do with a conflict between two or more competing principles; they involve right versus right. In everyday life we often face an ethical dilemma of this kind related, for example, to whether it is right to enforce justice or to be merciful. In evaluation, there might be a conflict between respecting individual confidentiality and honoring a commitment to the overall public good. In the second kind of dilemma it is usually clear to an individual what he or she should do, but external factors make it difficult to honor the ethical principle:

> Consider the case of an evaluator being pressured by a stakeholder to write a report that portrays the accomplishments of the stakeholder's program more positively than is warranted by the data. The conflict here is between the principle of honesty/integrity and the political influence that the stakeholder is attempting to exert. . . . The problem is that the ethical course of action is often a risky course of action for that individual.[41]

To provide some guidance for evaluation practitioners, most all associations and societies have developed a set of ethical guidelines or principles. These are not actual directives on how to solve the kinds of dilemmas discussed above. Rather, they are usually brief, broad statements designed to alert professionals to critical components of professional integrity. As is the case with standards for evaluations, codes of ethics or statements of ethical principles are guidelines, not rules, and failure to follow them does not involve any official sanctioning procedure on the part of any evaluation association or organization.

In some cases, statements of principles mix both ethical considerations and scientific virtues. For example, the principles guiding the evaluation policy of DFID are independence, transparency, quality, utility, and ethics.[42] Statements of ethical principles vary in their level of detail and whether they address only evaluators or other parties to an evaluation. The Canadian Evaluation Society's Guidelines for Ethical Conduct are quite brief and cover evaluator *competence* in the provision of services, acting with *integrity* in relationships with stakeholders, and *accountability* for their performance and product.[43] The Australasian Evaluation Society Guidelines for the Ethical Conduct of Evaluation, on the other hand, spell out principles with respect to the responsibilities of both commissioners of evaluation and evaluators for commissioning and preparing an evaluation as well as evaluator responsibilities for conducting and reporting the results of an evaluation.[44] In all, there are six principles and an extensive list of guidelines for each principle. Table 10 displays the AEA's Guiding Prin-

Table 10. American Evaluation Association's Guiding Principles for Evaluators

Principle	Short Definition
A. Systematic Inquiry	Evaluators conduct systematic, data-based inquiries
B. Competence	Evaluators provide competent performance to stakeholders
C. Integrity and Honesty	Evaluators display honesty and integrity in their own behavior and attempt to ensure the honesty and integrity of the entire evaluation process
D. Respect for People	Evaluators respect the security, dignity, and self-worth of respondents, program participants, clients, and other evaluation stakeholders
E. Responsibilities for the General and Public Welfare	Evaluators articulate and take into account the diversity of general and public interests and values that may be related to the evaluation

Source: American Evaluation Association. "American Evaluation Association Guiding Principles for Evaluators." Available at http://www.eval.org/p/cm/ld/fid=51CA: Sage.

ciples for Evaluators, clearly intended as a guide to ethical behavior, but the principles are also consonant with advice on appropriate evaluator behavior that appears in the Program Evaluation Standards and in statements of standards and practice guidelines from other evaluation associations.[45]

As one might expect, most of the controversy in the AEA surrounding the value of these principles as a guide to practice has largely focused on the fifth principle, Responsibilities for the General and Public Welfare. The others are less provocative and fairly commonplace as guiding ethical principles—commitment to evidence (scientific integrity or systematic inquiry), competence, personal integrity, honesty, and respect for persons. The fifth principle opens up but leaves unanswered just what the public good, public interest, or the general welfare of society means.[46] And, as we saw in Chapter 5, there is considerable disagreement within the field of evaluation regarding how evaluation is to best serve society. The occasion of disagreement over the interpretation of the fifth Guiding Principle is an entry point of sorts to three important issues surrounding whether evaluation practice is appropriate, fair, and just.[47]

First, ethical concerns as represented in professional guidelines or codes are framed, for the most part, in terms of individual behavior, ignoring a broader focus on the normative influence of social institutions and organized social practices. Both our institutions (the economy, politics, the family, education, etc.) and social practices (teaching, evaluation, administration, nursing, etc.) embody and specify cultural values in terms of what is right and wrong, good and bad. Institutions and practices mediate our relations with others and the world. They are not simply formal and informal arrangements of groups of people but patterns of normative, moral expectations. Thus, ethics in evaluation is not simply a matter of individual professional conduct but also of the normative orientations of institutional evaluation practices in society. This is essentially the point made in Chapter 5, where part of the discussion focused on how evaluation practices are wedded to particular conceptions of governance as well as to particular ethical and political points of view on what is the most appropriate, fair, and just way to connect evaluation to democratic ideals.

Second, consider the ethical imperative of cultural competence in evaluation as explained earlier in this chapter. The cultural competence movement has grown out of concerns for attending to the needs and interests of an increasingly diverse, multicultural society and the challenges of ensuring social equity in terms of access, quality, and outcomes of human service programs (e.g., health care, education, social services). The movement emphasizes awareness of and sensitivity to the beliefs, values, and ways of life of cultural groups different than one's own.[48] Cultural competence is evident when evaluators engage in self-reflection to examine their own culturally based assumptions, their understanding of the worldviews of culturally different participants and stakeholders in the evaluation, and the use of appropriate evaluation strategies and skills in working with culturally diverse groups. Diversity may be in terms of race, ethnicity, gender, religion, socioeconomics, or other factors pertinent to the evaluation context.

The implications of this notion of cultural competence for understanding ethics in evaluation can be interpreted in both weak (or "thin") and strong (or "thick") ways. These ways are not necessarily incompatible, but they do speak to different ethical postures and considerations. A weak or thin interpretation of cultural competence calls for evaluators to develop the moral virtues of sensitivity, empathy, and respect for others. Ethicists describe this as having a narrative imagination and "the ability to think what it might be like to be in the shoes of a person different from oneself, to be an intelligent reader of that person's story, and to understand the emotions and wishes and desires that someone so placed might have."[49] Cultivating this moral capacity for empathetic identification with those different from oneself is a reasonable ethical obligation for any professional. For evaluators whose work crosses boundaries of language, gender, class, ethnicity, and nations it seems to be an imperative for competent practice.

A strong or thick interpretation, however, goes beyond having this ethical virtue. It holds that the imperative for evaluators is to scrutinize their own culture for its distinctive norms that shape attitudes, values, and practices and to assess how these understandings are built into their methodologies, as well as into the interventions, programs, and policies they are evaluating that may be inhibiting a genuine understanding of stakeholders' perceptions of the value of an intervention, program, or policy. For example, consider the evaluation of medical interventions. As one commentator has noted, "there is a distinctive 'Americanness' in the optimistic belief in medical science and technology, in their limitless progress and promise, their vigorous application, and their power to 'overcome' disease, that pervades our society."[50] To what extent is it an ethical obligation of evaluators charged with assessing the effectiveness of Western medical interventions in minority cultures to question the underlying assumptions of the culture of biomedicine that some patients may not share?

Third, in a world in which transnational and globalizing forces influence most, if not all, of the practices of evaluation in significant ways, it is important to examine what these developments signify for standards of ethical behavior. The global circulation of ideas and ideologies and the development of international conventions and national cooperative agreements heighten our awareness of a longstanding tension in ways of thinking about ethics and morality. On the one hand, there is the cosmopolitan view that there are universal moral norms or principles. This way of thinking is reflected, for example, in the United Nations Declaration of Human Rights and the Geneva Convention. Here, no distinction is to be made in the moral obligations of persons by virtue of the national or cultural borders within which they reside. On the other hand, there is the cultural relativist view that moral judgments and moral norms are inextricable from the cultural circumstances in which they take shape. In other words, the meaning of acting ethically (being just, fair, honest, etc.) is shaped, in a significant way, by how persons are situated in cultural contexts. These two views are not necessarily incompatible. Nor is it the case that the latter view is equivalent to saying that there is no right or wrong or that moral terms have no meaning outside specific cultures. Rather, "the broad outlines of what we count as an ethical system must be drawn in universal terms, [yet] the detail in any general picture of a 'good human life' must be filled in by some thick cultural context."[51]

For evaluators, the issue is how to take account of this tension given the growing interest in the transnational features that increasingly characterize the practice of evaluation—for example, assessing policies and programs that transcend national and cultural boundaries and developing sector-wide evaluation standards that go beyond, and may also conflict with, ethical principles and standards promoted by national evaluation associations. Can we reasonably argue for something like a cross-cultural professional ethic for evaluators, and, if so, what norms would it reflect? How should we interpret the ethical principle that evaluators "take responsibility for the general and public welfare"? Does taking responsibility mean that evaluators ought to act in defense of local cultures and thus resist the cultural homogenization that results from the global influences of intergovernmental organizations such as OECD, UNESCO, the

World Bank, and the European Union?[52] Should evaluators who work in the vast terrain of international aid and development adopt a particularly activist global ethic that emphasizes global justice, environmental stewardship, social interdependence, and reverence for place, an ethic that derives its bearings from careful consideration of the problems engendered by the advance of science and technology?

Conclusion: Professionalism Reexamined

A common perspective on the education of evaluation practitioners is that it requires understanding a core body of knowledge and ways of reasoning that define the practice, coupled with a skill-based apprenticeship where one acquires the craft know-how characteristic of the practice. Hence the typical focus on models and approaches of the major evaluation theorists, along with training in social science methods and their application in evaluation, coupled with awareness of codes of professional ethical conduct. In addition to acquiring familiarity with this knowledge and skill base, this perspective emphasizes training to develop three capacities: (1) to make technical judgments, (2) to make procedural judgments, and (3) to be reflective.[53] Technical judgments are about how to apply existing knowledge and skills to routine tasks, for example, "How do I design instruments to measure both satisfaction with the program services that were provided to program participants as well as the kinds of knowledge and skills they gained as a result of receiving those services?" Procedural judgments involve comparing skills and tools available to determine which works best for the task at hand, for example, "How to I best visually represent the results of this evaluation to this client?" The capacity to be reflective means that practitioners are thinking carefully about tasks they face and asking whether their existing knowledge is adequate to address those tasks, whether they should seek ways to enhance their skills and knowledge, and whether innovation and new ways of tackling a task should be considered.

Training in these three capacities is acquired within the context of standards for both professional products (i.e., standards for evaluating the evaluation) and professional conduct (i.e., ethical guidelines). The latter encompass personal virtues such as honesty, integrity, and respect in dealing with others, as well as cognitive or intellectual virtues that include objectivity, skepticism, transparency of reasoning, and reliance on evidence.

The many lists of evaluator competencies and capabilities that are available for inspection from major evaluation associations and societies all contain some reference to desirable dispositions and attitudes such as "applying professional standards," "upholding ethical standards," "respecting clients and other stakeholders," "striving for integrity, honesty, and independence of thought," "being critically self-aware and pursuing self-development," and so on.

Professionalism in evaluation (and the professionalization of the practice), however, means something more than what is captured in lists of competencies or capabilities dealing with systematic inquiry, technical practice, project management, and attention to particular dispositions, attitudes, and ethical behaviors (see Table 8) or in the discussion about credentialing, certification, or licensure. We do not need to enter the long and complicated debate about what constitutes a profession and whether evaluation at present actually qualifies as such in order to grasp the point about the connection between preparation for a field of practice and the norms that define a profession. But we do need to understand that it is a profession's social ends and civic foundations more so than its technical demands that define it:

> The commitment to serve the public interest sets the terms of the essential compact between the profession and society, providing the basis for the profession's autonomy and public esteem. Although other occupational fields may require high levels of knowledge and skill, they cannot be considered professions unless they are centrally defined as serving some important aspect of the common good. Thus, the relationship between the professions and the general society is inherently ethical at its core.[54]

Understanding professionalism means making sense of competencies in the context of the profession's fundamental purposes that are embodied in its conception of its social roles and responsibilities. It means wrestling with how that purpose relates to notions of community, responsibility, and identity.[55] Community is a matter of understanding the context in which professional practice unfolds and in which the evaluator performs a role. What place does the profession (and the professional) occupy in a wider community? Responsibility is a matter of grasping that as a professional one does what one does on behalf of others, and thus involves making sense of what it means to serve the client, other stakeholders, and the public. Identity is matter of answering the question, "what does it mean to be a particular kind of person whose action is founded on certain kinds of knowledge and skill, oriented by particular kinds of responsibility?"[56] Answers to these questions point to the public purposes and ethical norms that constitute the very idea of a profession.

Evaluators ought to function and be seen in society as more than a particular kind of technical expert.[57] They ought to convey to their clients and the public at large the idea of evaluation as a practical, intellectual disposition and outlook on social and political life. Through their engagement with those who commission and fund evaluation work, those who direct and manage programs, those who craft social policies, and those who are the intended beneficiaries of efforts to solve social problems, evaluators ought to teach that evaluation is about experimenting, social criticism, constant questioning, objective appraisal, candor, intellectual honesty, and modesty in our claims to know what is of value. They ought to embody in their work the viewpoint that reasoned evaluative criticism plays a central role in the achievement, maintenance, and enhancement of the good society. In conducting their work they should embrace the complexity of social problems and the concomitant limitations on our ability to predict, plan, and control interventions designed to address them. Because they above all other professionals are skilled in judging the value of attempts at social problem solving in complex circumstances, evaluators ought to advocate for an experimenting society committed to innovation, social reality testing, learning, self-criticism, and the avoidance of self-deception. Yet they must be ever mindful that an experimenting society is not one in which policymakers, program directors, and their performance monitoring allies seek to manage social and economic affairs in an apolitical, managerialist, and scientized manner. Social problem solving, policymaking, and evaluation are not exercises in social technology, and an experimenting society is an evaluating society, not an audit society. Education for an evaluation profession conceived with this kind of ethical core is the focus of the comments in the Epilogue that follows.

Epilogue

A central premise of this book is that the pursuit of professional practice in evaluation requires developing a life of the mind for practice. This thesis involves the recognition that although knowledge and skills involved in the choice and application of models, methods, and techniques are necessary to do good work, professional practice is best characterized by the capacity for discretionary judgment and a sense of identity linked to a realization of the social purpose of the practice. Judgment is a situated, practice-based form of reasoning that differs from both means-end reasoning and rational calculation. Although sites where practice is conducted may yield concrete practical and working knowledge, one who possesses a life of the mind for practice realizes that engagement with a body of theoretical knowledge, concepts, principles, and insights (presented in the previous chapters as the landscape of issues in evaluation) best guides discretionary judgment.[1] Furthermore, it is generally recognized that the development of expert judgment also involves aspects of character including emotional involvement, discernment, and habits of thought closely wedded to the practitioner's understanding of and commitment to the social good that the practice is intended to serve.[2]

The notion of "a life of the mind for practice" unites two ideas—thought and action. To focus only on the former—"the life of the mind"—is to be concerned exactly, but narrowly, with cultivating the capacity for rational thought and intellectualism (a notion often negatively associated with the idea of "too much thinking"). To focus only on the latter—"for practice"—is to be concerned primarily with knowledge and skills required for the customary and habitual performance of well-defined tasks. "A life of the mind for practice" intentionally brings together theoretical understanding and practical reason, putting both to work in developing good judgment and taking a wise course of action.

My concern is what happens to the notion of preparing a life of the mind for practice as evaluation becomes increasingly viewed as little more than an extensive collection of practical guides, toolkits, and techniques for data collection, presentation, and reporting. Even more worrisome, what happens to that notion as evaluation becomes defined primarily by its role and function in bureaucratic and managerial systems—as a tool for quality assurance, performance management, and for assessing conformance to standards or benchmarks? Evaluation practice so conceived is the province of the technician who principally relies on following procedures or scripts and correctly applying methods. Of course, if the field is content with developing highly skilled technicians who will operate effectively in systems that employ technologies of measurement and evaluation, then my concern about developing professionals who exhibit the characteristics of a life of the mind for practice is moot. Yet many signs point toward strong interest in the continued professionalization of the evaluation field. Thus, we might at least entertain my hypothesis while acknowledging it requires more thorough empirical investigation.

If we tentatively accept the idea that evaluation practice is becoming more technical than professional, and if we are concerned with ways in which such a trend might be reversed, then one important consideration is how individuals are prepared for the practice. More specifically, where it is that one can develop "a life of the mind for practice?" In recent years, it appears that, for a variety of reasons not least of which is response to market demand, routes to learning about the practice are less characterized by full-time university graduate education programs and more by means such as certificate programs, workshops, institutes, short courses, and professional training sessions offered by evaluation societies and associations (and some of the latter make use of opportunities afforded by technologies such as webinars enabling "on-the job" or "just-in-time" learning).[3] The primary content of these types of training is evaluation models, methods, and practical issues encountered in planning and conducting an evaluation, although one also finds the occasional workshop or one-day course in evaluation ethics and professional standards.[4]

No doubt these approaches to training are valuable for a variety of personal and professional reasons to those who avail themselves of these opportunities. Yet one can reasonably ask whether training provided through a one- or two-day workshop, a weeklong institute, or a certificate comprised of a collection of three or four courses that includes an introduction to evaluation and a methods course or two is adequate preparation for professional practice. At times it seems that getting this kind of training in models, techniques, and methods of evaluation is a bit like deciding what to wear even before you have been invited to the party.

As demonstrated in the previous chapters, the field of evaluation is contested space; it displays considerable variability in conceptions of its social purpose, its choice of methods, the roles of its practitioners, its political stance, its understanding of how the utility of evaluation is to be understood, and so on. In light of that heterogeneous and challenging state of affairs, I suggest that the field of evaluation might be best served at present if it devoted greater effort to encouraging educational opportunities that combined instruction in the rational capacity for critically appraising knowledge of evaluation methods, concepts, principles, and theories with an exploration of moral commitment. Moral commitment signifies attention to the social purpose of the practice—its very ethical core, as suggested in Chapter 7.

Individuals seeking to become evaluators (and perhaps many who currently practice) might be encouraged to ask, "What are the intellectual and practical (moral, political) commitments that I am capable of and competent to perform when it comes to conducting studies of the value of social programs and discussing the meaning of evaluation with a variety of different stakeholders (including clients, program staff, beneficiaries, the public)?" From that question a host of related questions follow including, "Where do I stand on the matter of how evaluation serves democratic aims and social justice?" "Whose interests in evaluation should I serve?" "Is it possible for me to take an independent, objective stance as an evaluator—one that resists capture by managerial or other vested interests?" "How do I interpret the concern with causality in social programs?" "How should the evaluation results that I produce play a role in decisions about social policy and social programming?" "What are the strengths and weaknesses of my methodological commitments, and how do they relate to my understanding of the public purpose of the practice?" "How do I justify my choice of criteria and a values basis for judgments of the merit of programs and policies?" It is in light of answers to these kinds of questions that the study of evaluation models and methods and attention to evaluation abilities, skills, and aptitudes—that is, the "know-how" that comprises evaluator competencies—acquire a particular salience and relevance.

The central issue is how aspiring evaluators will learn both to ask and to develop answers to questions such as these, while, at the same time, they are acquiring necessary technical knowledge and skills. In short, where can they best learn about a life of the mind for professional evaluation practice? This can be done best in university where a liberal education can be joined to specialized training. Of course, one can easily be too glib about such an assertion. A university education for the profession that effectively marries education in practical reason with specialized skills and knowledge in evaluation faces serious challenges stemming from vulnerabilities inherent in the very idea of professionalism in contemporary society and from the character of university education itself.

Even in the most established professions there is considerable anxiety about the erosion of the ideal of professionalism. Market-driven philosophies turn doctors into providers; for an increasing number of lawyers justice has become privatized and restricted to the interests of their paying clients;[5] the very mention of Enron and Arthur Andersen signifies a breakdown in the logic of professionalism in (some) accounting firms;[6] organizational consultants are viewed as vendors and their relationships to clients are cast as cost-driven, commodity-based, transactional exchanges.[7] Demands for greater productivity in all professions from nursing to engineering "tend to drain the intrinsic meaning from professional work."[8] Add to this the kind of burnout, cynicism, and acceptance of mediocre practice that can accompany the loss of faith in the capacity of a profession to achieve its essential purpose.[9] If these are profound concerns in the established professions, then one is led to wonder what to make of the meaning and status of the professional ideal as it might be formulated and taught in the emerging evaluation profession.

Moreover, university education in evaluation is beset by several kinds of problems.[10] Academic departments tend to be silos and thus work against the kind of interdisciplinary awareness of concepts, theories, and methods that evaluation practice demands. (For example, a student in political science will learn how political scientists think about evaluation and policy analysis but not likely be exposed to how psychologists or economists think about the same phenomena, let alone how those in professional schools of education, business, social work, and nursing approach the matter.) If one studies evaluation in a professional school one runs the risk that the curriculum lacks breadth and depth, leaving one ill prepared methodologically and equally unaware of the enterprise of evaluation outside the boundaries of the particular profession in which one is studying. Finally, it is no secret that universities, particularly state universities, given their financial pressures and demands to demonstrate value for money, are increasingly succumbing to vocationalism.

However, despite all these concerns, we still look to universities as places that can offer a type of education that prepares one to exercise professional judgment. They are the places that can (and should) provide preparation in theoretical knowledge and practical reason—and that cultivate the central ideal that the life of the mind is essential to effective professional practice. They are sites where we expect to find both students and practicing professionals engaged intellectually and motivationally in the core issues of the practice and the leading edge of a profession's work.

Of course, we must ask whether the current curriculum for evaluation education in university-based programs adequately prepares students in this way for a life of the mind for practice. Here, data are sparse. We know that university-based graduate programs have little difficulty in offering introductory and advanced courses in evaluation that cover evaluation models as well as practical issues and concerns in planning and conducting an evaluation, coupled with courses in specific skills of research design and analysis of qualitative and quantitative data.[11] Many also offer some form of field experience either through required internships, a practicum, or graduate assistantships on evaluation projects.[12] All of this is necessary but not sufficient. Research conducted as part of the Preparation for the Professions Program undertaken by the Carnegie Foundation for the Advancement of Teaching[13] revealed that the following qualities make for sustainable, lifelong growth in professional competence and commitment:

- Deep engagement with the profession's public purposes, along with a sense of meaning and satisfaction from one's work that is grounded in or aligned with those purposes.

- Strong professional identity. That is, an identity as a . . . professional in which the field's mission and standards (integrity and conscientiousness, for example) are essential features of one's conception of the field and the self as a member of that field.

- Habits of interpretation or salience through which complex situations are understood or framed at least in part in moral terms, that is, in terms of the field's purposes and standards.

- Habitual patterns of behavioral response to . . . clients, subordinates, authorities, and peers that are well aligned with the profession's standards and ideals rather than with corrosive counter-norms or overriding self-interest.

- The capacity and inclination to contribute to the ethical quality of the profession and its institutions. This includes a sense of moral agency in relation to morally questionable aspects of the institutional context and the moral imagination and courage to create more constructive institutional structures or practices.[14]

Whether existing university programs that prepare evaluators foster these qualities essential to a life of the mind for practice is an unanswered question. However, the future of evaluation, as a professional practice committed to promoting the public good through judging the value of human activity, depends on their ability to do so.

Notes

Prologue

1. Stone (2001: 1).

2. This is a unique form of policy evaluation where the unit of analysis is agency or organizational strategy as opposed to a single program or policy; see Patrizi and Patton (2010). The evaluation examines an organization's strategic perspective (how the organization thinks about itself and whether within the organization there is a consistent view) and its strategic position (where it aims to have effect and contribute to outcomes) and how well aligned understandings of this perspective are across different constituencies of the organization including its leadership, staff, funders, partners, and so on. The strategy to be evaluated could well be a particular organization's own evaluation strategy.

3. Theodoulou and Kofinis (2003).

4. *African Evaluation Journal; American Journal of Evaluation; Canadian Journal of Program Evaluation; Educational Evaluation and Policy Analysis; Educational Research and Evaluation; Evaluation and the Health Professions; Evaluation Journal of Australasia; Evaluation and Program Planning; Evaluation Review; Evaluation: The International Journal of Theory, Research and Practice; International Journal of Evaluation and Research in Education; International Journal of Educational Evaluation for Health Professions; Japanese Journal of Evaluation Studies; Journal of MultiDisciplinary Evaluation; LeGes* (journal of the Swiss Evaluation Society); *New Directions for Evaluation; Practical Assessment, Research, and Evaluation; Studies in Educational Evaluation; Zeitschrift für Evaluation.* Of course, papers on evaluation are also published in discipline-specific journals, e.g., *Journal of Community Psychology, American Journal of Public Health,* and the *Journal of Policy Analysis and Management.*

5. See the list of evaluation organizations at the web site of the International

Organisation for Cooperation in Evaluation (IOCE) at http://www.ioce.net/en/index.php. *See also Rugh (2013).*

6. Stevahn, King, Ghere, and Minnema (2005: 46).

7. See the list of U.S. universities offering master's degrees, doctoral degrees, and/or certificates in evaluation at http://www.eval.org/p/cm/ld/fid=43. There are professional master's programs in evaluation in Austria, Germany, Denmark, and Spain.

8. For example, Auburn University, Tufts University, University of Minnesota, and the Evaluator's Institute at George Washington University.

9. At this writing, entering the phrase "evaluation toolkit" in a Google search yielded almost 1.4 million hits and included toolkits prepared by a wide variety of actors in field—the World Bank, The Centers for Disease Control and Prevention, FSG (a consulting firm); the Global Fund to Fight AIDS, Malaria, and Tuberculosis; the Coalition for Community Schools; the W.K. Kellogg Foundation; and the Agency for Healthcare Research and Quality (AHRQ) National Resource Center, to name but a few.

10. Indirect evidence of the growing significance of these training resources for preparing evaluators comes from trends in the composition of the membership of the American Evaluation Association—the largest evaluation membership organization in the world, with approximately 7,800 members. Studies of the membership in recent years have revealed that practitioner and "accidental" pathways into the profession are four times more prevalent than "academic" pathways. Moreover, the association reports that only 31% of its membership identifies as college or university affiliated.

11. Schwandt (2008).

12. Sullivan (2004).

13. Argyris (2004).

14. Hummelbrunner and Reynolds (2013).

15. Sullivan and Rosen (2008b: 91).

16. Schön (1987: 6)

17. Practical knowledge is "brought into play in the concrete, dealing with this situation now, that may be perfectly standard and typical—that is to say, of a type that has often been met previously and for which there is an already established and well-rehearsed procedure—but that may *not* be exactly to type but rather may deviate in an indefinite number of respects from what is standard or conventional. Judgment, then, is in the first instance an ability to recognize situations, cases, or problems of this kind . . . and to deal adequately with them. A person of judgment respects the particularity of the case—and thus does not impose on it the procrustean application of the general rule. At the same time, such a person will try to find a way of brining this particularity into some relationship . . . with established norms or procedures. . . . Thus a person of judg-

ment is not a maverick with a nose for the unusual, who is indifferent to the body of general knowledge codified in rules, formulae, and procedures (without familiarity with these how could she or he even recognize the atypicality of the present instance?). To the contrary, a person of judgment is a keen student of the general stock of knowledge. . . . The adeptness of the person of judgment . . . lies neither in knowledge of the general as such nor in an entirely unprincipled dealing with particulars. Rather, it lies precisely in the mediation between general and particular, bringing both into illuminating connection with one another." Dunne and Pendlebury (2003: 198).

18. Smith (2008: 2).

19. Mathison (2005); Patton (2008); Rossi, Lipsey, and Freeman (2004); Ryan and Cousins (2009); Shaw, Greene, and Mark (2006).

20. Shadish, Cook, and Leviton (1991: 35).

21. Cronbach and Suppes (1969).

Chapter 1

1. Patton (2001: 330).

2. Love (2013).

3. Lewis (2004).

4. Kahneman (2011: 223).

5. Polkinghorne (2004).

6. Polkinghorne (2004).

7. Greenhalgh (2002).

8. Day (2009).

9. See, e.g., the Cochrane Summary "Audit and Feedback: Effects on Professional Practice and Patient Outcomes" at http://summaries.cochrane.org/ CD000259/audit-and-feedback-effects-on-professional-practice-and-patient -outcomes.

10. See, for example, the website for the Community Sustainability Engagement Evaluation Toolbox . . . "a one-stop-site for the evaluation of community sustainability engagement projects. . . . The toolbox brings together a number of best-practice evaluation methods packaged into a comprehensive, user-friendly, how-to format." http://evaluationtoolbox.net.au

11. Buller (2012); Feuer, Floden, Chudowsky, and Ahn, (2013); Hannum (2004); McGann (2006); for best practices in evaluating public health programs, see the Canadian Best Practices Portal at http://cbpp-pcpe.phac-aspc.gc.ca

12. Julnes and Rog (2007a: 4).

13. Julnes and Rog (2007a); Julnes (2012a).

14. See Davidson (2005); House (1993); Scriven (1991, 2007b).

15. Scriven (1991); see also Davidson (2014a).

16. Davidson (2005); Scriven (2013).

17. Fournier (2005: 140).

18. Rossi, Lipsey, and Freeman (2004: 2).

19. Rossi (2013: 110). Those who practice evaluation research acknowledge that they do indeed make judgments as part of their findings. These judgments cover the appraisal of the need for a program, the soundness of its program theory, the clarity and strength of its implementation, its outcomes, and its efficiency; each of these appraisals involves matters of both fact and value.

20. W.K. Kellogg Foundation (2004: 2, 3).

21. United Nations Development Programme (2011).

22. U.S. Government Accountability Office (2012: 3).

23. Department for International Development (2013b: 5).

24. Scriven (2003).

25. The World Bank views M&E systems as essential to good government and useful at all stages of the policy process—from setting priorities and budgeting, to implementation and management of interventions, to demonstrating accountability through achievement of objectives; see, e.g., Lopez-Acevedo, Krause, and Mackay (2012). In view of the worldwide focus on government and organizational accountability and the overwhelming interest in improving organizational performance and managing for results, monitoring and evaluation are increasingly viewed as a comprehensive system for results-based management (RBM), especially in the extensive field of evaluation for development; see United Nations Development Group (2011); Kusek and Rist (2004); Wholey, Hatry, and Newcomer (2004); and Asian Development Bank (2006).

26. There is a growing interest in better understanding how the practices of performance management and evaluation are interrelated given that both are efforts to provide public agencies with information to help them improve the effectiveness and efficiency of the services they provide; see Newcomer and Scheirer (2001); Rist (2006). For an overview of the differences and complementarities between program evaluation and performance measurement, see Hunter and Nielsen (2013).

27. See the overview of the debate in Patton (2008: 420–469). See also a brief history of the development of qualitative approaches to evaluation in Schwandt and Cash (2014).

28. Stake (2004: xv).

29. Greene (2007); Reichardt and Rallis (1994).

30. See, e.g., Michael Bamberger (2012), "Introduction to Mixed Methods in Impact Evaluation" a Guidance Note developed by Interaction with support from the Rockefeller Foundation at http://www.interaction.org/sites/default/files/Mixed%20Methods%20in%20Impact%20Evaluation%20(English).pdf

31. For a discussion of the pressure to use scientifically based evaluation meth-

ods, see the brief recap in Julnes and Rog (2007a); for the international movement, see, e.g., Lipsey and Noonan (2009); White (2009a); for the current view
of the controversy, see Stern et al. (2012).

32. Compare, for example, Schwandt and Burgon (2006) to Mark and Henry
(2006).

33. Julnes and Rog (2007b).

34. King (2005).

35. Cullen, Coryn, and Rugh (2011).

36. Cousins and Whitmore (1998).

37. U.S. Agency for International Development (USAID) Center for Development Information and Evaluation(1996), Institute of Development Studies
(1998).

38. Dozois, Langlois, and Blanchet-Cohen (2010); Gamble (2008); Patton
(2010).

39. Patton (2008) quoted in Dozois, Langlois, and Blanchet-Cohen (2010: 15).

40. An analogous issue here is the relative merit of using internal versus external evaluators. Internal evaluators are part of the organization that houses
the program being evaluated and are directly accountable to that organization.
External evaluators are outside, third-party experts hired to do the evaluation.
An internal evaluator is likely to (a) have a deeper understanding of the context
and politics in which a program is embedded, and thus be in a better position to
design an evaluation approach that is sensitive to those circumstances; (b) have
developed relationships with program staff that might help reduce the anxiety
associated with being evaluated by an "outsider"; (c) contribute more than an
external evaluator to building an evaluation culture within an organization by
serving as an advocate for the role evaluation can play in organizational improvement. Conversely, external evaluators are likely to be perceived as more objective given their independence from the organization. Because the allegiance of
external evaluators is more closely tied to a community of professionals outside
the organization in which a program being evaluated is embedded, they may
bring fresh and innovative ways of viewing the program in question. Questions
of evaluator independence and the objectivity and credibility of the evaluator's
findings relative to the internal versus external position of the evaluator have
been debated for decades. However, there is no logically compelling reason why
internal evaluation must *necessarily* be less objective than its external counterpart
in rendering judgments of the value of a program or policy. Internal evaluators can produce high-quality, objective, warranted, defensible evaluative findings provided that procedures and structures are in place within an organization
to ensure their independence. See, e.g., Volkov and Baron (2011); Love (2005);
Sonnichsen (2000). The most significant issue is political, namely, whether and
how an internal evaluation unit is protected from influence from the manage-

ment of an organization that is charged with overseeing the development and implementation of programs. In the United States, the Government Accountability Office (GAO) has established and continues to maintain its reputation as an independent, nonpartisan agency in the legislative branch of the U.S. Congress conducting evaluations. At the United Nations, the United Nations Development Program (UNDP) Independent Evaluation Group has sought to establish its independence from UNDP management by reporting not to the Senior Administrator overseeing the operations of the UNDP but to the Executive Board; by giving that Board the authority to hire the director of the Evaluation Group; and by making it a condition of employment that after her or his term of service the Director of the Evaluation Group cannot take another job in the United Nations.

41. See, e.g., the American Indian Higher Education Consortium Indigenous Evaluation Framework at http://portal3.aihec.org/sites/Indigeval/Pages/Default .aspx; CommunityNet Aeotearoa at http://www.community.net.nz/how-toguides /community-research/publications-resources/maorievaluation.htm; see also Anderson et al. (2012).

42. Rodin and MacPherson (2012: 13).

43. Stern (2006).

44. Shadish, Cook, and Leviton (1991).

45. Smith (2008).

46. Bernstein (1991: 335–336).

47. This idea of a critical versus an empty or sloganeering pluralism is discussed with respect to claims on behalf of methodological pluralism in political science research in Topper (2005: 186–188).

Chapter 2

1. Shadish, Cook, and Leviton (1991: 30).

2. Thompson (2000).

3. Schön (1983); Schön (1987).

4. Polkinghorne (2004).

5. See, for example, the TRASI database of the Foundation Center at http:// trasi.foundationcenter.org/. It contains over 150 tools, methods, and best practices for evaluation. The American Evaluation Association (AEA) also offers "AEA365 Tip-a-Day Email Alerts," which it describes as "highlighting hot tips, cool tricks, rad resources, and lessons learned for and from evaluators."

6. Rittel and Webber (1973).

7. Mitroff and Silvers (2010); Weber and Khademian (2008).

8. Schön (1983: 68).

9. Polkinghorne (2004).

10. Wagenaar (2004).

11. Carr (1995).

12. Shadish, Cook, and Leviton (1991: 64).

13. See, for example, Mark (2008).

14. See the discussion of evaluator role in King and Stevahn (2002), Patton (2008: 210ff.), Stake (2004: 31ff.).

15. There are other classification efforts as well. Stufflebeam (2001a) organizes models into three categories: questions and/or methods-oriented approaches, improvement/accountability approaches, and social agenda/advocacy approaches. Fitzpatrick, Sanders, and Worthen (2011) sort evaluation approaches into expertise and consumer-oriented, program-oriented, decision-oriented, and participant-oriented. House (1980) analyzed approaches based on their epistemological and ethical premises.

16. Alkin (2013b).

17. The very existence of multiple means of classifying models of evaluation reveals that the task of classification or categorization itself is a theoretical exercise—it is an effort to produce general knowledge about what evaluation is based on, an author's assumptions about what qualifies as an evaluation approach, and what constitutes suitable criteria on which to compare and contrast approaches. Thus, when examining these various schemes, we can be as concerned with the rationale and adequacy of the scheme itself as with the characteristics of the approaches it analyzes.

18. Shadish (1998: 1).

19. Patton (2008: 199).

20. Patton (2008: 201).

21. Alkin's (2013b) approach is a step in the right direction here. However, comparative and critical analysis of the actual views of various theorists on matters of valuing, methods, and use is not a feature of this work. Rather, for each theorist, a brief characterization of her or his work is offered as justification for the placement on one of the three "branches" of the theory tree.

22. Donaldson and Lipsey (2006); Rossi, Lispey, and Freeman (2004).

23. Specifying program theory can be undertaken for many reasons. It can be used for planning a program or intervention—the planning can be based on a situation analysis as well as logical analysis of what the program is attempting to do and the social science evidence that is available to suggest whether this is likely to happen. In planning a program, evaluators might examine relevant substantive theory in the social-behavioral sciences, both to understand the problem being addressed by the program or intervention in question and to learn what knowledge already exists about how the problem has been addressed. Program theory can be used to help stakeholders develop a common understanding of the program and to communicate what the program is about to outsiders. It can

be used to guide monitoring and evaluation. Finally, because program theory is amenable to testing by systematic, empirical research, it can contribute to an evidence base of interventions; see Chen (2013); Donaldson (2007); Donaldson and Lipsey (2006); Funnell and Rogers (2011: 58-67); White (2009b).

24. Anderson (2005); Funnell and Rogers (2011).

25. Coryn (2008); Coryn, Noakes, Westine, and Schröter (2011); Scriven (1998); Stufflebeam and Shinkfield (2007). Even defenders of the approach argue that it probably should not be a routine part of every evaluation because "in many programs and for many purposes, an investigation of theoretical assumptions is too elaborate, too demanding, and probably irrelevant. What many program sponsors and managers want to know can be discovered by simpler and less probing strategies." Weiss (2000: 44).

26. Funnell and Rogers (2011: 74–90).

27. MacPherson et al. (2013).

28. Funnell and Rogers (2011: 89).

29. Patton (2008: 375).

30. Butler and Allen (2008); Hargreaves (2010); Hayes (2008); Leischow et al. (2008); Mowles (2014); Ramalingam and Jones (2008); Rogers (2008).

31. Williams and Hummelbrunner (2010).

32. Patton (2008: 360–379).

33. Sterman (2006: 509).

34. For a brief overview of such theories and how they can be used in program theory–based evaluation, see Funnell and Rogers (2011: 319–349). See also Taplin and Clark (2012) and the Center for Theory of Change at http://www.theoryofchange.org

35. Forti (2012).

36. See the overview of backwards mapping at http://www.theoryofchange.org/what-is-theory-of-change/how-does-theory-of-change-work/example/backwards-mapping/

37. Stein and Valters (2012).

38. Baker and Bruner (2006); Preskill and Torres (1999).

39. Preskill (2013).

40. Demers (2007); Rogers and Williams (2006).

41. Stern et al. (2012).

42. This is the debate over a realist view of causality in evaluation championed initially by Pawson and Tilley (1997).

43. Cook, Scriven, Coryn, and Evergreen (2010); Mark and Henry (2006); White (2009a).

44. Schwartz, Forss, and Marra (2011); see also the special issue on Contribution Analysis in *Evaluation: The International Journal of Theory, Research and Practice* 2012 (July), 18(3).

45. Beach and Pedersen (2013); Befani, Ledermann, and Sager (2007); Earl, Carden, and Smutylo (2001); Scriven (1974); White and Phillips (2012).

46. These are eight international development goals officially established following the Millennium Summit of the United Nations in 2000. The 189 United Nations member states and 23 international organizations have agreed to achieve these goals by the year 2015. The goals are (1) eradicating extreme poverty and hunger, (2) achieving universal primary education, (3) promoting gender equity and empowering women, (4) reducing child mortality rates, (5) improving maternal health, (6) combating HIV/AIDS, malaria, and other diseases, (7) ensuring environmental sustainability, (8) developing a global partnership for development.

47. Fetterman and Wandersman (2005); House and Howe (1999, 2000); Mertens (2009).

48. Hood (2002).

49. Ottoson and Hawe (2009).

50. Chelimsky (2013: 92).

Chapter 3

1. Julnes (2012b: 3–4, emphasis in the original).

2. See Davidson (2005: 85–97); House and Howe (1999); Julnes (2012b); Scriven (2012).

3. House and Howe (1999: 5).

4. House and Howe (1999: 9).

5. Patton (2008: 114–116).

6. There is some disagreement in the field about the use of these terms. Some evaluators do not sharply distinguish between merit and worth in this way, preferring instead to say that merit is about effectiveness and worth about costs and that the distinction that really matters is between *absolute* merit and worth—the quality of a given program in and of itself—and *relative* merit and worth—the quality of a program in comparison to other options or alternatives. When programs (or any other objects of evaluation) are compared and ranked from high to low in terms of their quality, we are engaging an assessment of relative value. On the other hand, when a program is graded in terms of its performance on a set of criteria, we are engaging in an assessment of absolute value. The evaluation of products in *Consumer Reports* involves both grading and ranking. See Scriven (1991).

7. Mark, Henry, and Julnes (2000: 289).

8. Explicit specification of criteria is one of the professional standards for evaluation: "Evaluations should clarify and specify the individual and cultural values underpinning purposes, processes, and judgments" (Yarbrough, Shulha, Hopson, and Caruthers, 2011).

9. Rushefsky (2008).

10. Patton (2012).

11. The following example and the discussion of problems with using program objectives as the basis of criteria is drawn from Davidson (2005: 24–27).

12. See DAC Criteria for Evaluating Development Assistance, http://www.oecd.org/dac/evaluation/daccriteriaforevaluatingdevelopmentassistance.htm

13. Society for Prevention Research (n.d.: 1, 7).

14. An *efficacious* intervention will have been tested in at least two rigorous trials that (a) involved defined samples from defined populations, (b) used psychometrically sound measures and data collection procedures, (c) analyzed their data with rigorous statistical approaches, (d) showed consistent positive effects (without serious iatrogenic effects), and (e) reported at least one significant long-term follow-up. An *effective* intervention under these standards will not only meet all standards for efficacious interventions, but also will have (a) manuals, appropriate training, and technical support available to allow third parties to adopt and implement the intervention; (b) been evaluated under real-world conditions in studies that included sound measurement of the level of implementation and engagement of the target audience (in both the intervention and control conditions); (c) indicated the practical importance of intervention outcome effects; and (d) clearly demonstrated to whom intervention findings can be generalized. See Flay et al. (2005: 151).

15. See, for example, the papers discussing impact evaluation available at International Initiative on Impact Evaluation (3ie) http://www.3ieimpact.org/ as well as the World Bank's definition of impact assessment at http://web.world bank.org/WBSITE/EXTERNAL/TOPICS/EXTEDUCATION/0,,contentM DK:20885241menuPK:2448393pagePK:210058piPK:210062theSitePK:282386,00 .html

16. See the OECD's Development Assistance Committee (DAC) Criteria for Evaluating Development Assistance at http://www.oecd.org/dac/evaluation/dac criteriaforevaluatingdevelopmentassistance.htm; see also Chianca (2008).

17. See the UNDP *Handbook on Planning, Monitoring and Evaluating for Development Results* at http://web.undp.org/evaluation/handbook/ch7-4.html

18. Bamberger and Segone (2011); Segone (2012).

19. See Levin and McEwan (2001); Yates (1996, 2012).

20. This is one arena where the lines between the professional practice of evaluation and the fields of organization consulting and development begin to be blurred; see, e.g., McKinsey & Company's initiative Learning for Social Impact at http://lsi.mckinsey.com/ and FSG's Strategy for Impact activities at http://www.fsg.org/

21. Rockefeller Foundation (2003: 2).

22. See http://www.socialimpactassessment.com/index.asp

23. Mulgan (2010: 38).

24. See, e.g., the Foundation Center's website Tools and Resources for Assessing Social Impact (TRASI) at http://trasi.foundationcenter.org/

25. Wood and Leighton (2010); Rockefeller Foundation (2003); http://www.thesroinetwork.org/

26. Tuan (2008: 24).

27. See the Sustainability Evaluation Checklist at the Western Michigan University Checklists project at http://www.wmich.edu/evalctr/checklists/. See the Program Sustainability Assessment Tool at https://sustaintool.org/assess

28. Cultural relevance and responsiveness is also properly regarded as an ethical obligation of the evaluator. That obligation entails not only an evaluator's understanding of program-community alignment, but also an evaluator's reflexive examination of her or his own cultural position and beliefs, and how all of this is expressed in the way an evaluator designs and conducts a program evaluation and interprets and reports findings of program effectiveness.

29. See http://www.healthypeople.gov/2020/default.aspx

30. Shipman (2012: 61–62).

31. Watkins, Meiers, and Visser (2012).

32. Rossi, Lipsey, and Freeman (2004: 102). For other discussions of this kind of systematic study, see Altschuld and Kumar (2010); Altschuld and Watkin (2000).

33. Each annual World Bank report focuses on a different area of development; see http://ieg.worldbank.org/Data/reports/impact_evaluation.pdf. UNDP's *Human Development Reports* are explained at http://hdr.undp.org/en/. They rely on dozens of individual and composite indicators in different sectors of society (education, gender, health, security, poverty, sustainability, etc.).

34. The distinction between needs and wants that originates with Scriven is explained in Davidson (2005: 33–41).

35. For a brief discussion of the use of these tools in values inquiry, see Mark, Henry, and Julnes (2000: 303–313).

36. See, e.g., Hurteau, Houle, and Mongiat (2009).

37. See Scriven (1994). In a study of evaluation practitioners who rated the importance of 49 evaluation competencies, the competency of "making judgments" was rated the second lowest on average of all the competencies, indicating that not all respondents believe that to evaluate is to judge; see King, Stevahn, Ghere, and Minnema (2001).

38. Davidson (2014b: 4).

39. The "how-to" of these approaches is too detailed to discuss here. See Davidson (2005: 151–187) for an explanation and illustration of both qualitative and quantitative weighting methodologies; see also Scriven (1994).

40. Stake (2004: 6, and 159–160).

41. Stake (2004: 171).

42. The discussion surrounding a holistic approach to determining quality is more conceptual than technical, but see Stake (2004: 159–179) and Stake and Schwandt (2006).

43. Stake (2004: 178).

44. House (1995: 34).

45. Gastil (2000: 22).

46. Burchardt (2012).

47. House and Howe (1999: 93).

48. Barber (1988: 200).

49. Barber (1988: 200).

50. House and Howe (1999: 51).

51. Robert and Zeckhauser (2011).

52. Shipman (2012: 60).

53. Cronbach et al. (1980).

54. Weiss (1979, 1999).

55. Alkin (2013a).

56. See Alkin (2013a: 290–291); also Rog, Fitzpatrick, and Conner (2012) for an overview of these contextual considerations. A recent effort aims to develop a framework that facilitates matching means of determining criteria to particular contextual considerations including stakeholder decisions and the amount of precision desired in measuring performance on criteria (Julnes, 2012a).

57. Alkin, Vo, and Christie (2012: 39, emphasis added).

Chapter 4

1. Paul and Elder (2014: 2).

2. Scriven (2007a).

3. Some of the material in this chapter is drawn from Schwandt (2009).

4. Dewey (1910); see also Baker and Bruner (2006).

5. One account (Patton, 2008: 154) discusses "evaluative thinking" as a combination of dispositions (e.g., be clear, accountable, specific, intentional, and systematic) and skills (focus and prioritize, make assumptions explicit, separate statements of fact from interpretations and judgments, etc.)

6. Paul and Elder (2014).

7. There is considerable debate about whether the critical thinking skills shown in Table 4.1 transfer from one context to another—that is, whether they are generic or domain-specific—and the evidence on either side of the argument is mixed; see Lai (2011: 15–16).

8. Lai (2011); Lewis and Smith (1993).

9. Facione (1990: 2).

10. Donaldson (2009: 249).

11. Haack (2003: 23).

12. Chelimsky (2007); Reiss (2011).

13. Chelimsky (2007: 19).

14. Housing-first is an evidence-based practice that views housing for the homeless as a tool for ending homelessness rather than a reward that a homeless person earns when he or she recovers from an addiction or successfully enrolls for a long period of time in treatment for a mental health problem, and so on. See, e.g., http://www.endhomelessness.org/pages/housing_first

15. Braverman (2013).

16. Cartwright (2007b).

17. Case-controlled studies are a type of observation study often used in epidemiological research. Two existing groups differing in some outcome of interest are compared; for example, people who smoke compared to people who do not smoke evaluated on the basis of which group has the higher incidence of lung cancer (the outcome of interest).

18. Cartwright (2007a; 2011a).

19. Abeysinghe and Parkhurst (2013: 12).

20. Cartwright (2007a: 11).

21. Cartwright (2006; 2009).

22. For a philosopher's view that evidence is relative to an argument, see Cartwright (2011b).

23. Department for International Development (2013a).

24. Dunworth, Hannaway, Holanhan, and Turner, (2008: 7).

25. Davies, Nutley, and Smith (2000).

26. Upshur (2002: 114).

27. Prewitt, Schwandt, and Straf (2012: 4).

28. Spillane and Miele (2007).

29. See the World Bank's Development Impact Evaluation Initiative at http://ieg.worldbank.org/Data/reports/impact_evaluation.pdf

30. See Mark and Henry (2006); Stern et al. (2012).

31. The controversy is particular sharp in the field of international development evaluation, where there is disagreement not only about best methods but also about the meaning of impact evaluation itself. For example, the Organisation for Economic Cooperation and Development/Development Assistance Committee (OECD/DAC, (004) defines impacts as the positive and negative, primary and secondary long-term effects produced by a development intervention, directly or indirectly, intended or unintended. The definition produced by the International Initiative for Impact Evaluation (3ie) (2008: 2) is more restricted: Rigorous impact evaluation studies measure the net change in

outcomes for a particular group of people that can be attributed to a specific program using the best methodology available, feasible, and appropriate to the evaluation question being investigated and to the specific context.

32. Macinko and Silver (2012: 1698).

33. Ramalingam (2013).

34. These are often referred to by several different names including social experiments, randomized controlled trials, randomized controlled experiments, and random assignment studies.

35. See, e.g., http://blogs.worldbank.org/publicsphere/lant-pritchett-v-rand omistas-nature-evidence-wonkwar-brewing; http://socialscienceandhealth .blogspot.com/; and Parker (2010).

36. Mark and Henry (2006).

37. Schorr and Farrow (2011: 24).

38. Stern et al. (2012: 38).

39. Mayne (2011: 54); see also the special issue on contribution analysis in *Evaluation: the International Journal of Theory, Research and Practice* (July 2012), 18(3).

40. Rothman and Greenland (2005).

41. Schorr (2012: 50).

42. Braverman (2013); see also the checklist of criteria for selecting indicators at MacDonald (2013).

43. Bamberger, Rugh, and Mabry (2010).

44. Schorr and Farrow (2011: 41).

45. Schorr and Farrow (2011).

46. Majone (1989).

47. Majone (1989: 22).

48. House (1980: 173).

49. Blair (1995: 76–77).

50. Walton (1989).

51. Lupia (2013).

52. Cialdini (2009).

53. Walton, Reed, and Macagno (2008).

54. Zelik, Patterson, and Woods (2010).

Chapter 5

1. Cronbach et al. (1980: 3).

2. In the English language we distinguish between *policy* and *politics*; however, in German, Danish, and Swedish there is one word for both, i.e., *politik*; this is also the case in Spanish (*política*) and French (*politique*). Policymaking in Span-

ish and French is simply the "doing" of politics (*la formulacion de políticas* or *l'élaboration des politiques*).

3. The value of a policy or program may be established ex post (retrospectively)—examining outcomes of a program or policy after it has been implemented—or ex ante (prospectively)—examining potential outcomes using predictive tools.

4. Prewitt, Schwandt, and Straf (2012).

5. See the EvalPartners website at http://www.mymande.org/evalpartners/the -international-evaluation-partnership-initiatives

6. Blase (1991); Malen (1994).

7. Guzman and Feria (2002).

8. Weaver and Cousins (2004).

9. Roche and Kelly (2012: 3).

10. Weiss (1993: 94).

11. Nutley, Walter, and Davies (2007).

12. Nutley and Webb (2000).

13. Majone (1989: 12).

14. Stone (2002: 376).

15. Nutley, Walter, and Davies (2007: 93–94).

16. Stone (2002: 305).

17. Stone (2002: 7, 8).

18. Stone (2002).

19. Weiss (1979).

20. Pielke (2007: 35).

21. Beer, Ingargiola, and Beer (2012).

22. Organizational Research Services (2010); Reisman, Gienapp, and Stachowiak (2007).

23. Stachowiak (2013).

24. See, e.g., the Institute on Governance at http://iog.ca/

25. United Nations Development Programme (1997). To this list others add "rights-based"—good governance does not infringe on the legal and customary rights of individuals or communities, and "subsidiarity"—authority and responsibility for decision making is delegated to the lowest possible level with the relevant capacity, thereby promoting public participation and accountability in decision making.

26. Chelimsky (2008: 401).

27. Chelimsky (2006: 39).

28. Betts and Wedgwood (2011); World Bank (1994).

29. Kushner and Norris (2007).

30. Sanderson (2001).

31. National Performance Management Advisory Commission (2010: vii).

32. van der Meer (2007: 167).
33. Henkel (1991); see also Taylor (2005).
34. Power (1997: 4); see also Dahler-Larsen (2012: 169ff.).
35. Dahler-Larsen (2012); Leeuw and Furubo (2008). According to Dahler-Larsen (2013: 31) these evaluation systems have the following ideal-typical characteristics: "They are fairly permanent, repetitive, and routine-based. They generalize forms of evaluation and/or their results across time and space. Evaluation systems are decreasingly dependent on the values and ideas and styles of individual evaluators. Instead, they embody evaluation epistemologies or institutionalized types of thinking, and they are supported by general and abstract tools such as verification processes, documentation processes, indicators, criteria, standards, benchmarks, testing systems, information technology and handbooks that can be used in fairly standardized ways across different substantial areas of activity. Evaluation systems allow the handling of information about large amounts of public activities in a systematic, integrated, and comparable way. Evaluation systems are embedded in organizational procedures of verification [and] . . . run by organizations . . . [and] produce streams of evaluative information (Rist & Stame, 2006) rather than stand-alone evaluation reports."
36. See "FACT SHEET on the President's Plan to Make College More Affordable: A Better Bargain for the Middle Class" released by the White House on August 22, 2013, at http://www.whitehouse.gov/the-press-office/2013/08/22/fact-sheet-president-s-plan-make-college-more-affordable-better-bargain-
37. Rodwin (2001: 440).
38. Rodwin (2001: 441).
39. Ozga, Dahler-Larsen, Segerholm, and Simola (2011).
40. Davies, Newcomer, and Soydan (2006).
41. The key Evaluation Policy Task Force document is "An Evaluation Roadmap for More Effective Government," available at http://www.eval.org/p/cm/ld/fid=129
42. Squires and Measor (2005).
43. Maltz ([1984] 2001: 18).
44. Weiss (1993).
45. Cordray and Lipsey (1986).
46. Bovens, 't Hart, and Kuipers (2006).
47. Datta (2011).
48. Datta (2011).
49. Dryzek (1993).
50. Majone (1989).
51. Datta (2011).
52. Datta (2011).
53. Fischer (2003: 185).

54. Greene (2006).
55. Segone (2012).
56. Fischer (2003).
57. This example is adapted from Fischer (2003: 196–197).
58. Mathison (2000).
59. Simons (2010).
60. Barber (1984).
61. Bohman and Rehg (1997).

Chapter 6

1. Rossi, Lipsey, and Freeman (2004: 412).
2. It was around this time that notable publications in the knowledge utilization literature began to appear, including Cohen and Lindblom (1979); Floden and Weiner (1978); Lynn (1978); Weiss (1977); and Weiss and Bucuvalas (1980).
3. See, e.g., Coburn and Turner (2012); Marsh, Payne, and Hamilton (2006).
4. See, e.g., Boruch and Rui (2008); Haskins and Baron (2011).
5. See, e.g., Forester (1984); Huberman (1987, 1994); Lomas (1993); Sabatier and Jenkins-Smith (1993).
6. See, e.g., Cousins and Leithwood, 1986; Johnson et al. (2009); Ledermann (2012); Shulha and Cousins (1997).
7. There is a small literature on what constitutes misuse of evaluation, for example when an evaluation is commissioned simply to give the appearance of objectively assessing program effects, when a funder is committed to a program regardless of what the evaluative evidence might reveal, or when an evaluator manipulates data or changes findings to satisfy a client. See Alkin and Coyle (1988); Stevens and Dial (1994); Palumbo (1994); Patton (2008: 105–107).
8. Weiss (1980, 1981).
9. Kirkhart (2000: 7).
10. Contandriopoulos, Lemire, Denis, and Tremblay (2010).
11. Contandriopoulos, Lemire, Denis, and Tremblay (2010: 459).
12. Contandriopoulos, Lemire, Denis, and Tremblay (2010: 459).
13. Prewitt, Schwandt, and Straf (2012: 55). See also Contandriopoulos and Brouselle (2012: 63), who argue, "To be relevant, usable and meaningful, evidence needs to be embedded in what political science calls 'policy options' and what we generically describe here as action proposals. Action proposals are assertions that employ rhetoric to embed information into arguments to support a causal link between a given course of action and anticipated consequences."
14. Henry and Mark (2003); Mark and Henry (2004).
15. Cook and Brown (1999: 386–387).
16. Coburn and Turner (2012); Spillane (2012).

17. Hutchins (1995).

18. Spillane and Miele (2007: 48–49)

19. Nutley, Walter, and Davies (2007: 36).

20. Weiss (1979: 427): "A problem exists and a decision has to be made, information or understanding is lacking either to generate a solution to the problem or to select among alternative solutions, research provides the missing knowledge. With the gap filled, a decision is reached."

21. Nutley, Walter, and Davies (2007); Pielke (2007).

22. Weiss (1978: 77).

23. Weiss (1979: 430).

24. Patton (2008: 104).

25. Floden and Weiner (1978: 16).

26. Herbst (2003: 484); quoted in Boswell (2008: 472).

27. See Dahler-Larsen (2012, Chapters 1 and 2)

28. Boswell (2008).

29. Dahler-Larsen (2012: 67).

30. Boswell (2008: 473).

31. Patton (2008: 155).

32. See also the idea of "evaluative inquiry for learning in organizations" in Preskill (2013).

33. Yarbrough, Shulha, Hopson, and Caruthers (2011: 5).

34. Preskill and Boyle (2008: 444).

35. Cousins, Goh, Elliott, and Bourgeois (2014: 17).

36. Contandriopoulos, Lemire, Denis, and Tremblay (2010: 450).

37. Sutherland et al. (2012).

38. Green, Ottoson, García, and Hiatt (2009); Contandriopoulos, Lemire, Denis, and Tremblay (2010).

39. Contandriopoulos, Lemire, Denis, and Tremblay (2010: 468).

40. Caplan (1979).

41. Kingdon (1995: 228).

42. Bonbright (2102).

43. Spillane and Miele (2007).

44. Contandriopoulos, Lemire, Denis, and Tremblay (2010).

45. Pielke (2007).

46. Contandriopoulos, Lemire, Denis, and Tremblay (2010: 461).

47. Contandriopoulos and Brousselle (2012: 65).

48. Contandriopoulos, Lemire, Denis, and Tremblay. (2010: 463).

49. Conklin, Hallsworth, Hatziandreu, and Grant (2008).

50. Wandersman et al. (2008).

51. Weiss (1999).

52. Havelock (1969). See also Pielke (2007), who refers to this as the linear

reservoir model: knowledge generated by science flows into a reservoir from which society then draws to create benefits.

53. See, for example, in health care the National Guideline Clearinghouse at http://www.guideline.gov/. In social service, education, and criminal justice fields, registries of best practices or model programs as found, for example, in the work of the International Campbell Collaboration often replace guidelines.

54. Nutley, Walter, and Davies (2007: 119).

55. See "More about Knowledge Translation at CIHR" at http://www.cihr-irsc.gc.ca/e/39033.html#Synthesis. See also Lomas (2000) and Sudsawad (2007) for discussion of the CIHR model and others.

56. Bogenschneider and Corbett (2010); Coburn (1998).

57. Wandersman et al. (2008). For another example combining ideas from systems thinking with transdisciplinary research, see Leischow et al. (2008).

58. Patton (2008: 173).

59. Patton (2008: 37).

60. Patton (2013b).

61. Empowerment evaluation (Fetterman and Wandersman, 2005) is said to rest on the following ten principles: improvement, community ownership, inclusion, democratic participation, social justice, community knowledge, evidence-based strategies, capacity building, organizational learning, and accountability.

62. Wandersman (2003).

63. Schorr and Farrow (2011: iv).

64. UNESCO (2005: 210).

65. See, e.g., Baccaro and Papadakis (2008); Biegelbauer and Hansen (2011); Fischer (2003); Maasen and Weingart (2005).

66. Johnson et al. (2009: 389).

67. Bonbright (2102).

Chapter 7

1. Cronbach et al. (1980: 9).

2. Gargani (2011).

3. Almost from the beginning of evaluation forming itself as an organized practice in the United States (late 1970s onward), its standing as a profession was a matter of concern. See, e.g., Merwin and Weiner (1985); Morell and Flaherty (1978).

4. Picciotto (2011: 170); see also Worthen (1994).

5. Rossi, Lipsey, and Freeman (2004: 394).

6. For an overview of different approaches to developing competencies, see Wilcox and King (2014); that article is part of a special issue of the *Canadian Journal of Program Evaluation* on "Professionalizing Evaluation."

7. Epstein and Hundert (2002: 226).

8. Schön (1983).

9. Epstein and Hundert (2002: 228).

10. Toulemonde (1995).

11. UKES Evaluation Capabilities Framework 2012 is available at https://www
.evaluation.org.uk/about-us/publications

12. See "Results of the 2011 Evaluation Capabilities Survey" at http://euro
peanevaluation.org/sites/default/files/surveys/EES_Capabilities_Survey_Evalu
ation_0.pdf

13. The convenor of the UKES working group (Simons, 2013: 4) that developed their framework argued, "The wider connotation of capability takes us
beyond the specific focus on the individual having to meet all the skills required
for any one evaluation to consider what combination of skills and knowledge is
required to conduct a quality evaluation and in different contexts."

14. Available at http://www.evaluationcanada.ca/site.cgi?s=50&ss=8&_
lang=EN

15. Stevahn, King, Ghere, and Minnema (2005).

16. Available on AEA's website at http://www.eval.org/p/cm/ld/fid=51

17. Available on AEA's website at http://www.eval.org/p/cm/ld/fid=92. See
also SenGupta, Hopson, and Thompson-Robinson (2004).

18. See "Evaluator Competencies 2011" p. 10 at http://www.anzea.org.nz/wp
-content/uploads/2013/05/110801_anzea_evaluator_competencies_final.pdf

19. For one perspective on whether competencies might support efforts to
certify, credential, or license evaluators, or become the basis for accreditation of
training programs, see Altschuld (2005).

20. Morra Imas (2010).

21. See IDEAS "Competencies for Development Evaluators, Managers, and Commissioners" at http://www.ideas-int.org/documents/file_list
.cfm?DocsSubCatID=48

22. See the DeGEval document at http://www.degeval.de/publikationen/
requirement-profiles-for-evaluators/; see the AES document at http://www.aes
.asn.au/professional-learning/pl-resources.html

23. See DFID "Evaluation Department: Technical Competency Framework"
at https://www.gov.uk/government/publications/dfid-technical-competency
-frameworks

24. The Japanese Evaluation Society's approach to credentialing is described
in Wilcox and King (2014). See the CES approach at https://www.cesprofession
aldesignation.ca/CES/login.jsp; also Cousins, Cullen, Malik, and Maicher (2009).

25. See the discussion of this VEPR system and relevant documents at http://
europeanevaluation.org/community/thematic-working-groups/twg-3-profes
sionalization-evaluation

26. Yarbrough, Shulha, Hopson, and Caruthers (2011).

27. The *Program Evaluation Standards* were developed in the U.S., and AEA members have served on and chaired the task forces, review panels, and validation panels that developed the standards through all its revisions. The AEA does not officially endorse these standards, although it supports the work of the Joint Committee.

28. OECD/DAC (2010: 5).

29. Council of the Inspectors General on Integrity and Efficiency (2011: 15).

30. Council of the Inspectors General on Integrity and Efficiency (2011: 18).

31. United Nations Evaluation Group (2005).

32. Scriven (2009).

33. Yarborough, Shulha, Hopson, and Caruthers (2011: 226).

34. See the Evaluation Checklist Project at http://www.wmich.edu/evalctr/checklists/evaluation-checklists/

35. See the UNDP IEO material on quality assurance at http://web.undp.org/evaluation/evaluation-office.shtml#advisory-panel

36. Hageboeck, Frumkin, and Monschien (2013).

37. Patton (2013a).

38. Stufflebeam (2001b).

39. Scriven (2009: iv).

40. Morris (2008: 4).

41. Morris (2008: 4)

42. Department for International Development (2013b).

43. See the CES ethical guidelines at http://www.evaluationcanada.ca/site.cgi?s=5&ss=4&_lang=en

44. See the AES web site for the document http://www.aes.asn.au

45. For the full text of these guiding principles, see http://www.eval.org/p/cm/ld/fid=51

46. Cooksy (2009); Morris (2008, 2009).

47. Some of the material that follows is drawn from Schwandt (2007).

48. See, e.g., Hopson (2003, 2009); The Colorado Trust (2002).

49. Nussbaum (1997: 11).

50. Fox (2005: 1317).

51. Fleischacker (1999: 109)

52. See, e.g., Ozga, Dahler-Larsen, Segerholm, and Simola (2011) for an examination of the way in which the continuous production of performance data and the preoccupation with quality assurance has developed into a form of governance of education in Europe.

53. McDavid, Huse, and Hawthorn (2013: 453).

54. Colby and Sullivan (2008: 405).

55. Sullivan and Rosen (2008a: 47).

56. Sullivan and Rosen (2008b: 19).

57. See Schwandt (2008) for a fuller explication of the ideas that follow.

Epilogue

1. Freidson (2001: 95).

2. Benner, Tanner, and Chesla (2009); Sullivan (2004).

3. Data on the decline of university-based education programs are controversial. A 2002 study by Engle, Altschuld, and Kim (2006) reported a 60 percent decline in such programs since 1980. A study by LaVelle and Donaldson (2010) reported a doubling of such programs in the period 2006–2008. However, their data are questionable because they included not just programs in evaluation, but also programs in research methodology, social policy, educational leadership, educational psychology, psychology, sociology, public policy, and educational policy, as long as those programs listed two or more courses with the word "evaluation" in the title. Whether having such courses available literally constitutes a program of training in evaluation is questionable.

4. For example, see the requirements for the Certificate in Evaluation Practice (CEP) at The Evaluators' Institute, https://tei.gwu.edu/certificate-evaluation -practice-cep; the Certificate of Advanced Study in Evaluation at Claremont University at http://www.cgu.edu/pages/4883.asp; and the requirements for the three- or four-course certificate programs in evaluation at Boston University, American University, Tufts University, the University of Illinois at Chicago, and the University of Minnesota.

5. Lord Phillips of Sudbury (2004).

6. Suddaby, Gendron, and Lam (2007).

7. Church and Waclawski (1998).

8. Colby and Sullivan (2008: 413).

9. Colby and Sullivan (2008: 414).

10. Problems in the education of evaluators such as those that follow have also been identified by Rossi, Lipsey, and Freeman (2004).

11. Davies and MacKay (2014).

12. LaVelle and Donaldson (2010).

13. See http://www.carnegiefoundation.org/previous-work/professional-grad uate-education; also Sullivan and Rosen (2008a, 2008b).

14. Colby and Sullivan (2008: 415).

Bibliography

Abeysinghe, Sudeepa, and Justin O. Parkhurst. 2013. "Better Evidence for Policy: From Hierarchies to Appropriateness." Working Paper #2. London School of Hygiene and Tropical Medicine, GRIP-Health Programme. Available at http://www.lshtm.ac.uk/groups/griphealth/resources/better_evidence_for_policy:_from_hierarchies_to_appropriateness.pdf

Alkin, Marvin C. 2013a. "Context-Sensitive Evaluation." In Marvin C. Alkin (ed.), *Evaluation Roots: A Wider Perspective of Theorists' Views and Influences* 2nd ed. Los Angeles: Sage, 283–292.

Alkin, Marvin C. (ed.). 2013b. *Evaluation Roots: A Wider Perspective of Theorists' Views and Influences* 2nd ed. Los Angeles: Sage.

Alkin, Marvin C., and Karin Coyle. 1988. "Thoughts on Evaluation Utilization, Misutilization and Non-utilization." *Studies in Educational Evaluation* 14: 331–340.

Alkin, Marvin C., Anne Vo, and Christina Christie. 2012. "The Evaluator's Role in Valuing: Who and with Whom." In George Julnes (ed.), *Promoting Valuation in the Public Interest: Informing Policies for Judging Value in Evaluation. New Directions for Evaluation* 133: 29–42. San Francisco: Jossey-Bass.

Altschuld, James W. 2005. "Certification, Credentialing, Licensure, Competencies, and the Like: Issues Confronting the Field of Evaluation." *Canadian Journal of Program Evaluation* 20: 157–168.

Altschuld, James W., and David D. Kumar. 2010. *Needs Assessment: An Overview.* Thousand Oaks, CA: Sage.

Altschuld, James W., and Belle Ruth Watkin. 2000. *From Needs Assessment to Action: Transforming Needs into Solution Strategies.* Thousand Oaks, CA: Sage.

Anderson, Andrea. 2005. *The Community Builder's Approach to Theory of Change: A Practical Guide to Theory and Development.* New York: The Aspen Institute Roundtable on Community Change.

Anderson, Clara, et al. 2012. "It Is Only New Because It Has Been Missing for So Long: Indigenous Evaluation Capacity Building." *American Journal of Evaluation* 33: 566–582.

Argyris, Chris. 2004. *Reasons and Rationalizations: The Limits to Organizational Knowledge.* Oxford, UK: Oxford University Press.

Asian Development Bank. 2006. *An Introduction to Results Management: Principles, Implications, and Applications.* Metro Manila, The Philippines: Asian Development Bank.

Baccaro, Lucio, and Konstantinos Papadakis. 2008. *The Promise and Perils of Participatory Policy Making.* Geneva, Switzerland: International Labour Organization, Institute for Labour Studies.

Baker, Anita, and Beth Bruner. 2006. "Evaluation Capacity and Evaluative Thinking in Organizations." Rochester, NY: The Bruner Foundation. Available at http://www.evaluativethinking.org/sub_page.php?page =manuals

Bamberger, Michael, Jim Rugh, and Linda Mabry. 2010. *Real World Evaluation: Working Under Budget, Time, Data, and Political Constraints* 2nd ed. Los Angeles: Sage.

Bamberger, Michael, and Marco Segone (eds.). 2011. *How to Design and Manage Equity-Focused Evaluations.* New York: UNICEF Evaluation Office.

Barber, Benjamin. 1984. *Strong Democracy: Participatory Politics for a New Age.* Berkeley: University of California Press.Barber, Benjamin. 1988. *The Conquest of Politics.* Princeton, NJ: Princeton University Press.

Beach, Derek, and Rasmus Brun Pedersen. 2013. *Process-Tracing Methods: Foundations and Guidelines.* Ann Arbor, MI: University of Michigan Press.

Beer, Tanya, Pilar Stella Ingargiola, and Meghann Flynn Beer. 2012. *Advocacy and Public Policy Grantmaking: Matching Process to Purpose.* Denver, CO: The Colorado Trust. Available at http://www.evaluationinnovation.org/sites/default/files/Advocacy%20Public%20Policy%20Grantmaking.pdf

Befani, Barbara, Simone Ledermann, and Fritz Sager. 2007. "Realistic Evaluation and QCA: Conceptual Parallels and an Empirical Application." *Evaluation: The International Journal of Theory, Research and Practice* 13: 171–192.

Benner, Patricia, Christine A. Tanner, and Catherine A. Chesla. 2009. *Expertise in Nursing: Practice, Caring, Clinical Judgment and Ethics.* New York: Springer.

Bernstein, Richard J. 1991. *The New Constellation: The Ethical-Political Horizons of Modernity/Postmodernity.* Cambridge, MA: MIT Press.

Betts, Julia, and Helen Wedgwood. 2011. "Effective Institutions and Good Governance for Development: Evidence on Progress and the Role of Aid. *Evaluation Insights* No. 4. Available at http://www.oecd.org/dac/evaluation/evaluation insights.htm

Biegelbauer, Peter, and Janus Hansen. 2011. "Democratic Theory and Citizen

Participation: Democracy Models in the Evaluation of Public Participation in Science and Technology." *Science and Public Policy* 38: 589–597.

Blair, J. Anthony. 1995. "Informal Logic and Reasoning in Evaluation. In Deborah Fournier (ed.), *Reasoning in Evaluation: Inferential Links and Leaps. New Directions for Evaluation* 68: 71–80. San Francisco: Jossey-Bass.

Blase, Joseph. 1991. *The Politics of Life in Schools: Power, Conflict, and Cooperation.* London: Sage.

Bogenschneider, Karen, and Thomas J. Corbett. 2010. *Evidence-Based Policymaking: Insights from Policy-Minded Researchers and Research-Minded Policymakers.* New York: Routledge.

Bohman, James, and William Rehg (eds.). 1997. *Deliberative Democracy: Essays on Reason and Politics.* Cambridge, MA: The MIT Press.

Bonbright, David. 2012. "Use of Impact Evaluation Results." Impact Evaluation Notes No. 4. Washington, DC: Interaction. Available at http://www.interaction .org/impact-evaluation-notes

Boruch, Robert, and Ning Rui. 2008. "From Randomized Controlled Trials to Evidence Grading Schemes: Current State of Evidence-Based Practice in Social Sciences." *Journal of Evidence-Based Medicine* 1: 41–49.

Boswell, Christina. 2008. "The Political Functions of Expert Knowledge: Knowledge and Legitimation in European Union Immigration Policy." *European Journal of Public Policy* 15: 471–488.

Bovens, Mark, Paul 't Hart, and Sanneke Kuipers. 2006. "The Politics of Policy Evaluation." In Michael Moran, Martin Rein, and Robert E. Goodin (eds.), *The Oxford Handbook of Public Policy.* Oxford, UK: Oxford University Press, 317–333.

Braverman, Marc T. 2013. "Negotiating Measurement: Methodological and Interpersonal Considerations in the Choice and Interpretation of Instruments." *American Journal of Evaluation* 34: 99–114.

Buller, Jeffrey. 2012. *Best Practices in Faculty Evaluation.* San Francisco: Jossey-Bass.Butler, Michael R., and Peter M. Allen. 2008. "Understanding Policy Implementation Processes as Self-Organizing Systems." *Public Management Review* 10: 421–440.

Burchardt, Tania. 2012. "Deliberative Research as a Tool to Make Value Judgments." Paper No. CASE/159. Centre for Analysis of Social Exclusion, London School of Economics and Political Science. Available at http://sticerd .ac.uk/case/_new/publications/year.asp?pubyear=2012

Caplan, Nathan. 1979. "The Two Communities Theory and Knowledge Utilization." *American Behavioral Scientist* 22: 459–470.

Carr, Wilfred. 1995. *For Education.* Buckingham, UK: Open University Press.

Cartwright, Nancy. 2006. "Well-Ordered Science: Evidence for Use." *Philosophy of Science* 73: 981–990.

Cartwright, Nancy. 2007a. "Are RCTs the Gold Standard?" *Biosocieties* 2(2): 11–20.

Cartwright, Nancy. 2007b. *Hunting Causes and Using Them*. Cambridge, UK: Cambridge University Press.

Cartwright, Nancy. 2009. "Evidence-Based Policy: What's to Be Done About Relevance?" *Philosophical Studies* 143: 127–136.

Cartwright, Nancy. 2011a. "A Philosopher's View of the Long Road from RCTs to Effectiveness." *The Lancet* 377: 1400–1401.

Cartwright, Nancy. 2011b. "Predicting What Will Happen When We Act: What Counts as Warrant?" *Preventive Medicine* 53: 221–224.

Chelimsky, Eleanor. 2006. "The Purposes of Evaluation in a Democratic Society." In Ian Shaw, Jennifer C. Greene, and Melvin M. Mark (eds.), *Handbook of Evaluation*. London: Sage, 33–55.

Chelimsky, Eleanor. 2007. "Factors Influencing the Choice of Methods in Federal Evaluation Practice." In George Julnes and Deborah Rog (eds.), *Informing Federal Policies on Evaluation Methodology. New Directions for Evaluation* 113, 13–33. San Francisco: Jossey-Bass.

Chelimsky, Eleanor. 2008. "A Clash of Cultures: Improving the 'Fit' Between Evaluative Independence and the Political Requirements of a Democratic Society." *American Journal of Evaluation* 29: 400–415.

Chelimsky, Eleanor. 2013. "Balancing Evaluation Theory and Practice in the Real World." *American Journal of Evaluation* 34: 91–98.

Chen, Huey T. 2013. "The Roots and Growth of Theory-Driven Evaluations: An Integrated Perspective for Assessing Viability, Effectuality, and Transferability." In Marvin C. Alkin (ed.), *Evaluation Roots: Tracing Theorists' Views and Reflections* 2nd ed. Los Angeles: Sage, 113–129.

Chianca, Thomas. 2008. "The OECD/DAC Criteria for International Development Evaluations: An Assessment and Ideas for Improvement." *Journal of MultiDisciplinary Evaluation* 5: 41–51.

Church, Allan H., and Janine Waclawski. 1998. "The Vendor Mind-Set: The Devolution from Organizational Consultant to Street Peddler." *Consulting Psychology Journal* 50: 87–100.

Cialdini, Robert B. 2009. *Influence: The Psychology of Persuasion*. Rev. ed. New York: Harper Collins.

Coburn, Andrew. 1998. "The Role of Health Services Research in Developing State Health Policy." *Health Affairs* 17: 139–151.

Coburn, Cynthia E., and Erica O. Turner. 2012. "The Practice of Data Use: An Introduction." *American Journal of Education* 118: 99–111.

Cohen, Keith, and Charles Lindblom. 1979. *Usable Knowledge: Social Science and Social Problem Solving*. New Haven, CT: Yale University Press.

Colby, Anne, and William M. Sullivan. 2008. "Formation of Professionalism and Purpose Perspective from the Preparation for the Professions Program." *University of St. Thomas Law Journal* 5: 404–427.

The Colorado Trust. 2002. "Keys to Cultural Competency: A Literature Review for Evaluators of Recent Immigrant and Refugee Service Programs in Colorado." Denver: The Colorado Trust.

Conklin, Annalijn, Michael Hallsworth, Evi Hatziandreu, and Jonathan Grant. 2008. *Briefing on Linkage and Exchange Facilitating Diffusion of Innovation in Health Services.* Santa Monica, CA: RAND.

Contandriopoulos, Damien, and Astrid Brousselle. 2012. "Evaluation Models and Evaluation Use." *Evaluation* 18: 61–77.

Contandriopoulos, Damien, Marc Lemire, Jean-Louis Denis, and Émile Tremblay. 2010. "Knowledge Exchange Processes in Organizations and Policy Arenas: A Narrative Systematic Review of the Literature." *The Milbank Quarterly* 88: 444–483.

Cook, Scott D. N., and John Seely Brown. 1999. "Bridging Epistemologies: The Generative Dance Between Organizational Knowledge and Organizational Knowing." *Organization Science* 10: 381–400.

Cook, Thomas D., Michael Scriven, Chris L. S. Coryn, and Stephanie D. H. Evergreen. 2010. "Contemporary Thinking About Causation in Evaluation: A Dialogue with Tom Cook and Michael Scriven." *American Journal of Evaluation* 31: 105–117.

Cooksy, Leslie J. 2009. "Reflections of Guiding Principle E: Responsibilities for General and Public Welfare." *American Journal of Evaluation* 30: 217–219.

Cordray, David, and Mark Lipsey. 1986. "Introduction: Evaluation Studies in 1986—Program Evaluation and Program Research." In David Cordray and Mark Lipsey (eds.), *Evaluation Studies Review Annual,* Vol. 11. Newbury Park, CA: Sage, 17–44.

Coryn, Chris L. S. 2008. "Program Theory-Driven Evaluation Science [Review of *Program Theory-Driven Evaluation Science*, by S. I. Donaldson]. *American Journal of Evaluation* 29: 215–220.

Coryn, Chris L. S., Lindsay A. Noakes, Carl D. Westine, and Daniela C. Schröter. 2011. "A Systematic Review of Theory-Driven Evaluation Practice from 1990 to 2009." *American Journal of Evaluation* 32: 199–226.

Council of the Inspectors General on Integrity and Efficiency. 2011. Quality Standards for Inspection and Evaluation. Washington, DC: U.S. Government Printing Office. Available at http://www.ignet.gov/pande/standards/oeistds11 .pdf

Cousins, J. Bradley, Jim Cullen, Sumbal Malik, and Brigitte Maicher. 2009. "Debating Professional Designations for Evaluators: Reflections on the Canadian Process." *Journal of Multidisciplinary Evaluation* 6(11): 71–82.

Cousins, J. Bradley, Swee C. Goh, Catherine J. Elliott, and Isabelle Bourgeois.

2014. "Framing the Capacity to Do and Use Evaluation." In J. Bradley Cousins and Isabelle Bourgeois (eds.), *Organizational Capacity to Do and Use Evaluation. New Directions for Evaluation* 141: 7–23. San Francisco: Jossey-Bass.

Cousins, J. Bradley, and Keith A. Leithwood. 1986. "Current Empirical Research on Evaluation Utilization." *Review of Educational Research* 56: 331–364.

Cousins, J. Bradley, and Elizabeth Whitmore. 1998. "Framing Participatory Evaluation." In Elizabeth Whitmore (ed.), *Understanding and Practicing Participatory Evaluation. New Directions for Evaluation* 80: 5–23. San Francisco: Jossey-Bass.

Cronbach, Lee J., et al. 1980. *Toward Reform of Program Evaluation*. San Francisco: Jossey-Bass.

Cronbach, Lee J., and Patrick Suppes (eds.). 1969. *Disciplined Inquiry for Education*. New York: MacMillan.

Cullen, Anne E., Chris L. S. Coryn, and Jim Rugh. 2011. "The Politics and Consequences of Including Stakeholders in International Development Evaluation." *American Journal of Evaluation* 32: 345–361.

Dahler-Larsen, Peter. 2012. *The Evaluation Society*. Stanford, CA: Stanford University Press.

Dahler-Larsen, Peter. 2013. "Evaluation as Situational or a Universal Good? Why Evaluability Assessment for Evaluation Systems Is a Good Idea, What It Might Look Like in Practice, and Why It Is Not Fashionable." *Scandinavian Journal of Public Administration* 16: 29–46.

Datta, Lois-ellin. 2011. "Politics and Evaluation: More Than Methodology." *American Journal of Evaluation* 32: 273–294.

Davidson, E. Jane. 2005. *Evaluation Methodology Basics: The Nuts and Bolts of Sound Evaluation*. Los Angeles: Sage.

Davidson, E. Jane. 2014a. "How 'Beauty' Can Bring Truth and Justice to Life." In James C. Griffith and Bianca Montrosse-Moorhead (eds.), *Revisiting, Truth, Beauty, and Justice: Evaluating with Validity in the 21st Century. New Directions for Evaluation* 142: 31–43. San Francisco: Jossey- Bass.

Davidson, E. Jane. 2014b. "It's the Very Core of Evaluation and Makes or Breaks Our Work: So Why Is It in Hardly Anyone's Toolkit?" *Evaluation Connections*, The European Evaluation Society Newsletter. Available at http://europeanevaluation.org/sites/default/files/ees_newsletter/ees-newsletter -2014-03-march-08.pdf

Davies, Huw T. O., Sandra M. Nutley, and Peter C. Smith. 2000. *What Works: Evidence-Based Policy and Practice in Public Services*. Bristol, UK: The Policy Press.

Davies, Philip, Kathryn Newcomer, and Haluk Soydan. 2006. "Government as Structural Context for Evaluation." In Ian Shaw, Jennifer C. Greene, and Melvin M. Mark (eds.), *Handbook of Evaluation*. London: Sage, 163–183.

Davies, Randall, and Kathryn MacKay. 2014. "Evaluator Training: Content and Topic Valuation in University Evaluation Courses." *American Journal of Evaluation* 35: 419–429.

Day, Lisa. 2009. "Evidence-Based Practice, Rule-Following, and Expertise." *American Journal of Critical Care* 18: 479–482.

Department for International Development (DFID). 2013a. "How to Note: Assessing the Strength of Evidence". London: Department for International Development. Available at http://www.gov.uk/government/publications/how -to-note-assessing-the-strength-of-evidence

Department for International Development (DFID). 2013b. "International Development Evaluation Policy." London: Department for International Development. Available at http://www.gov.uk/government/publications/dfid -evaluation-policy-2013

Demers, Christane. 2007. *Organizational Change Theories: A Synthesis*. Thousand Oaks, CA: Sage.

Dewey, John. 1910. *How We Think*. Lexington, MA: D.C. Heath.

Donaldson, Stewart I. 2007. *Program Theory-Driven Evaluation Science: Strategies and Applications*. Mahwah, NJ: Lawrence Erlbaum.

Donaldson, Stewart I. 2009. "Epilogue: A Practitioner's Guide for Gathering Credible Evidence in the Evidence-Based Global Society." In Stewart I. Donaldson, Christina A. Christie, and Melvin M. Mark (eds.), *What Counts as Credible Evidence in Applied Research and Evaluation Practice?* Thousand Oaks, CA: Sage, 239–251.

Donaldson, Stewart I., and Mark W. Lipsey. 2006. "Roles for Theory in Contemporary Evaluation Practice: Developing Practical Knowledge." In Ian Shaw, Jennifer C. Greene, and Melvin M. Mark (eds.), *Handbook of Evaluation*. London: Sage, 56–75.

Dozois, Elizabeth, Marc Langlois, and Natasha Blanchet-Cohen. 2010. *DE 201: A Practitioner's Guide to Developmental Evaluation*. Montreal, Canada: The J.W. McConnell Family Foundation. Available at http://www.mcconnellfoun dation.ca/en/resources/publication/de-201-a-practitioner-s-guide-to-develop mental-evaluation

Dryzek, John S. 1993. "From Science to Argument." In Frank Fischer and John Forester (eds.), *The Argumentative Turn in Policy Analysis and Planning*. Durham, NC: Duke University Press, 213–232.

Dunne, Joseph, and Shirley Pendlebury. 2003. "Practical Reason." In Nigel Blake, Paul Smeyers, Richard Smith, and Paul Standish (eds.), *The Blackwell Guide to the Philosophy of Education*. Oxford, UK: Blackwell, 194–211.

Dunworth, Terry, Jane Hannaway, John Holanhan, and Margery Austin Turner. 2008. *The Case for Evidence-Based Policy: Beyond Ideology, Politics, and Guess-*

work. Rev. ed. Washington, DC: The Urban Institute. Available at http://
www.urban.org/url.cfm?ID=901189

Earl, Sarah, Fred Carden, and Terry Smutylo. 2001. *Outcome Mapping: Building
Learning and Reflection into Development Programs*. Ottawa, Ontario: International Development Research Centre.

Engle, Molly, James W. Altschuld, and Yung-Chul Kim. 2006. "2002 Survey of
Evaluation Preparation Programs: An Update of the 1992 American Evaluation
Association Sponsored Study." *American Journal of Evaluation* 27(3): 353–359.

Epstein, Ronald M., and Edward M. Hundert. 2002. "Defining and Assessing
Professional Competence." *Journal of the American Medical Association* 287:
226–235.

Facione, Peter. 1990. "Critical Thinking: A Statement of Expert Consensus for
Purposes of Educational Assessment and Instruction." Millbrae, CA: The
California Academic Press. Available at http://assessment.aas.duke.edu/docu
ments/Delphi_Report.pdf

Fetterman, David M., and Abraham Wandersman (eds.). 2005. *Empowerment
Evaluation: Principles in Practice*. New York: Guilford.

Feuer, Michael J., Robert E. Floden, Naomi Chudowsky, and Judie Ahn. 2013.
Evaluation of Teacher Preparation Programs. Washington, DC: National Academy of Education.

Fischer, Frank. 2003. *Reframing Public Policy: Discursive Politics and Deliberative
Practices*. Oxford, UK: Oxford University Press.

Fitzpatrick, Jody L., James R. Sanders, and Blaine R. Worthen. 2011. *Program
Evaluation: Alternative Approaches and Practical Guidelines* 4th ed. New York:
Pearson.

Flay, Brian R., et al. 2005. "Standards for Evidence: Criteria for Efficacy, Effectiveness and Dissemination." *Prevention Science* 6: 151–175.

Fleischacker, Samuel. 1999. "From Cultural Diversity to Universal Ethics: Three
Models." *Cultural Dynamics* 11: 105–128.

Floden, Robert E., and Stephen S. Weiner. 1978. "Rationality to Ritual: The
Multiple Roles of Evaluation in Governmental Processes." *Policy Sciences* 9:
9–18.

Forester, John. 1984. "Bounded Rationality and the Politics of Muddling
Through." *Public Administration Review* 44: 23–31.

Forti, Matthew. 2012. "Six Theories of Change Pitfalls to Avoid." *Stanford Social Innovation Review* Blog. Available at http://www.ssireview.org/blog/entry/
six_theory_of_change_pitfalls_to_avoid

Fournier, Deborah. 2005. "Evaluation." In Sandra Mathison (ed.), *Encyclopedia
of Evaluation*. Thousand Oaks, CA: Sage, 139–140.

Fox, Renée C. 2005. "Cultural Competence and the Culture of Medicine." *New
England Journal of Medicine* 353: 1316–1319.

Freidson, Eliot. 2001. *Professionalism: The Third Logic*. Chicago: University of Chicago Press.

Funnell, Sue C., and Patricia J. Rogers. 2011. *Purposeful Program Theory: Effective Use of Theories of Change and Logic Models*. San Francisco: Jossey-Bass.

Gamble, Jamie A. A. 2008. *A Developmental Evaluation Primer*. Montreal, Canada: The J.W. McConnell Family Foundation. Available at http://www.mc connellfoundation.ca/en/resources/publication/a-developmental-evaluation -primer

Gargani, John. 2011. "More Than 25 Years of the *American Journal of Evaluation*: The Recollections of Past Editors in Their Own Words." *American Journal of Evaluation* 32: 428–447.

Gastil, John. 2000. *By Popular Demand*. Berkeley: University of California Press.

Green, Lawrence W., Judith M. Ottoson, César García, and Robert A. Hiatt. 2009. "Diffusion Theory and Knowledge Dissemination, Utilization, and Integration in Public Health." *Annual Review of Public Health* 30: 151–174.

Greene, Jennifer C. 2006. "Evaluation, Democracy, and Social Change." In Ian Shaw, Jennifer C. Greene, and Melvin M. Mark (eds.), *Handbook of Evaluation*. London: Sage, 118–140.

Greene, Jennifer C. 2007. *Mixed Methods in Social Inquiry*. San Francisco: Jossey-Bass.

Greenhalgh, Trisha. 2002. "Intuition and Evidence—Uneasy Bedfellows?" *British Journal of General Practice* 52: 395–400.

Guba, Egon, and Yvonna S. Lincoln. 1989. *Fourth Generation Evaluation*. Newbury Park, CA: Sage.

Guzman, Biana, and Aida Feria. 2002. "Community-Based Organizations and State Initiatives: The Negotiation Process of Program Evaluation." In Rakesh Mohan, David J. Bernstein, and Maria Whitsett (eds.), *Responding to Sponsors and Stakeholders in Complex Evaluation Environments. New Directions for Evaluation* 95: 57–62. San Francisco: Jossey-Bass.

Haack, Susan. 2003. *Defending Science—Within Reason: Between Scientism and Cynicism*. Amherst, NY: Prometheus.

Hageboeck, Molly, Micah Frumkin, and Stephanie Monschien. 2013. *Meta-Evaluation of Quality and Coverage of USAID Evaluations 2009–2012*. Washington, DC: USAID. Available at http://usaidlearninglab.org/library/meta -evaluation-quality-and-coverage-usaid-evaluations-2009-2012

Hannum, Kelly. 2004. "Best Practices: Choosing the Right Methods for Evaluation." *Leadership in Action* 23: 14–19.

Hargreaves, Margaret B. 2010. "Evaluating System Change: A Planning Guide." Methods Brief. Princeton, NJ: Mathematica Policy Research, Inc.

Haskins, Ron, and Jon Baron. 2011. "Building the Connection Between Policy and Evidence: The Obama Evidence-Based Initiatives." London: NESTA.

Available at http://www.brookings.edu/research/reports/2011/09/07-evidence
-based-policy-haskins

Havelock, Ronald G. 1969. *Planning for Innovation Through the Dissemination
and Utilization of Knowledge.* Ann Arbor, MI: Center for Research on Utilization of Scientific Knowledge, University of Michigan.

Hayes, Philip. 2008. "Complexity Theory and Evaluation in Public Management." *Public Management Review* 10: 401–419.

Henkel, Mary. 1991. "The New 'Evaluative State.'" *Public Administration* 69:
121–136.

Henry, Gary T., and Melvin M. Mark. 2003. "Beyond Use: Understanding Evaluation's Influence on Attitudes and Actions." *American Journal of Evaluation*
24: 293–314.

Herbst, Susan. 2003. "Political Authority in a Mediated Age." *Theory and Society*
32: 481–503.

Hood, Paul. 2002. "Perspectives on Knowledge Utilization in Education." San
Francisco: WestEd. Available at http://www.wested.org/online_pubs/perspec
tives.pdf

Hopson, Rodney. 2003. "Overview of Multicultural and Culturally Compe-
tent Program Evaluation." Oakland, CA: Social Policy Research Associates.
Available at http://www.calendow.org/uploadedFiles/Publications/Evaluation/
Multicultural_Health_Evaluation/OverviewBook.pdf

Hopson, Rodney. 2009. "Reclaiming Knowledge at the Margins: Culturally Re-
sponsive Evaluation in the Current Evaluation Moment." In Katherine E.
Ryan and J. Bradley Cousins (eds.), *Handbook of Educational Evaluation.* Los
Angeles: Sage, 429–446.

House, Ernest R. 1980. *Evaluating with Validity.* Beverly Hills, CA: Sage.

House, Ernest R. 1993. *Professional Evaluation: Social Impact and Political Consequences.* Newbury Park, CA: Sage.

House, Ernest R. 1995. "Putting Things Together Coherently: Logic and Justice." In Deborah M. Fournier (ed.), *Reasoning in Evaluation: Inferential Links
and Leaps. New Directions for Evaluation* 68: 33–48. San Francisco: Jossey-Bass.

House, Ernest R., and Kenneth Howe. 1999. *Values in Evaluation and Social
Research.* Newbury Park, CA: Sage.

House, Ernest R., and Kenneth Howe. 2000. "Deliberative Democratic Evaluation." In Katherine E. Ryan and Lizanne DeStefano (eds.), *Evaluation as
a Democratic Process: Promoting Inclusion, Dialogue, and Deliberation. New
Directions for Evaluation* 85: 3–12. San Francisco: Jossey-Bass.

Huberman, Michael. 1987. "Steps Toward an Integrated Model of Research Utilization." *Knowledge: Creation, Diffusion, Utilization* 8: 586–611.

Huberman, Michael. 1994. "Research Utilization: The State of the Art." *Knowledge, Technology & Policy* 7(4): 13–33.

Hummelbrunner, Richard, and Martin Reynolds. 2013, June. "Systems Thinking, Learning and Values in Evaluation." *Evaluation Connections (Newsletter of the European Evaluation Society)*. Available at http://www.europeanevaluation .org/sites/default/files/ees_newsletter/ees-newsletter-2013-06-june.pdf

Hunter, David E. K., and Steffen Bohni Nielsen. 2013. "Performance Management and Evaluation: Exploring Complementarities." In Steffen Bohni Nielsen and David E. K. Hunter (eds.), *Performance Management and Evaluation. New Directions for Evaluation* 137: 7–17. San Francisco: Jossey-Bass.

Hurteau, Marthe, Sylvain Houle, and Stéphanie Mongiat. 2009. "How Legitimate and Justified Are Judgments in Evaluation?" *Evaluation* 15: 307–319.

Hutchins, Edwin. 1995. *Cognition in the Wild*. Cambridge, MA: The MIT Press.

Institute of Development Studies. 1998. "Participatory Monitoring and Evaluation: Learning from Change." IDS Policy Briefing Issue 12. Available at http://www.ids.ac.uk/index.cfm?objectid=01D512C5-5056-8171-7BA528050E140ED9

International Initiative for Impact Evaluation (3ie). 2008. "Founding Document for Establishing the International Initiative for Impact Evaluation." Available at http://www.3ieimpact.org/strategy/pdfs/3ieFoundingDocument30 June2008.pdf

Johnson, Kelli, et al. 2009. "Research on Evaluation Use: A Review of the Empirical Literature from 1986 to 2005." *American Journal of Evaluation* 30: 377–410.

Jonsen, Albert R., and Stephen Toulmin. 1998. *The Abuse of Casuistry*. Berkeley: University of California Press.

Julnes, George. 2012a. "Developing Policies to Support Valuing in the Public Interest." In George Julnes (ed.), *Promoting Valuation in the Public interest: Informing Policies for Judging Value in Evaluation. New Directions for Evaluation* 133: 109–129. San Francisco: Jossey-Bass.

Julnes, George. 2012b. "Managing Valuation." In George Julnes (ed.), *Promoting Valuation in the Public Interest: Informing Policies for Judging Value in Evaluation. New Directions for Evaluation* 133: 3–15. San Francisco: Jossey-Bass.

Julnes, George, and Debra J. Rog. 2007a. "Current Federal Policies and Controversies over Methodology in Evaluation." In George Julnes and Debra J. Rog (eds.), *Informing Federal Policies on Evaluation Methodology: Building the Evidence Base for Method Choice in Government Sponsored Evaluation. New Directions for Evaluation* 113: 4–12. San Francisco: Jossey-Bass.

Julnes, George, and Debra J. Rog. 2007b. "Pragmatic Support for Policies on Methodology." In George Julnes and Debra J. Rog (eds.), *Informing Federal Policies on Evaluation Methodology: Building the Evidence Base for Method Choice in Government Sponsored Evaluation. New Directions for Evaluation* 113: 129–147. San Francisco: Jossey-Bass.

Kahneman, Daniel. 2011. *Thinking, Fast and Slow*. New York: Farrar, Straus & Giroux.

Khandker, Shahidur R., Gayatri B. Koolwal, and Hussain A. Samad. 2010. *Handbook on Impact Evaluation: Quantitative Methods and Practices*. Washington, DC: The World Bank.

King, Jean A. 2005. "Participatory Evaluation." In Sandra Mathison (ed.), *Encyclopedia of Evaluation*. Thousand Oaks, CA: Sage, 291–294.

King, Jean A., and Laurie Stevahn. 2002. "Three Frameworks for Considering Evaluator Role." In Katherine Ryan and Thomas Schwandt (eds.), *Exploring Evaluator Role and Identity*. New York: Information Age Press, 1–16.

King, Jean A., Laurie Stevahn, Gail Ghere, and Jane Minnema. 2001. "Toward a Taxonomy of Essential Evaluator Competencies." *American Journal of Evaluation* 22: 229–247.

Kingdon, John. 1995. *Agendas, Alternatives, and Public Policies* 2nd ed. New York: Harper Collins.

Kirkhart, Karen. 2000. "Reconceptualizing Evaluation Use: An Integrated Theory of Influence." In Valerie Caracelli and Hallie Preskill (eds.), *The Expanding Scope of Evaluation Use*. New Directions for Evaluation 88: 5–23. San Francisco: Jossey Bass.

Kusek, Jody Zall, and Ray C. Rist. 2004. *Ten Steps to a Results-Based Monitoring and Evaluation System*. Washington, DC: The World Bank.

Kushner, Saville, and Nigel Norris (eds.). 2007. *Dilemmas of Engagement: Evaluation and the New Public Management*. San Diego, CA: Elsevier.

Lai, Emily R. 2011. "Critical Thinking: A Literature Review." Pearson Research Report. Available at http://www.pearsonassessments.com/hai/images/tmrs/criticalthinkingreviewfinal.pdf

LaVelle, John M., and Stewart I. Donaldson. 2010. "University-Based Evaluation Training Programs in the United States 1980–2008: An Empirical Examination." *American Journal of Evaluation* 31: 9–23.

Ledermann, Simone. 2012. "Exploring the Necessary Conditions for Evaluation Use in Program Change." *American Journal of Evaluation* 33: 159–178.

Leeuw, Frans L., and Jan-Eric Furubo. 2008. "Evaluation Systems: What Are They? Why Study Them?" *Evaluation: The International Journal of Theory, Research and Practice* 14: 157–169.

Leischow, Scott J., et al. 2008. "Systems Thinking to Improve the Public's Health." *American Journal of Preventive Medicine* 35: S196–S203.

Levin, Henry M., and P. J. McEwan. 2001. *Cost-Effectiveness Analysis: Methods and Applications* 2nd ed. Thousand Oaks, CA: Sage.

Lewis, Arthur, and David Smith. 1993. "Defining Higher Order Thinking." *Theory into Practice* 32: 131–137.

Lewis, Michael. 2004. *Moneyball: The Art of Winning an Unfair Game*. New York: Norton.

Lipsey, Mark W., and Eammon Noonan (eds.). 2009. "Better Evidence for a Better World." International Initiative for Impact Evaluation (3ie) Working Paper No. 2. New Delhi: International Initiative for Impact Evaluation. Available at http://www.3ieimpact.org/en/evaluation/working-papers/

Lomas, Jonathan. 1993. "Diffusion, Dissemination, and Implementation: Who Should Do What?" *Annals of the New York Academy of Sciences* 703: 226–235.

Lomas, Jonathan. 2000. "Using 'Linkage and Exchange' to Move Research into Policy at a Canadian Foundation." *Health Affairs* 19(3): 236–240.

Lopez-Acevedo, Gladys, Philipp Krause, and Keith Mackay (eds.). 2012. *Building Better Policies: The Nuts and Bolts of Monitoring and Evaluation Systems*. Washington, DC: The World Bank. Available at http://documents.world bank.org/curated/en/2012/04/16234384/building-better-policies-nuts-bolts-monitoring-evaluation-systems

Lord Phillips of Sudbury. 2004. "Are the Liberal Professions Dead, and If So, Does It Matter?" *Clinical Medicine* 4: 7–9.

Love, Arnold. 2005. "Internal Evaluation." In Sandra Mathison (ed.), *Encyclopedia of Evaluation*. Thousand Oaks, CA: Sage, 206–207.

Love, Tom. 2013. "Variation in Medical Practice: Literature Review and Discussion." Sapere Research Group. Wellington, NZ: Health Quality & Safety Commission. Available at https://www.hqsc.govt.nz/assets/Health-Quality-Evaluation/PR/variation-literature-review-Oct-2013.pdf

Lupia, Arthur. 2013. "Communicating Science in Politicized Environments." *Proceedings of the National Academy of Sciences* 110: 14048–14054.

Lynn, Laurence (ed.). 1978. *Knowledge and Policy: The Uncertain Connection*. Washington, DC: The National Academies Press.

Maasen, Sabine, and Peter Weingart (eds.). 2005. *Democratization of Expertise? Exploring Novel Forms of Scientific Advice in Political Decision-Making*. Dordrecht, The Netherlands: Springer.

MacDonald, Goldie. 2013. "Criteria for Selection of High-Performing Indicators: A Checklist to Inform Monitoring and Evaluation." Available at http://www.wmich.edu/evalctr/checklists/evaluation-checklists/

Macinko, James, and Diana Silver. 2012. "Improving State Health Policy Assessment: An Agenda for Measurement and Analysis." *American Journal of Public Health* 102: 1697–1705.

MacPherson, Nancy, et al. 2013. "Key Findings and Lessons Learned from an Evaluation of the Rockefeller Foundation's Disease Surveillance Networks Initiative." *Emerging Health Threats Journal* 6: 1–5.

Majone, Giandomenico. 1989. *Evidence, Argument, and Persuasion in the Policy Process*. New Haven, CT: Yale University Press.

Malen, Betty. 1994. "The Micropolitics of Education: Mapping the Multiple Dimensions of Power Relations in School Politics." *Journal of Education Policy* 9: 147–167.

Maltz, Michael D. [1984] 2001. *Recidivism*. Originally published by Academic Press, Inc., Orlando, Florida. Internet edition available at http://www.uic .edu/depts/lib/forr/pdf/crimjust/recidivism.pdf

Mark, Melvin M. 2005. "Evaluation Theory or What Are Evaluation Methods for?" *The Evaluation Exchange* XI(2): 2–3. Available at http://www.hfrp.org/ var/hfrp/storage/original/application/d6517d4c8da2c9f1fb3dffe3e8b68ce4.pdf

Mark, Melvin. M. 2008. "Building a Better Evidence Base for Evaluation Theory: Beyond General Calls to a Framework of Types of Research on Evaluation." In Nick L. Smith and Paul R. Brandon (eds.), *Fundamental Issues in Evaluation*. New York: Guilford, 111–134.

Mark, Melvin M., and Gary T. Henry. 2004. "The Mechanisms and Outcomes of Evaluation Influence." *Evaluation* 1: 35–57.

Mark, Melvin M., and Gary T. Henry. 2006. "Methods for Policy-Making and Knowledge Development Evaluations." In Ian Shaw, Jennifer C. Greene, and Melvin M. Mark (eds.), *Handbook of Evaluation*. London: Sage, 317–339.

Mark, Melvin M., Gary T. Henry, and George Julnes. 2000. *Evaluation: An Integrated Framework for Understanding, Guiding, and Improving Public Policies and Programs*. San Francisco: Jossey-Bass.

Marsh, Julie A., John F. Payne, and Laura S. Hamilton. 2006. "Making Sense of Data-Driven Decision Making in Education." Santa Monica, CA: RAND. Available at http://www.rand.org/pubs/occasional_papers/OP170.html

Mathison, Sandra. 2000. "Deliberation, Evaluation, and Democracy." In Katherine E. Ryan and Lizanne DeStefano (eds.), *Evaluation as Democratic Process: Promoting Inclusion, Dialogue, and Deliberation. New Directions for Evaluation* 85: 85–89. San Francisco: Jossey-Bass.

Mathison, Sandra (ed.). 2005. *Encyclopedia of Evaluation*. Newbury Park, CA: Sage.Mayne, John. 2011. "Contribution Analysis: Addressing Cause and Effect." In Kim Forss, Mita Marra, and Robert Schwartz (eds.), *Evaluating the Complex*. Piscataway, NJ: Transaction Publishers, 53–96.

McDavid, James C., Irene Huse, and Laura R. L. Hawthorn. 2013. *Program Evaluation and Performance Measurement*. Los Angeles: Sage.

McGann, James G. 2006. "Best Practices for Funding and Evaluating Think Tanks and Policy Research." Prepared for the William and Flora Hewlett Foundation. Ambler, PA: McGann Associates. Available at http://www.hew lett.org/uploads/files/BestPracticesforFundingandEvaluatingThinkTanks.pdf

Mertens, Donna. 2009. *Transformative Research and Evaluation*. New York: Guilford Press.

Merwin, Jack C., and Paul H. Weiner. 1985. "Evaluation: A Profession?" *Educational Evaluation and Policy Analysis* 7: 253–259.

Mitroff, Ian I., and Abraham Silvers. 2010. *Dirty Rotten Strategies: How We Trick Ourselves into Solving the Wrong Problems Precisely*. Stanford, CA: Stanford University Press.

Morell, Jonathan, and Eugenie W. Flaherty. 1978. "Evaluation: Manifestations of a New Field." *Evaluation and Program Planning* 1: 1–10.

Morra Imas, Linda G. 2010. "The Movement for Global Competencies for Development Evaluators." Paper presented at the Annual Meeting of the CES, Victoria, BC. Available at http://www.ideas-int.org/documents/file_list.cfm ?DocsSubCatID=48

Morris, Michael (ed.). 2008. *Evaluation Ethics for Best Practice: Cases and Commentaries*. New York: Guilford.

Morris, Michael. 2009. "The Fifth Guiding Principle: Beacon, Banality, or Pandora's Box?" *American Journal of Evaluation* 30: 220–224.

Mowles, Chris. 2014. "Complex, but Not Quite Complex Enough: The Turn to the Complexity Sciences in Evaluation Scholarship." *Evaluation* 20: 160–175.

Mulgan, Geoff. 2010. "Measuring Social Value." *Stanford Social Innovation Review* (Summer) 6: 38–43. Available at http://www.ssireview.org/articles/entry/measuring_social_value

National Performance Management Advisory Commission. 2010. "A Performance Management Framework for State and Local Government: From Measurement and Reporting to Management and Improving." Chicago: National Performance Management Advisory Commission. Available at http://www.nasbo.org/publications-data/reports/performance-management-framework-state-and-local-government-measurement-an

Newcomer, Kathryn E., and Mary Ann Scheirer. 2001. "Using Evaluation to Support Performance Management: A Guide for Federal Executives." Arlington, VA: PricewaterhouseCoopers the Business of Government Series.

Nutley, Sandra, Isabel Walter, and Huw T. O. Davies. 2007. *Using Evidence: How Research Can Inform Public Services*. Bristol, UK: The Policy Press.

Nutley, Sandra, and Jeff Webb. 2000. "Evidence and the Policy Process." In Huw T. O. Davies, Sandra M. Nutley, and Peter C. Smith (eds.), *What Works? Evidence-Based Policy and Practice in Public Services*. Bristol, UK: The Policy Press, 13–41.

Organisation for Economic Cooperation and Development/Development Assistance Committee (OECD/DAC). 2004. *Glossary of Key Terms in Evaluation and Results Based Management*. Paris: OECD. Available at http://www.oecd.org/dac/evaluation/glossaryofkeytermsinevaluationandresultsbasedmanagement.htm

Organisation for Economic Cooperation and Development/Development Assistance Committee (OECD/DCA). 2010. *Quality Standards for Development Evaluation.* Available at http://www.oecd.org/dac/evaluation/qualitystan dardsfordevelopmentevaluation.htm

Organizational Research Services. 2010. *Advocacy and Policy Change Evaluation: A Primer.* Available at http://www .organizationalresearch.com/publications_ and_resources_advocacy.aspx

Ottoson, Judith M., and Penelope Hawe (eds.) 2009. *Knowledge Utilization, Diffusion, Implementation, Transfer, and Translation: Implications for Evaluation. New Directions for Evaluation* 124. San Francisco: Jossey-Bass.

Ozga, Jenny, Peter Dahler-Larsen, Christina Segerholm, and Hannu Simola (eds.). 2011. *Fabricating Quality in Education: Data and Governance in Europe.* London: Routledge.

Palumbo, Dennis J. 1994. "The Political Roots of Misuse of Evaluation." In Carla J. Stevens and Micah Dial (eds.), *Preventing the Misuse of Evaluation. New Directions for Evaluation* 64: 15–23.

Parker, Ian. 2010. "The Poverty Lab: Transforming Development Economics, One Experiment at a Time." *The New Yorker,* May 17.

Patrizi, Patricia A., and Michael Quinn Patton (eds.). 2010. *Evaluating Strategy. New Directions for Evaluation* 128. San Francisco: Jossey-Bass.

Patton, Michael Q. 2001. "Evaluation, Knowledge Management, Best Practices, and High Quality Lessons Learned." *American Journal of Evaluation* 22: 329–336.

Patton, Michael Q. 2008. *Utilization-Focused Evaluation* 4th ed. Newbury Park, CA: Sage.

Patton, Michael Q. 2010. *Developmental Evaluation: Applying Complexity Concepts to Enhance Innovation and Use.* New York: Guilford Press.

Patton, Michael Q. 2012. "Contextual Pragmatics of Valuing." In George Julnes (ed.), *Promoting Valuation in the Public Interest: Informing Policies for Judging Value in Evaluation. New Directions for Evaluation* 133: 97–108. San Francisco: Jossey-Bass.

Patton, Michael Q. 2013a. "Meta-Evaluation: Evaluating the Evaluation of the Paris Declaration." *Canadian Journal of Program Evaluation* 27: 147–171.

Patton, Michael Q. 2013b. "The Roots of Utilization-Focused Evaluation." In Marvin C. Alkin (ed.), *Evaluation Roots: A Wider Perspective of Theorists' Views and Influences* 2nd ed. Los Angeles: Sage, 293–303.

Paul, Richard, and Linda Elder. 2014. *Critical Thinking: Tools for Taking Charge of Your Professional and Personal Life* 2nd ed. Upper Saddle River, NJ: Pearson Education.

Pawson, Ray, and Nick Tilly. 1997. *Realistic Evaluation.* London: Sage.

Picciotto, Robert. 2011. "The Logic of Evaluation Professionalism." *Evaluation* 17: 165–180.

Pielke, Roger A., Jr. 2007. *The Honest Broker: Making Sense of Science in Policy and Politics*. Cambridge, UK: Cambridge University Press.

Polkinghorne, Donald. 2004. *Practice and the Human Sciences*. Albany, NY: SUNY Press.

Power, Michael. 1997. *The Audit Society: Rituals of Verification*. Oxford, UK: Oxford University Press.

Preskill, Hallie. 2013. "The Transformative Power of Evaluation: Passion, Purpose, and Practice." In Marvin C. Alkin (ed.), *Evaluation Roots: A Wider Perspective of Theorists' Views and Influences*. Los Angeles: Sage, 323–333.

Preskill, Hallie, and Shanelle Boyle. 2008. "A Multidisciplinary Model of Evaluation Capacity Building." *American Journal of Evaluation* 29: 443–459.

Preskill, Hallie, and Rosalie Torres. 1999. *Evaluative Inquiry for Learning in Organizations*. Thousand Oaks, CA: Sage.

Prewitt, Kenneth, Thomas A. Schwandt, and Miron L. Straf. 2012. *Using Science as Evidence in Public Policy*. National Research Council, Committee on the Use of Social Science Knowledge in Public Policy. Washington, DC: The National Academies Press.

Ramalingam, Ben. 2013. *Aid on the Edge of Chaos*. Oxford, UK: Oxford University Press.

Ramalingam, Ben, and Harry Jones with Toussaint Reba and John Young. (2008). "Exploring the Science of Complexity: Ideas and Implications for Development and Humanitarian Efforts" 2nd ed. Working paper 285. London: Overseas Development Institute.

Reichardt, Charles S., and Sharon F. Rallis (eds.). 1994. *The Qualitative-Quantitative Debate: New Perspectives. New Directions for Program Evaluation* 61. San Francisco: Jossey-Bass.

Reisman, Jane, Anne Gienapp, and Sarah Stachowiak. 2007. *A Guide to Measuring Advocacy and Policy*. Baltimore, MD: The Annie E. Casey Foundation. Available at http://www.aecf.org/KnowledgeCenter/Publications. aspx?pubguid=%7B4977C910-1A39-44BD-A106-1FC8D81EB792%7D

Reiss, Julian. 2011. "Empirical Evidence: Its Nature and Sources." In Ian C. Jarvie and Jesus Zamora-Bonilla (eds.), *The SAGE Handbook of the Philosophy of Social Science*. London: Sage, 551–576.

Rist, Ray C. 2006. "The 'E' in Monitoring and Evaluation: Using Evaluation Knowledge to Support a Results-Based Management System." In Ray C. Rist and Nicoletta Stame (eds.), *From Studies to Streams: Managing Evaluation Systems*. New Brunswick, NJ: Transaction Publishers, 3–22.

Rittel, Horst, and Melvin Webber. 1973. "Dilemmas in a General Theory of Planning." *Policy Sciences* 4: 155–169. *Source: wicked problems*

Robert, Christopher, and Richard Zeckhauser. 2011. "The Methodology of Normative Policy Analysis." *Journal of Policy Analysis and Management* 30: 613–643.

Roche, Chris, and Linda Kelly. 2012. "Monitoring and Evaluation When Politics Matter." Background Paper 12. University of Birmingham, Developmental Leadership Program. Available at http://publications.dlprog.org/Monitoring %20and%20Evaluation%20when%20Politics%20Matters.pdf

Rockefeller Foundation. 2003. *Social Impact Assessment: A Discussion Among Grantmakers.* New York: Rockefeller Foundation. Available at http://www .riseproject.org/Social%20Impact%20Assessment.pdf

Rodin, Judith, and Nancy MacPherson. 2012. "Shared Outcomes: How the Rockefeller Foundation Is Approaching Evaluation with Developing Country Partners." Sponsored supplement to the *Stanford Social Innovation Review.* Available at http://www.ssireview.org/articles/entry/shared_outcomes

Rodwin, Marc A. 2001. "Commentary: The Politics of Evidence-Based Medicine." *Journal of Health Politics, Policy and Law* 26: 439–446.

Rog, Deborah, Jody L. Fitzpatrick, and Ross F. Conner (eds.). 2012. *Context: A Framework for Its Influence on Evaluation Practice. New Directions for Evaluation* 135. San Francisco: Jossey-Bass.

Rogers, Patricia J. 2008. "Using Program Theory to Evaluate Complicated and Complex Aspects of Interventions." *Evaluation: The International Journal of Theory, Research and Practice* 14: 29–48.

Rogers, Patricia J., and Bob Williams. 2006. "Evaluation for Practice Improvement and Organizational Learning." In Ian Shaw, Jennifer C. Greene, and Melvin M. Mark (eds.), *Handbook of Evaluation.* London: Sage, 76–97.

Rossi, Peter H. 2013. "My Views of Evaluation and Their Origins." In Marvin C. Alkin (ed.), *Evaluation Roots: Tracing Theorists' Views and Reflections* 2nd ed. Los Angeles: Sage, 106–112.

Rossi, Peter H., Mark W. Lipsey, and Howard E. Freeman. 2004. *Evaluation: A Systematic Approach* 7th ed. Newbury Park, CA: Sage.

Rothman, Kenneth J., and Sander Greenland. 2005. "Causation and Causal Inference in Epidemiology." *American Journal of Public Health*, Supplement 1, 95(S1): 144–150.

Rugh, Jim. 2013, June. "The Growth and Evolving Capacities of Voluntary Organizations for Professional Evaluation." *Evaluation Connections* (Newsletter of the European Evaluation Society). Available at http://www.europeanevalu ation.org/sites/default/files/ees_newsletter/ees-newsletter-2013-06-june.pdf

Rushefsky, Mark E. 2008. *Public Policy in the United States: At the Dawn of the Twenty-First Century* 4th ed. Armonk, NJ: M.E. Sharpe.

Ryan, Katherine E., and J. Bradley Cousins (eds.). 2009. *Handbook of Educational Evaluation.* Los Angeles: Sage.

Sabatier, Paul. A., and Hank C. Jenkins-Smith. 1993. *Policy Change and Learning: An Advocacy Coalition Approach.* Boulder, CO: Westview Press.

Sanderson, Ian. 2001. "Performance Management, Evaluation and Learning in 'Modern' Local Government." *Public Administration* 79: 297–313.

Schorr, Lisbeth B. 2012. "Broader Evidence for Bigger Impact." *Stanford Social Innovation Review* 1 (Fall): 50–55.

Schorr, Lisbeth B., and Frank Farrow. 2011. "Expanding the Evidence Universe: Doing Better by Knowing More." Paper prepared for the 2011 Harold Richman Public Policy Symposium. Washington, DC: Center for the Study of Social Policy. Available at http://lisbethschorr.org/doc/ExpandingtheEvidence UniverseRichmanSymposiumPaper.pdf

Schön, Donald. 1983. *The Reflective Practitioner: How Professionals Think in Action.* New York: Basic Books.

Schön, Donald. 1987. *Educating the Reflective Practitioner.* San Francisco: Jossey-Bass.

Schwandt, Thomas A. 2007. "Expanding the Conversation on Evaluation Ethics." *Evaluation and Program Planning* 30: 400–403.

Schwandt, Thomas A. 2008. "Educating for Intelligent Belief in Evaluation." *American Journal of Evaluation* 29: 139–150.

Schwandt, Thomas A. 2009. "Toward a Practical Theory of Evidence for Evaluation." In Stewart I. Donaldson, Christina A. Christie, and Melvin M. Mark (eds.), *What Counts as Credible Evidence in Applied Research and Evaluation Practice.* Los Angeles: Sage, 197–212.

Schwandt, Thomas A., and Holli Burgon. 2006. "Evaluation and the Study of Lived Experience." In Ian Shaw, Jennifer C. Greene, and Melvin M. Mark (eds.), *Handbook of Evaluation.* London: Sage, 98–117.

Schwandt, Thomas A., and Timothy Cash. 2014. "The Origins, Meaning and Significance of Qualitative Inquiry in Evaluation." In Leslie Goodyear, Eric Barela, Jennifer Jewiss, and Janet Usinger (eds.), *Qualitative Inquiry in Evaluation: From Theory to Practice.* San Francisco: Jossey-Bass, 3–24.

Schwartz, Robert, Kim Forss, and Mita Marra (eds.). 2011. *Evaluating the Complex.* New Brunswick, NJ: Transaction Publishers.

Scriven, Michael. 1974. "Maximizing the Power of Causal Investigations: The Modus Operandi Method." In W. James Popham (ed.), *Evaluation in Education: Current Applications.* Berkeley, CA: McCutchan Publishing, 68–84.

Scriven, Michael. 1991. *Evaluation Thesaurus* 4th ed. Newbury Park, CA: Sage.

Scriven, Michael. 1994. "The Final Synthesis." *Evaluation Practice* 15: 367–382.

Scriven, Michael. 1998. "Minimalist Theory: The Least Theory That Practice Requires. *American Journal of Evaluation* 19: 57–70.

Scriven, Michael. 2003. "Evaluation in the New Millennium: The Transdisciplinary Vision." In Stuart Donaldson and Michael Scriven (eds.), *Evaluating Social Programs and Problems.* Mahwah, NJ: Lawrence Erlbaum, 19–42.

Scriven, Michael. 2007a. "Evaluation as a Cognitive Process." *Journal of Multidisciplinary Evaluation* 4(8): 74–75.

Scriven, Michael. 2007b. "The Logic of Evaluation." In H. V. Hansen et al. (eds.), *Dissensus and the Search for Common Ground.* Windsor, ON: OSSA, 1–16. CD-ROM. Available at http://www.coris.uniroma1.it/news/files/Scriven _Logic_evaluation.pdf

Scriven, Michael. 2009. "Meta-Evaluation Revisited." *Journal of MultiDisciplinary Evaluation* 6(11): iii-viii.

Scriven, Michael. 2012. "The Logic of Valuing." In George Julnes (ed.), *Promoting Valuation in the Public Interest: Informing Policies for Judging Value in Evaluation. New Directions for Evaluation* 133: 17–28. San Francisco: Jossey-Bass.

Scriven, Michael. 2013. "Conceptual Revolutions in Evaluation: Past, Present, and Future." In Marvin C. Alkin (ed.), *Evaluation Roots* 2nd ed. Los Angeles: Sage, 167–179.

Segone, Marco (ed.). 2012. *Evaluation for Equitable Development Results.* New York: UNICEF Evaluation Office. Available at http://www.mymande.org/ selected-books

SenGupta, Saumitra, Rodney Hopson, and Melva Thompson-Robinson. 2004. "Cultural Competence in Evaluation: An Overview." In Melva Thompson-Robinson, Rodney Hopson, and Saumitra SenGupta (eds.), *In Search of Cultural Competence in Evaluation. New Directions for Evaluation* 102: 5–19. San Francisco: Jossey-Bass.

Shadish, William R. 1998. "Evaluation Theory Is Who We Are." *American Journal of Evaluation* 19: 1–19.

Shadish, William R., Thomas D. Cook, and Laura C. Leviton. 1991. *Foundations of Program Evaluation: Theories of Practice.* Newbury Park, CA: Sage.

Shaw, Ian, Jennifer C. Greene, and Melvin M. Mark (eds.). 2006. *Handbook of Evaluation.* London: Sage.

Shipman, Stephanie. 2012. "The Role of Context in Valuing Federal Programs." In George Julnes (ed.), *Promoting Valuation in the Public Interest: Informing Policies for Judging Value in Evaluation. New Directions for Evaluation* 133: 53–61. San Francisco: Jossey-Bass.

Shulha, Lyn M., and J. Bradley Cousins. 1997. "Evaluation Use: Theory, Research, and Practice Since 1986." *Evaluation Practice* 18: 195–208.

Simons, Helen. 2010. "Democratic Evaluation: Theory and Practice." Paper prepared for the Virtual Conference on Methodology in Programme Evaluation. University of the Witwatersrand, Johannesburg: Wits Programme Evaluation Group.

Simons, Helen. 2013, September. "Why Do We Need an Evaluation Capabilities Framework?" *Evaluation Connections*, the European Evaluation Society Newsletter. Available at http://europeanevaluation.org/sites/default/files/ees_news letter/ees-newsletter-2013-09-september-04.pdf

Smith, Nick L. 2008. "Fundamental Issues in Evaluation." In Nick L. Smith and Paul R. Brandon (eds.), *Fundamental Issues in Evaluation*. New York: Guilford, 1–23.

Society for Prevention Research (n.d.). "Standards for Evidence: Criteria for Efficacy, Effectiveness and Dissemination." Available at http://www.preventionresearch.org/advocacy/#SofE

Sonnichsen, Richard. 2000. *High Impact Internal Evaluation*. Thousand Oaks, CA: Sage.Spillane, James P. 2012. "Data in Practice: Conceptualizing the Data-Based Decision-Making Phenomena." *American Journal of Education* 118: 113–141.

Spillane, James P., and David B. Miele. 2007. "Evidence in Practice: A Framing of the Terrain." In Pamela A. Moss (ed.), *Evidence and Decision Making: 106th Yearbook of the National Society for the Study of Education* (Part I). Malden, MA: Blackwell, 46–73.

Squires, Peter, and Lynda Measor. 2005. "Below Decks on the Youth Justice Flagship: The Politics of Evaluation." In David Taylor and Susan Balloch (eds.), *The Politics of Evaluation: Participation and Policy Implementation*. Bristol, UK: The Policy Press, 21–40.

Stachowiak, Sarah. 2013. *Pathways for Change: 10 Theories to Inform Advocacy and Policy Change Efforts*. Washington, DC: Center for Evaluation Innovation. Available at http://www.evaluationinnovation.org/sites/default/files/Path ways%20for%20Change.pdf

Stake, Robert E. 2004. *Standards-Based and Responsive Evaluation*. Newbury Park, CA: Sage.Stake, Robert E., and Thomas A. Schwandt. 2006. "On Discerning Quality in Evaluation." In Ian Shaw, Jennifer C. Greene, and Melvin M. Mark (eds.), *Handbook of Evaluation*. London: Sage, 404–418.

Stein, Danielle, and Craig Valters. 2012. *Understanding Theory of Change in International Development*. London: Justice and Security Research Programme, International Development Department, London School of Economics and Political Science. Available at http://www.theoryofchange.org/wp-content/uploads/toco_library/pdf/UNDERSTANDINGTHEORYOFChangeStein ValtersPN.pdf

Sterman, John D. 2006. "Learning from Evidence in a Complex World." *American Journal of Public Health* 96: 505–514.

Stern, Elliot. 2006. "Contextual Challenges for Evaluation Practice." In Ian Shaw, Jennifer C. Greene, and Melvin M. Mark (eds.), *Handbook of Evaluation*. London: Sage, 292–314.

Stern, Elliot, et al.. 2012. "Broadening the Range of Designs and Methods for Impact Evaluations." Working Paper 38. London: Department for Interna-

tional Development. Available at http://r4d.dfid.gov.uk/Output/189575/De
fault.aspx

Stevahn, Laurie, Jean King, Gail Ghere, and Jane Minnema. 2005. "Establishing
Essential Competencies for Program Evaluators." *American Journal of Evaluation* 26: 43–59.

Stevens, Carla J., and Micah Dial. 1994. "What Constitutes Misuse?" In Carla J.
Stevens and Micah Dial (eds.), *Preventing the Misuse of Evaluation. New Directions for Evaluation* 64: 3–13.

Stone, Deborah. 2002. *The Policy Paradox: The Art of Political Decision Making.*
Rev. ed. New York: W.W. Norton.

Stone, Diane. 2001. "Getting Research into Policy?" Paper presented to the third
Annual Global Development Network Conference on Blending Local and
Global Knowledge, Rio de Janeiro. Available at http://www.reut-institute.org
/Data/Uploads/PDFVer/20080225%20-Getting%20research%20into%20
Policy_1.pdf

Stufflebeam, Daniel. 2001a. *Evaluation Models. New Directions for Evaluation* 89.
San Francisco: Jossey-Bass.

Stufflebeam, Daniel. 2001b. "The Metaevaluation Imperative." *American Journal
of Evaluation* 22: 183–209.

Stufflebeam, Daniel, and Anthony J. Shinkfield. 2007. *Evaluation Theory, Models, and Applications.* San Francisco: Jossey-Bass.

Suddaby, Roy, Yves Gendron, and Helen Lam. 2007. "Accounting for Enron:
Locating the Source of Ethical Failure in the Accounting Profession." Paper
presented at the Canadian Academic Accounting Association annual meeting,
Halifax, NS, May 31. Available at http://www.google.com/search?client=safari
&rls=en&q=ersion+of+professionalism+in+accounting&ie=UTF-8&oe=UTF
-8#q=suddaby+accounting+for+enron&rls=en

Sudsawad, Pimaji. 2007. *Knowledge Translation: Introduction to Models, Strategies, and Measures.* Austin, TX: Southwest Educational Development Laboratory, National Center for Dissemination of Disability Research. Available at
http://www.ncddr.org/kt/products/ktintro/

Sullivan, William M. 2004. *Work and Integrity: The Crisis and Promise of Professionalism in America* 2nd ed. San Francisco: Jossey-Bass.

Sullivan, William M., and Matthew Rosen. 2008a. "A Life of the Mind for Practice." *Change* (March/April): 44–47.

Sullivan, William M., and Matthew Rosen. 2008b. *A New Agenda for Higher
Education: Shaping a Life of the Mind for Practice.* San Francisco: Jossey-Bass.

Sutherland, William J., et al. 2012. "A Collaboratively-Derived Science-Policy
Research Agenda." *PLoS ONE* 7(3): 1–5.

Taplin, Dana H., and Hèlene Clark. 2012. *Theory of Change Basics: A Primer of*

Theory of Change. New York: ActKnowledge. Available at http://www.theory ofchange.org/wp-content/uploads/toco_library/pdf/ToCBasics.pdf

Taylor, David. 2005. "Governing Through Evidence: Participation and Power in Policy Evaluation." *Journal of Social Policy* 34: 601–618.

Theodoulou, Stella Z., and Chris Kofinis. 2003. *The Art of the Game: Understanding Public Policy.* Belmont, CA: Wadsworth.

Thompson, Neil. 2000. *Theory and Practice in Human Services.* Buckingham, UK: Open University Press.

Topper, Keith. 2005. *The Disorder of Political Inquiry.* Cambridge, MA: Harvard University Press.

Toulemonde, Jacques. 1995. "The Emergence of an Evaluation Profession in European Countries: The Case of Structural Policies." *Knowledge and Policy* 8: 43–54.

Tuan, Melinda T. 2008. "Measuring and/or Estimating Social Value Creation: Insights into Eight Integrated Cost Approaches." Prepared for Bill & Melinda Gates Foundation Impact Planning and Improvement. Available at http:// evpa.eu.com/wp-content/uploads/2010/09/Measuring-social-value-creation -Bill-Gates.pdf

United Nations Development Group (UNDG). 2011. *Results-Based Management Handbook.* New York: United Nations Development Programme. Available at http://www.ilo.org/public/english/bureau/program/dwcp/download/undg _rbm1011.pdf

United Nations Development Programme (UNDP). 1997. "Governance for Sustainable Human Development." Available at http://mirror.undp.org/magnet/ policy/

United Nations Development Programme (UNDP). 2009. *Handbook on Planning, Monitoring and Evaluating for Development Results.* New York: United Nations Development Programme.

United Nations Development Programme (UNDP). 2011. "The Evaluation Policy of UNDP." Available at http://web.undp.org/evaluation/policy.htm#iv

United Nations Educational, Scientific, and Cultural Organization (UNESCO). 2005. *Towards Knowledge Societies.* Paris: UNESCO. Available at http://www .unesco.org/new/en/communication-and-information/resources/publications -and-communication-materials/publications/full-list/towards-knowledge-so cieties-unesco-world-report/

United Nations Evaluation Group (UNEG). 2005. *Standards for Evaluation in the UN System.* Available at http://www.unevaluation.org/normsandstan dards/index.jsp?doc_cat_source_id=4

United States Agency for International Development (USAID) Center for Development Information and Evaluation. 1996. "Conducting a Participatory Evaluation." Available at http://pdf.usaid.gov/pdf_docs/PNABS539.pdf

United States Government Accountability Office (USGAO). 2012. *Designing Evaluation, 2012 revision*. GAO-12-208G. Washington, DC: U.S. Government Accountability Office.

Upshur, Ross E. G. 2002. "If Not Evidence, Then What? Or Does Medicine Really Need an Evidence Base?" *Journal of Evaluation in Clinical Practice* 8: 113–119.

van der Meer, Frans-Bauke L. 2007. "New Public Management and Evaluation." In Christopher Pollitt, Sandra van Thiel, and Vincent Homburg (eds.), *The New Public Management in Europe*. Basingstoke, UK: Palgrave Macmillan, 165–180.

Volkov, Boris B., and Michelle E. Baron (eds.). 2011. *Internal Evaluation in the 21st Century. New Directions for Evaluation* 132. San Francisco: Jossey-Bass.

Wagenaar, Hendrik. 2004. "'Knowing' the Rules: Administrative Work as Practice." *Public Administration Review* 64: 643–655.

Walton, Douglas N. 1989. *Informal Logic: A Handbook for Critical Argumentation*. Cambridge, UK: Cambridge University Press.

Walton, Douglas N., Christopher Reed, and Fabrizio Macagno. 2008. *Argumentation Schemes*. Cambridge, UK: Cambridge University Press.

Wandersman, Abraham. 2003. "Community Science: Bridging the Gap Between Science and Practice with Community-Centered Models." *American Journal of Community Psychology* 31: 227–242.

Wandersman, Abraham, et al. 2008. "Bridging the Gap Between Prevention Research and Practice: The Interactive Systems Framework for Dissemination and Implementation." *American Journal of Community Psychology* 41: 171–181.

Watkins, Ryan, Maurya West Meiers, and Yusra Laila Visser. 2012. *A Guide to Assessing Needs: Essential Tools for Collecting Information, Making Decisions, and Achieving Development Results*. Washington, DC: The World Bank. Available at http://www.needsassessment.org/

Weaver, Lynda, and J. Bradley Cousins. 2004. "Unpacking the Participatory Process." *Journal of MultiDisciplinary Evaluation* 1(1): 19–40. Available at http://journals.sfu.ca/jmde/index.php/jmde_1/issue/view/19

Weber, Edward P., and Anne M. Khademian. 2008. "Wicked Problems, Knowledge Challenges, and Collaborative Capacity Builders in Network Settings." *Public Administration Review* 68: 334–349.

Weiss, Carol Hirschon (ed.). 1977. *Using Social Research in Public Policy Making*. Lexington, MA: Lexington Books.

Weiss, Carol Hirschon. 1978. "Improving the Linkage Between Social Research and Public Policy." In Laurence E. Lynn (ed.), *Knowledge and Policy: The Uncertain Connection*. Washington, DC: National Academies Press, 23–81.

Weiss, Carol Hirschon. 1979. "The Many Meanings of Research Utilization." *Public Administration Review* 39: 426–431.

Weiss, Carol Hirschon. 1980. "Knowledge Creep and Decision Accretion." *Knowledge: Creation, Utilization, Diffusion* 1: 381–404.

Weiss, Carol Hirschon. 1981. "Measuring the Use of Evaluation." In James A. Ciarlo (ed.), *Utilizing Evaluation: Concepts and Measurement Techniques.* Thousand Oaks, CA: Sage, 17–33.

Weiss, Carol Hirschon. 1993. "Where Politics and Evaluation Research Meet." *Evaluation Practice* 14: 93–106. (Originally published in *Evaluation* 1973, 1: 37–45.)

Weiss, Carol Hirschon. 1999. "The Interface Between Evaluation and Public Policy." *Evaluation* 5: 468–486.

Weiss, Carol Hirschon. 2000. "Which Links in Which Theories Shall We Evaluate?" In Anthony Petrosino, Patricia J. Rogers, Tracy A. Huebner, and Timothy Hasci (eds.), *Program Theory in Evaluation: Challenges and Opportunities. New Directions for Evaluation* 87: 35–45. San Francisco: Jossey-Bass.

Weiss, Carol Hirschon, and Michael J. Bucuvalas. 1980. *Social Science Research and Decision Making.* New York: Columbia University Press.

White, Howard. 2009a. "Some Reflections on Current Debates on Impact Evaluation." Working Paper 1. New Delhi: International Initiative for Impact Evaluation. Available at http://www.3ieimpact.org/en/evaluation/working -papers/working-paper-1/

White, Howard. 2009b. "Theory-Based Impact Evaluation: Principles and Practice." Working Paper 3. New Delhi: International Initiative for Impact Evaluation. Available at http://www.3ieimpact.org/en/evaluation/working-papers/ working-paper-3/

White, Howard, and Daniel Phillips. 2012. "Addressing Attribution of Cause and Effect in Small n Impact Evaluations: Towards an Integrated Framework." Working Paper 15. New Delhi: International Initiative for Impact Evaluation. Available at http://www.3ieimpact.org/media/filer/2012/06/29/ working_paper_15.pdf

Wholey, Joseph S., Harry Hatry, and Kathryn Newcomer (eds.). 2004. *Handbook of Practical Program Evaluation.* San Francisco: Jossey-Bass.

Wilcox, Yuanjing, and Jean King. 2014. "A Professional Grounding and History of the Development and Formal Use of Evaluator Competencies." *Canadian Journal of Program Evaluation* 28(3): 1–28.

Williams, Bob, and Richard Hummelbrunner. 2010. *Systems Concepts in Action: A Practitioner's Tool Kit.* Stanford, CA: Stanford University Press.

W.K. Kellogg Foundation. 2004. *Evaluation Handbook.* Battle Creek, MI: W.K. Kellogg Foundation. Available at http://www.wkkf.org/knowledge-center/ resources/2010/W-K-Kellogg-Foundation-Evaluation-Handbook.aspx

Wood, Claudia, and Daniel Leighton. 2010. *Measuring Social Value: The Gap Between Policy and Practice.* London: Demos. Available at http://www.demos.co.uk/publications/measuring-social-value

World Bank. 1994. *Governance: The World Bank's Experience. Development in Practice.* Washington, DC: The World Bank. Available at http://documents.world bank.org/curated/en/1994/05/698374/governance-world-banks-experience

Worthen, Blaine. 1994. "Is Evaluation a Mature Profession That Warrants the Preparation of Evaluation Professionals?" In James Altschuld and Molly Engle (eds.), *The Preparation of Professional Evaluators: Issues, Perspectives, Programs. New Directions for Evaluation* 62: 3–15.

Yarbrough, Donald. B., Lyn M. Shulha, Rodney K. Hopson, and F. A. Caruthers. 2011. *The Program Evaluation Standards: A Guide for Evaluators and Evaluation Users* 3rd ed. Thousand Oaks, CA: Sage.

Yates, Brian T. 1996. *Analyzing Costs, Procedures, Processes, and Outcomes in Human Services: An Introduction.* Thousand Oaks, CA: Sage.

Yates, Brian T. 2012. "Steps Around Common Pitfalls When Valuing Resources Used Versus Resources Produced." In George Julnes (ed.), *Promoting Valuation in the Public Interest: Informing Policies for Judging Value in Evaluation. New Directions for Evaluation* 133. San Francisco: Jossey-Bass, 43–52.

Zelik, Daniel J., Emily S. Patterson, and David D. Woods. 2010. "Measuring Attributes of Rigor in Information Analysis." In Emily S. Patterson and Janet E. Miller (eds.), *Macrocognition Metrics and Scenarios: Design and Evaluation for Real-World Teams.* Aldershot, UK: Ashgate.

Index